ENGLAND FROM CHAUCER
TO CAXTON

ENGLAND FROM CHAUCER TO CAXTON

BY

HENRY S. BENNETT

BOOKS FOR LIBRARIES PRESS
FREEPORT, NEW YORK

First Published 1928
Reprinted 1970

STANDARD BOOK NUMBER:
8369-5308-8

LIBRARY OF CONGRESS CATALOG CARD NUMBER:
77-114904

PRINTED IN THE UNITED STATES OF AMERICA

PREFACE

THE last two or three decades have shown a steadily increasing interest in the social history of our country as opposed to the traditional ' drum and trumpet ' history that for so long held the field. More and more we have turned from the accounts of wars and parliaments to seek the ordinary everyday occupations and recreations of men and women. An adequate understanding of these matters is hard to come by, for the necessary information is not to be gained from one source alone but must be sought for in many diverse quarters. Much still remains to be done : the medieval records preserved in the Public Record Office and in the great Libraries are at once the pride and the despair of the social historian. ' The lyf so short, the craft so long to lern ', is the rueful cry of the scholar as he surveys the incredibly numerous masses of documents which all need to be investigated and summarized before we can hope to know the whole story of English life in the Middle Ages.

But something short of this full knowledge we already have, and it is fairly readily available. The difficult and highly technical language which was used by the scribes who turned everything into Latin of a sort, and wrote it down in the greatly abbreviated form from which we patiently decipher it to-day is only one source of our information. Waiting for us is the whole field of medieval English literature—poetry, homilies, chronicles, romances—from all of which we may glean innumerable details and many glowing pictures of the life the poet saw about him every day. The joy with which the ordinary man greeted the spring, for example, is enshrined in the lines which Chaucer prefixes to the *Legende of Good Women* ; the noise and medley of the medieval street come before us in the closing lines of Langland's Prologue to the *Vision of Piers the Plowman* ; the excitement, colour and movement of the chase are re-created for us in passages of *Sir Gawaine and the Grene Knyght*. Turn where we will in contemporary literature different aspects of life and manners are displayed to us—not in the synthesis of the scholar, patiently assembling his details and reconstructing the past, but rather in the living images of the writer which do indeed reflect ' the very age and body of the time, his form and pressure.'

The present collection, then, is selected with this belief, and it is hoped that it will illustrate many phases of medieval life and thought. Inevitably in places the material is scanty : the artist's business is not primarily to provide for the social historian, and hence at times literature gives only a poor example of some social usage that may be far better illustrated from the documents of a court of law, or from the pages of an account book. With this proviso in mind, however, the reader will find most sides of medieval life reflected in the pages which follow. I have deliberately omitted Chaucer, except for one small extract, because his work is likely to be familiar in part at least to most readers. A fairly extensive search among fourteenth- and fifteenth-century writers has resulted in the selection of a comparatively small number of them as suitable to my purpose. Far too many writers drone on and on, content with their immediate purpose, and blind to the use their more skilful brothers can make of local colour and of contemporary custom. Hence if Lydgate and others seem to figure unduly in these pages it is not because his contemporaries and successors have been overlooked.

A work like this is only possible by reason of the generosity of editors and publishers, and I wish to record the great kindness I have received on all sides in asking permission to print. I am most indebted to Sir Israel Gollancz the

Director of the Early English Text Society and to the
individual editors for allowing me the fullest opportunities
to make use of the Society's publications. Indeed, without
such permission this volume would hardly have been
possible. I am also indebted to the Royal Historical
Society for permission to make extracts from the *Stonor
Letters* and from *Gregory's Chronicle*: to the Oxford
University Press for like permission in respect of Gower's
Confessio Amantis, C. L. Kingsford's *English Historical
Literature of the XVth Century* and *Pierce the Ploughman's
Crede*. Sir Israel Gollancz has also been good enough to
allow me to make use of his editions of *Winner and Waster*
and *The Parliament of the Three Ages*. I regret that I
have not been able to trace the present owners of the
copyright of the *Paston Letters*. Messrs. Constable & Co.,
who held the copyright in 1921, and who kindly allowed
me to print extracts from the letters in my book, *The
Pastons and their England*, inform me that they have no
record of the present ownership. I am, however, em-
boldened to make use of the letters, because I believe
that extracts will only whet the appetite and send my
readers to the originals themselves.

I have to acknowledge the help I have received from
Dr. Eileen Power, one of the Editors of this Series, and also
from Miss H. M. R. Murray, Director of English Studies
at Girton College ; and finally to record the constant
stimulus and encouragement generously given me by my
friend and master Dr. G. G. Coulton of S. John's College.
Whatever is of value in this compilation derives from him.

H. S. BENNETT.

EMMANUEL COLLEGE, CAMBRIDGE
November, 1927.

CONTENTS

ix

SECTION II. VILLAGE LIFE

SECTION III. TOWN LIFE

CONTENTS

SECTION IV. CHURCH LIFE

SECTION V.   FOREIGN LIFE

ENGLAND FROM
CHAUCER TO CAXTON

SECTION ONE

HOME LIFE

In attempting to view English life and manners from the time of Chaucer to that of Caxton, we may very conveniently start with a survey of family life ; for the family, whether free or serf, was the unit. However great the differences in medieval society were—such differences as those of rank and social standing, of occupations, of ideas, of ideals—the underlying elemental things which concerned all these people and influenced their thought are clear enough. Contemporary views upon such things as birth, death, marriage, are of the first importance in trying to understand the life of any period, and so we must begin with the formation, education and surroundings of the family.

' Love comes to every gentle heart,' sings Dante, but it also comes to those not of gentle birth, even to bailiffs ' rough as a boar '. We start then with some extracts to show the influence of love on various sections of the community. The cult of the Virgin and the idealization of women are inextricably mingled, and long before Chaucer's time an elaborate code had been evolved by which the gentle lover should be guided. The extracts from Malory and Gower well illustrate this courtly love, but it was something too fanciful and ethereal for most people ; and, indeed, at the best could only have been the pastime of bored and idle people. Everyday folk, especially those with lands and revenues to safeguard, were more practical, and openly bargained and argued in the most business-like way over their matrimonial ventures (see pages 17 and 26).

But at the same time, the best-laid schemes of far-seeing parents would go awry when determined young people took

1

a hand. Between the extravagances of chivalric love and
the hard-headed bargaining of moneyed men, landowners
and rich burgesses, we find genuine passion asserting itself
the more vividly because of its surroundings. Elizabeth
Paston and the family bailiff shatter the dream world of
chivalry as successfully and completely as they flout the
conventional resistance of the *bourgeoise*.

I. TRUE LOVE

*Our ideas· of medieval life are so largely coloured by our memories
of the romances and ballads that it seems fitting to begin with Malory's
famous outburst in praise of true love. Sir Thomas Malory, towards
the end of his chequered life, compiled from 'the French book' and other
sources the history of Arthur and the Round Table. It is the last,
most brilliant, flash of a dying era, and from it we can evoke the spirit
of the departed age of chivalry. The* Morte Darthur *was written about
1469, first published by Caxton in 1485, and reprinted from that edition
in 1889–91 in three volumes by H. O. Sommer. The following extract
is from Vol. I, p. 771 (Book XVIII, Chapter 25), of Sommer's edition.*

AND thus it past on from Candylmas untyl after Ester
that the moneth of May was come whan every lusty herte
begynneth to blosomme and to brynge forth fruyte ; for,
lyke as herbes and trees bryngen forth fruyte and florys-
shen in May, in lyke wyse every lusty herte that is in ony
maner a lover spryngeth and floryssheth in lusty dedes.
For it gyveth unto al lovers courage that lusty moneth
of May in some thyng to constrayne hym to some maner
of thyng more in that moneth than in ony other moneth
for dyverse causes. For thenne alle herbes and trees re-
newen a man and woman, and lyke-wyse lovers callen
ageyne to their mynde old gentilnes and old servyse. For
lyke as wynter rasure doth alway a-rase and deface grene
somer, soo fareth it by unstable love in man and woman.
For in many persons ther ys no stabylyte. For we may
see al day for a lytel blast of wynters rasure anone we
shalle deface and lay a-parte true love, for lytel or noughte
that cost moch thynge : this is no wysedome nor stabylyte,
but it is feblenes of nature and grete disworshyp who-
somever used this. Therfore lyke as May moneth floreth
and floryssheth in many gardyns soo in lyke wyse lete

every man of worship florysshe his herte in this world,
fyrst unto God, and next unto the joye of them that he
promysed his feythe unto, for there was never worshypful
man or worshypfull woman but they loved one better than
another, and worshyp in armes may never be foyled, but
fyrst reserve the honour to God, and secondly the quarel
must come of thy Lady, and suche love I calle vertuous
love. But now adayes men can not love seven nyghte
but they must have alle their desyres that love may not
endure by reason, for where they ben soone accorded and
hasty hete, soone it keleth. Ryghte soo fareth love now
adayes, sone hote, soone cold. Thys is noo stabylyte, but
the old love was not so. Men and wymmen coude love
to gyders seven yeres, and no lycours lustes were bitwene
them, and thenne was love, trouthe and feythfulnes, and
too in lyke wyse was used love in kynge Arthurs days.

Wherfor I lyken love now adayes unto somer and wynter,
for lyke as the one is hote, and the other cold, so fareth
love now adayes. Therfor alle ye that be lovers calle unto
your remembraunce the moneth of May, lyke as dyd quene
Guenever, for whom I make here a lytel mencyon that
whyle she lyved she was a true lover, and therfor she had
a good ende.

II. THE DEVOUT LOVER

*We may see this devout lover of whom Malory speaks at somewhat
closer quarters if we turn to the pages of Gower's* Confessio Amantis.
*The machinery of this poem contains the confessions of a young lover
who has to tell to the old priest Genius the sufferings and joys he has
experienced in the service of Venus whilst pursuing his suit for the
hand of his lady. Our extracts are taken from the definitive edition
of Gower's* Complete Works, *edited by G. C. Macaulay, of which the
English work, called the* Confessio Amantis. *fills Vols. II and III.
The* Confessio Amantis *was completed in its final version not later
than* 1393.

I

Lines 1122–1221 (*p*. 331)

Mi fader, evere yit er this
In every place, in every stede,
What so my lady hath me bede,

With al myn herte obedient
I have therto be diligent.
And if so is sche bidde noght,
What thing that thanne into my thoght
Comth ferst of that I mai suffise,
I bowe and profre my servise,
Somtime in chambre, somtime in halle,   10
Riht as I see the times falle.
And whan sche goth to hiere masse,
That time schal noght overpasse,
That I naproche hir ladihede,
In aunter ¹ if I mai hire lede
Unto the chapelle and ayein.
Thanne is noght al mi weie in vein,
Somdiel I mai the betre fare,
Whan I, that mai noght fiele hir bare,
Mai lede hire clothed in myn arm :   20
Bot afterward it doth me harm
Of pure ymaginacioun ;
For thanne this collacioun
I make unto miselven ofte,
And seie, ' Ha lord, hou sche is softe,
How sche is round, hou sche is smal !
Now wolde God I hadde hire al
Withoute danger at mi wille ! '
And thanne I sike ² and sitte stille,
Of that I see my best thoght   30
Is torned ydel into noght.
Bot for al that lete I ne mai,
Whanne I se time an other dai,
That I ne do my besinesse
Unto mi ladi worthinesse.
For I therto mi wit afaite ³
To se the times and awaite
What is to done and what to leve :
And so, whan time is, be hir leve,

---

¹ perchance.   ² sigh.   ³ prepare.

What thing sche bit me don, I do,   40
And wher sche bidt me gon, I go,
And whanne hir list to clepe,[1] I come.
Thus hath sche fulliche overcome
Min ydelnesse til I sterve,
So that I mot hire nedes serve,
For as men sein, nede hath no lawe.
Thus mot I nedly to hire drawe,
I serve, I bowe, I loke, I loute,
Min yhe [2] folweth hire aboute,
What so sche wole so wol I,   50
Whan sche wol sitte, I knele by,
And whan sche stant, than wol I stonde ;
Bot whan sche takth hir werk on honde
Of wevinge or enbrouderie,
Than can I noght bot muse and prie
Upon hir fingres longe and smale,
And now I thenke, and now I tale,
And now I singe, and now I sike,[3]
And thus mi contienance I pike.
And if it falle, as for a time   60
Hir liketh noght abide bime,
Bot besien hire on other thinges,
Than make I othre tariinges
To dreche [4] forth the longe dai,
For me is loth departe away.
And thanne I am so simple of port,
That forto feigne som desport
I pleie with hire litel hound
Now on the bedd, now on the ground,
Now with hir briddes in the cage ;   70
For there is non so litel page,
Ne yit so simple a chamberere,
That I ne make hem alle chere,
Al for thei scholde speke wel :
Thus mow ye sen mi besi whiel,

---

[1] call.   [2] eye.   [3] sigh.   [4] while away.

That goth noght ydeliche aboute.
And if hir list to riden oute
On pelrinage or other stede,
I come, thogh I be noght bede.
And take hire in min arm alofte   80
And sette hire in hire sadel softe,
And so forth lede hire be the bridel,
For that I wolde noght ben ydel.
And if hire list to ride in Char,
And thanne I mai therof be war,
Anon I schape me to ryde
Riht evene be the Chares side;
And as I mai, I speke among,
And otherwhile I singe a song,
Which Ovide in his bokes made,   90
And seide, ' O whiche sorwes glade,
O which wofull prosperite
Belongeth to the proprete
Of love, who so wole him serve !
And yif therfro mai noman swerve,
That he ne mot his lawe obeie.'
And thus I ryde forth mi weie,
And am riht besi overal
With herte and with mi body al,
As I have said you hier tofore.   100

II

Lines 2773–2881 (p. 376)

AT alle time if it befelle
So that I mihte come and duelle
In place ther my ladi were,
I was noght slow ne slepi there :
For thanne I dar wel undertake,
That whanne hir list on nyhtes wake
In chambre as to carole and daunce,
Me thenkth I mai me more avaunce,

If I mai gon upon hir hond,
Thanne if I wonne a kinges lond.   10
For whanne I mai hire hand beclippe,[1]
With such gladnesse I daunce and skippe,
Me thenkth I touche noght the flor ;
The Ro, which renneth on the Mor,
Is thanne noght so lyht as I :
So mow ye witen wel forthi,
That for the time slep I hate.
And whanne it falleth othergate,
So that hire like noght to daunce,
Bot on the Dees to caste chaunce   20
Or axe of love som demande,
Or elles that hir list comaunde
To rede and here of Troilus,
Riht as sche wole or so or thus,
I am al redi to consente.
And if so is that I mai hente [2]
Somtime among a good leisir,
So as I dar of mi desir
I telle a part ; bot whanne I preie,
Anon sche bidt me go mi weie   30
And seith it is ferr in the nyht ;
And I swere it is even liht.
Bot as it falleth ate laste,
Ther mai no worldes joie laste,
So mot I nedes fro hire wende
And of my wachche make an ende :
And if sche thanne hiede toke,
Hou pitousliche on hire I loke,
Whan that I schal my leve take,
Hire oghte of mercy forto slake   40
Hire daunger, which seith evere nay.
Bot he seith often, ' Have good day,'
That loth is forto take his leve :
Therfore, while I mai beleve,

<hr>

[1] kiss   [2] seize:

I tarie forth the nyht along,
For it is noght on me along
To slep that I so sone go,
Til that I mot algate so ;
And thanne I bidde Godd hire se,
And so doun knelende on mi kne   50
I take leve, and if I schal,
I kisse hire, and go forth withal.
And otherwhile, if that I dore,
Er I come fulli to the Dore,
I torne ayein and feigne a thing,
As thogh I hadde lost a Ring
Or somwhat elles, for I wolde
Kisse hire eftsones, if I scholde,
Bot selden is that I so spede.
And whanne I se that I mot nede   60
Departen, I departe, and thanne
With al myn herte I curse and banne
That evere slep was made for yhe ;
For, as me thenkth, I mihte dryhe [1]
Withoute slep to waken evere,
So that I scholde noght dissevere
Fro hire, in whom is al my liht :
And thanne I curse also the nyht
With al the will of mi corage,
And seie, ' Awey, thou blake ymage,   70
Which of thi derke cloudy face
Makst al the worldes lyht deface,
And causest unto slep a weie,
Be which I mot nou gon aweie
Out of mi ladi compaignie.
O slepi nyht, I thee defie,
And wolde that thou leye in presse
With Proserpine the goddesse
And with Pluto the helle king ;
For til I se the daies spring,   80

---

[1] endure.

I sette slep noght at a risshe.'
And with that word I sike and wisshe,
And seie, ' Ha, whi ne were it day ?
For yit mi ladu thanne I may
Beholde, thogh I do nomore.'
And efte I thenke forthermore,
To som man hou the niht doth ese,
Whan he hath thing that mai him plese
The longe nyhtes be his side,
Where as I faile and go beside. 90
Bot slep, I not wherof it serveth,
Of which noman his thonk deserveth
To gete him love in eny place,
Bot is an hindrere of his grace
And makth him ded as for a throwe,
Riht as a Stok were overthrowe.
And so, mi fader, in this wise
The slepi nyhtes I despise,
And evere amiddes of mi tale
I thenke upon the nyhtingale, 100
Which slepeth noght be weie of kinde
For love, in bokes as I finde.
Thus ate laste I go to bedde,
And yit min herte lith to wedde
With hire, wher as I cam fro ;
Thogh I departe, he wol noght so,
Ther is no lock mai schette him oute,
Him nedeth noght to gon aboute,
That perce mai the harde wall ;

III. ' THE COURSE OF TRUE LOVE . . .'

Now having seen the courtly-conventional side of love, we may ask what relation this really bears to the life of the ordinary man and woman in the fifteenth century. Our evidence as to the love-affairs of the rustics is tantalizingly scrappy. So long as they married within the manor and one of their own station they could do much as they liked, for it was worth no one's while to interfere. If they wanted to marry with a free man or woman, or with some one not living on the manor it was more difficult, but could generally be arranged by payment to the Lord of the Manor.

For the burgesses, the commercial families and the upper classes generally, things were not so simple. Love was a strictly rationed element in most matrimonial arrangements, and the following extracts will show some examples of the various factors that went to the making of marriage in those days. The well-known Norfolk family of the Pastons provide us with some illuminating information on this matter. The Pastons about the middle of the fifteenth century had ' arrived ' and cut an important figure in the county, so that the numerous sons and daughters of the family were an object of considerable interest to prospective fathers-in-law. We may read much of all this in the famous Paston Letters.

Here we have upwards of a thousand letters, most of them either written by, or written to, members of the Paston family. They enable us to examine at leisure almost every detail of the social life of their time. Unlike some later correspondences they were written with no thought of their being read outside the family circle ; and indeed the writers often ask that they shall be burnt, once they have been read. Hence their value : for the writers say frankly what is in their minds and allow us to fathom their secrets to an almost unbelievable degree. The letters here printed exhibit the inmost thoughts of Margery Paston and Richard Calle, the Pastons' bailiff, at a critical moment in their lives, when it had become necessary to avow openly that they were betrothed. The Paston Letters have been admirably edited by James Gairdner, first in 1872-5 in 3 volumes, again with a supplementary volume in 1901 ; and finally in a definitive library edition in 6 vols. in 1904. My references are to the 1872 edition.

I

[Richard Calle to Margery Paston. ' P.L.' No. 609]

1469

M<small>YN</small> owne lady and mastres, and be for God very trewe wyff, I with herte full sorowefull recomaunde me unto you, as he that can not be mery, nor nought shalbe tyll it be othewise with us then it is yet, for thys lyf that we lede nough is nowther plesur to Godde nor to the worlde, consederyng the gret bonde of matrymonye that is made be twix us, and also the greete love that hath be, and as I truste yet is be twix us, and as on my parte never gretter ; wherfor I beseche Almyghty Godde comfort us as sone as it plesyth Hym, for we that ought of very ryght to be moost

to gether ar moost asondre ; me semyth it is a m^{ll}.[1] yere
a goo son that I speke with you. I had lever thenne all
the goode in the worlde I myght be with you. Alas, alas !
goode lady, full litell remembre they what they doo that
kepe us thus asunder ; iiij. tymes in the yere ar they a
cursid that lette [2] matrymonye ; it causith many men to
deme in hem they have large consyence in other maters
as wele as herin. But what lady suffre as ye have do ;
and make you as mery as ye can, for I wys, lady, at the
longe wey Godde woll of Hys ryght wysnes helpe Hys
servants that meane truly, and wolde leve accordyng to
Hes lawys, &c.

I undrestende, lady, ye have hadde as moche sorwe for
me as any gentelwoman hath hadde in the worlde, as wolde
Godd all that sorwe that ye have hadde had rested upon
me, so that ye hadde be discharged of it, for I wis, lady,
it is to me a deethe to her [3] that ye be entreted other wise
thene ye ought to be. This is a peyneful lyfe that we lede.
I can not leve thus withoute it be a gret displesure to Godde.

Also like you to wete that I had sent you a letter be my
ladde from London, and he tolde me he myght not speeke
with you, ther was made so gret awayte upon hym and
upon you boothe. He told me John Threscher come to
hym in your name, and seide that ye sent hym to my ladde
for a letter or a token, weche I shulde have sent you, but
he truste hym not ; he wold not delyver hym noon. After
that he brought hym a rynge, seyng that ye sent it hym,
comaundyng hym that he schulde delyver the letter or
token to hym, weche I conceyve sethen [4] be my ladde it
was not be your sendyng, it was be my mastres and Sir
Jamys [5] a vys. Alas, what meane they ? I suppose they
deeme we be not ensuryd [6] to gether, and if they so doo I
merveyll, for then they ar not wele avised, remembryng
the pleynes [7] that I breke to my mastres at the begynnyng,
and I suppose be you bothe, and ye dede as ye ought to do

---

[1] thousand.   [2] forbid.   [3] hear.   [4] since.
[5] (Sir) James Gloys, the Pastons' domestic chaplain.
[6] betrothed.   [7] plainness.

of very ryght ; and if ye have do the contrare, as I have
be enformed ye have do, ye dede nouther concyensly [1]
nor to the plesure of Godde, withoute ye dede it for feere,
and for the tyme to please suche as were at that tyme a
boute you ; and if ye so dede it for this service it was a
resonable cause, consederyng the grete and importable [2]
callyng upon that ye hadde, and many an on-trewe tale
was made to you of me, weche God knowt I was never
gylty of.

My ladde tolde me that my mastres your modre axyd
hym if he hadde brought any letter to you, and many
other thyngs she bare hym on hande, [3] and a monge all
other at the last she seide to hym that I wolde not make
her prevy to the begynnyng, but she supposyd I wolde
at the endyng ; and as to that, God knowt sche knewe
furst of me and non other. I wott not what her mastreschip
meneth, for be my trowthe ther is no gentylwoman on
lyve that my herte tendreth more then it dothe her, nor
is lother to displese, savyng only your person, weche of
very ryght I ought to tendre and love beste, for I am bounde
therto be the lawe of Godde, and so wol do whyle that I
leve, what so ever falle of it. I supose, and ye telle hem
sadly [4] the trouthe, they wold not dampne ther soules for
us ; though I telle hem the trouthe they woll not be leve
me as weele as they woll do you ; and ther for, goode lady,
at the reverence of Godde be pleyne to hem and telle the
trouthe, and if they woll. in no wise agree therto, betwix
God, the Deelf, and them be it, and that perell that we
schuld be in, I beseche Godde it may lye upon them and
not upon us. I am hevy and sory to remembre ther disposicion, God sende them grace to gyde all thyngs weele,
as wele I wolde they dede ; Godde be ther gide, and sende
them peas and reste, &c.

I mervell moche that they schulde take this mater so
heedely as I undrestonde they doo, remembryng it is in
suche case as it can not be remedyed, and my desert upon

---

[1] conscientiously.   [2] unsupportable.   [3] insinuated.
[4] solemnly.

every be halfe it is for to be thought ther shulde be non obstacle a yenst it ; and also the worchipfull that is in them, is not in your mariage, it is in ther owne mariage, weche I beseche Godde sende hem suche as may be to ther worship and plesur to Godde, and to ther herts ease, for ell(es) were it gret pety. Mastres, I am aferde to write to you, for I undrestonde ye have schewyd my letters that I have sent you be for this tyme ; but I prey you lete no creatur se this letter. As sone as ye have redde it lete it be brent,[1] for I wolde no man schulde se it in no wise ; ye had no wrytyng from me this ij. yere, nor I wolle not sende you no mor, therfor I remytte all this matre to your wysdom. Almyghty Jesu preserve, kepe, and (give) you your hertys desire, weche I wotte weele schulde be to Goods plesur, &c.

Thys letter was wreten with as greete peyne as ever wrote I thynge in my lyfe, for in good feyth I have be ryght seke, and yet am not veryly weele at ease, God amend it, &c.

II

[John Paston to Sir John Paston. 'P.L.' No. 607]

SYR, plesyth it to undystand, that I conceyve, by your lettyr whyche that ye sent me by Jwde, that ye have herd of R[ichard] C[alle's] labor whyche he makyth by our ungracyous sustyrs assent ; but wher as they wryet that they have my good wyll ther in, savyng your reverence, they falsly lye of it, for they never spake to me of that mater, ner non othyr body in ther name. Lovell axyd me onys a qwestyon whedyr that I undyrstood how it was betwyx R.C. and my suster. I can thynk that it was by Callys menys, for when I axyd hym whedyr C. desyird hym to meve[2] me that qwestyon or not, he wold have gotyn it aweye by humys and by hays, but I wold not so be answeryd ; wherfor at the lest he told me that hys oldest sone desyird hym to spere[3] whedyr that R.C. wes

[1] burnt.   [2] ask.   [3] inquire.

swyr [1] of hyr or nowt, for he seyd that he knew a good
maryage for hyr, but I wot he lyeyd, for he is hole with
R. Cale in that mater. Wherfor to the entent that he
nor they sholl pyck no comfort of me, I answered hym,
that and [2] my fadyr, whom God asoyle,[3] wer a lyve, and
had consentyd ther to, and my modyr, and ye bothe, he
shold never have my good wyll for to make my sustyr to
selle kandyll [4] and mustard in Framlyngham ; and thus,
wythe mor whyche wer to longe to wryet to you, we
departyd. . . .

III

[Margaret Paston to Sir John Paston. ' P.L.' No. 617]

I GRETE zow [5] wel, and send zow Godds blyssyng and myn,
letyng zow wete that on Thurysday last was my moder and
I wer with my Lord [Bishop] of Norwych, and desyerd hym
that he woold no mor do in the mater towscheyng zowr syster,
tyl that ze and my brother and other that wern executors
to zowr fader mythe beyn her to geder, for they had the
rule of her as weel as I ; and he sayde playnly that he had
be requeryd so oftyn for to exameyn her, that he mythe
not nor woold no longar delay yt, and schargyd me, in
peyn of cursyng, that sche schuld not be deferred, but that
she xuld a per beforn hym the nexte day ; and I sayd
pleynly that I woold nowder bryng her nor send her ; and
than he sayd that he woold send for her hym sylfe, and
schargyd that she schuld be at her lyberte to cume wan he
sent for her ; and he seyd be hys trowthe that he woold
be as sory for her and [6] sche ded not welle, as he wold be
and [6] sche wer ryth ner of hys kyn, bothe for my moder
ys sake and myn, and other of her frendds, for he woost
welle that her demenyng had stekyd soor at our harts.
  My moder and I in formyd hym that we kowd never
onderstond be her sayyng, be no language that ever sche

---

[1] sure.   [2] if.   [3] pardon.   [4] candles.
[5] Margaret Paston often uses z to represent our y, and x to
represent sh.   [6] if.

had to hym, that neyther of hem wer bownd to other,
but that they myth schese [1] bothe. Than he seyd that he
woold sey to her as wele as he kowde, before that he
exameynd her ; and so that was told me be dyverse persones that he ded as welle and as pleynly as sche had be
rythe ner to hym, wych wer to long to wrythe at thys
tyme : her aftyr ye xalle wete, and hoo wer laberers ther
in. The schanseler [2] was not so gylty her in as I wend he
had ben.

On Fryday the Bysschope he sent for her be Asschefeld
and other than arn ryth sory of her demenyng. And the
Bysschop seyd to her ryth pleynly, and put her in re-
memberawns how she was born, wat kyn and frendds that
sche had, and xuld have mo yf sche wer rulyd and gydyd
aftyr hem ; and yf she ded not, wat rebuke, and schame,
and los yt xuld be to her, yf sche wer not gydyd be them,
and cause of forsakyng of her for any good, or helpe, or
kownfort that sche xuld have of hem ; and seyd that he
had hard sey, that sche loved schechecn [3] that her frend(es)
wer not plesyd with that sche xuld have, and therfor he
had her be ryth weel avysed how sche ded, and seyd that
he woold undyrstand the woords that sche had seyd to
hym, wheyther that mad matrimony or not. And sche
rehersyd wat sche had seyd, and seyd, yf thoo wordds mad
yt not suher, [4] she seyd boldly that sche wold make that
suerher [4] or than sche went thens, for sche seyd sche
thowgthe in her conschens sche was bownd, wat so ever
the wordds wern. Thes leud wordds greveth me and her
grandam as myche as alle the remnawnte. And than the
Bysschop and the Schawnseler bothe seyd that ther was
neyther I ner no frend of hers wold reseyve (her).

And than Calle was exameynd aparte be hym sylfe, that
her wordds and hys acordyd, and the tyme, and wher yt
xuld a [5] be don. And than the Bysschop sayd that he
supposyd that ther xuld be fownd other thynggs ageyns
hym that mythe cause the lettyng [6] ther of ; and ther for

---

[1] choose.　　[2] Chancellor.　　[3] such one.　　[4] sure
　　　　[5] have.　　　　　　　[6] forbidding.

he say he wold not be to hasty to geve sentens ther upon, and sayd that he wold geve overe day tyl the Wednsday or Thursday aftyr Mykylmes, and so yt tys delayyd. They woold an had her wyl performyd in haste, but the Bysschope seyd he woold non other wyse than he had seyd.

I was with my moder at her plase whan sche was exameynd, and wan I hard sey what her demenyng was, I schargyd my servaunts that sche xuld not be reseyved in my hows. I had zeve hir warnyng, sche mythe a be war a for, yf sche had a be grasyows ; [1] and I sent to on or ij. mor that they xuld not reseyve her yf sche cam ; sche was browthe a geyn to my place for to a be reseyved, and Sir Jamys tolde them that browthe her that I had schargyd hem alle and sche xuld not be reseyved ; and soo my Lord of Norwych hath set her at Roger Bests, to be ther tyle the day befor sayd, God knowyth fule evel ageyn hys [2] wyle and hys wyvys, yf they durst do other wyse. I am sory that they arn a cumyrd [3] with her, but zet I am better payed that sche isther for the whyle, that sche had ben in other place be cause of the sadnes [4] and good dysposysion of hys sylfe and hys wyfe, for sche xal not be sou'd (suffered ?) ther to pleye the brethele.[5] I pray zow and requer zow that ye take yt not pensyly,[6] for I wot wele yt gothe ryth ner zowr hart, and so doth yt to myn and to other ; but remembyr zow, and so do I, that we have lost of her but a brethele, and set yt the les to hart, for and sche had be good, wherso ever sche had be, yt xuld not aben as it is, for and he wer ded at thys owyr, she xuld never be at myn hart as sche was. As for the devors [7] that ze write to me of, I supose wat ze ment, but I scharge zow upon my blyssyng that ze do not, ner cause non other to do, that xuld offend God and zour conschens, for and ze do, or cause for to be do, God wul take vengawns ther upon, (and) ye xuld put zour sylfe and other in gret joparte ; [8] for wettyt [9] wele, sche xal ful sor repent her leudnes [10] her aftyr, and I pray God sche mute soo. I

[1] gracious.　[2] Best's.　[3] encumbered.　[4] discretion.　[5] wanton.
[6] pensively.　[7] divorce.　[8] jeopardy.　　[9] know it.　[10] wickedness.

pray zow for myn hard ys hese,[1] be ze of a good cownfort in alle thynggs ; I trust God xal helpe ryth wele, and I pray God so do in alle our maters. I wuld ze toke hed yf ther weher any labor mad in the kort of Cawntrybery [2] for the leud mater forsayd.

IV. A MEDIEVAL COURTSHIP

From the same Correspondence we are enabled to follow in detail the matrimonial adventures of another member of this family — John Paston, the brother of Sir John Paston. He had made many earlier efforts to find a wife : his letters for some years constantly contain references to this, and I have gathered together the whole story in The Pastons and their England. *Here we have his final attempt, in which he was more fortunate than he deserved to be.*

I

[John Paston to Margery Brews. ' P.L.' No. 774]

1476

MASTRESSE, thow so be that I, unaqweyntyd with yow as yet, tak up on me to be thus bold as to wryght on to yow with-ought your knowlage and leve, yet, mastress, for syche pore servyse as I now in my mynd owe yow, purposyng (ye not dyspleasyd) duryng my lyff to contenu the same, I beseche yow to pardon my boldness, and not to dysdeyn, but to accepte thys sympyll byll [3] to recomand me to yow in syche wyse as I best can or may imagyn to your most plesure. And, mastress, for sych report as I have herd of yow by many and dyverse persones, and specyally by my ryght trusty frend, Rychard Stratton, berer her-of, to whom I beseche yow to geve credence in syche maters as he shall on my behalve comon [4] with yow of, if it lyke you to lystyn hym, and that report causythe me to be the more bold to wryght on to yow, so as I do ; for I have herd oft tymys Rychard Stratton sey that ye can and wyll take every thyng well that is well ment, whom I beleve and trust as myche as fewe men leveing,

---

[1] heart's case.   [2] Court of Canterbury.   [3] letter.   [4] talk.

I ensuer yow by my trowthe. And, mastress, I beseche
yow to thynk non other wyse in me but that I wyll and
shall at all seasons be redy wythe Godes grace to accom-
plyshe all syche thynges as I have enformyd and desyerd
the seyd Rychard on my behalve to geve yow knowlage
of, but if [1] it so be that a geyn my wyll it come of
yow that I be cast off fro yowr servyse and not wyllyngly
by my desert, and that I am and wylbe yours and at your
comandmen in every wyse dwryng my lyff. Her I send
yow this bylle wretyn with my lewd [2] hand and sealyd
with my sygnet to remayn with yow for a wyttnesse ayentse
me, and to my shame and dyshonour if I contrary it. And,
mastress, I beseche yow, in easyng of the poore hert that
somtyme was at my rewle, whyche now is at yours, that
in as short tyme as can be that I may have knowlage of
your entent and hough ye wyll have me demeanyd in thys
mater, and I wylbe at all seasons redy to performe in thys
mater and all others your plesure, as ferforth as lythe
in my poore power to do or in all thers that ought wyll
do for me, with Godes grace, Whom I beseche to send yow
the accomplyshement of your most worchepfull desyers,
myn owne fayer lady, for I wyll no ferther labore but to
yow, on-to the tyme ye geve me leve, and tyll I be suer
that ye shall take no dysplesur with my ferther labore.

II

[Dame Elizabeth Brews to John Paston. 'P.L.' No. 781]

1476

RYGHT wurschypfull cosyn, I recommande me un (to)
yowe, &c. And I send my husbonde a bill of the mater
that ye knowe of, and he wrote an other bill to me agayn
towchyng the same mater; and he wold that ye schuld go
un to my maistresse yowr modur, and asaye [3] if ye myght
gete the hole £20 in to yowr handes, and then he wolde
be more gladd to marye with yowe, and will gyffe yowe

---

[1] unless. [2] unformed. [3] try.

an £100. And, cosyn, that day that sche is maryed, my
fadur will gyffe hyr 50 merks. But and [1] we acorde, I
schall gyffe yowe a grettere tresur, that is, a wytty gentylwoman, and if I sey it, bothe good and vertuos ; for if I
schuld take money for hyr, I wold not gyffe hyr for a £1,000.
But, cosyn, I trust yowe so meche that I wold thynke her
wele besett on yowe, and ye were worthe meche more.
And, cosyn, a lytyll after that ye were gone, come a man
from my cosyn Derby, and broght me wurde that suche
a chance fell that he myght not come at the day that was
set, as I schall let yowe undyrstond more pleynly, when
I speke with yowe, &c. But, cosyn, and it wold please
yowe to come agayn what dey that ye will set, I dare
undyrtake that they schall kepe the same day ; for I wold
be glad that, and myn husbond and ye myght acorde in
thys maryage, that it myght be my fortune to make and
ende in thys mater betwene my cosyns and yowe, that
yche of yowe myght love other in frendely wyse, &c. And,
cosyn, if thys byll please not yowr entent, I pray yowe
that it may be brent, &c.

No more unto yowe at thys tyme, but Almyghty Jesus
preserve yowe, &c.

By yowr cosyn,
Dame Elizabeth Brews.

III

[Dame Elizabeth Brews to John Paston. ' P.L.' No. 782]
February, 1477

To my wurschypfull cosyne, John Paston, be this bill
delyveryd, &c.

Cosyn, I recomande me un to yowe, thankyng yowe hertely
for the grette chere that ye made me and all my folkys,
the last tyme that I was at Norwych ; and ye promysyd
me, that ye wold never breke the mater to Margrery unto
suche tyme as ye and I were at a point. But ye hafe made

[1] if.

hyr suche advokett for yowe, that I may never hafe rest nyght ner day, for callyng and cryeng uppon to brynge the saide mater to effecte, &c.

And, cosyn, uppon Fryday is Sent Volentynes Day, and every brydde chesyth hym a make [1]; and yf it lyke yowe to come one Thursday at nyght, and so purvey yowe that ye may abyde there tyll Monday, I trusty to God, that ye schall so speke to myn husband ; and I schall prey that we schall bryng the mater to a conclusyon, &c. For, cosyn,

> It is but a sympill oke,
> That (is) cut down at the first stroke.

For ye will be resonabill, I trust to God, Whech hafe yowe ever in Hys mercyfull kepyng, &c.

> Be yowr cosyn, Dame Elizabeth Brews,
> otherwes schall be called, be Godds grace.

IV

[Margery Brews to John Paston. 'P.L.' No. 783]

February, 1477

Unto my ryght welebelovyd Voluntyn, John Paston, Squyer, be this bill delyvered, &c.

RYGHT reverent and wurschypfull, and my ryght welebeloved Voluntyne, I recomande me unto yowe, ffull hertely desyring to here of yowr welefare, whech I beseche Almyghty God long for to preserve un to Hys plesur, and yowr herts desyre. And yf it please yowe to here of my welefar, I am not in good heele of body, nor of herte, nor schall be tyll I her ffrom yowe ;

> For there wottys no creature what peyn that I endure,
> And for to be deede, I dare it not dyscure.[2]

And my lady my moder hath labored the mater to my

---

[1] mate.　　　　[2] discover.

ffadur full delygently, but sche can no mor gete then ye
knowe of, for the whech God knowyth I am full sory. But
yf that ye loffe me, as I tryste verely that ye do, ye will
not leffe me therefor ; for if that ye hade not halfe the
lyvelode that ye hafe, for to do the grettest labur that
any woman on lyve myght, I wold not forsake yowe.

And yf ye commande me to kepe me true wherever I go,
I wyse I will do all my myght yowe to love and never no mo.
 And yf my freends say, that I do amys,
  Thei schal not me let so for to do,
Myne herte me bydds ever more to love yowe
 Truly over all erthely thing.
And yf thei be never so wroth,
 I tryst it schall be better in tyme commyng.

No more to yowe at this tyme, but the Holy Trinite hafe
yowe in kepyng. And I besech yowe that this bill be not
seyn of none erthely creatur safe only your selffe, &c.

And thys letter was indyte at Topcroft, with full hevy
herte, &c.

By your own,
MARGERY BREWS.

V

[Margery Brews to John Paston. ' P.L.' No. 784]

February, 1477

To my ryght welebelovyd cosyn, John Paston, Swyer, be
this letter delyveryd, &c.

RYGHT wurschypfull and welebelovyd Volentyne, in my
moste umble wyse, I recommande me un to yowe, &c.
And hertely I thanke yowe for the lettur whech that ye
sende me be John Bekarton, wherby I undyrstonde and
knowe, that ye be purposyd to come to Topcroft in schorte
tyme, and withowte any erand or mater, but only to hafe
a conclusyon of the mater betwyx my fader and yowe ;
I wolde be most glad of any creatur on lyve, so that the

3

mater myght growe to effect. And ther as ye say, and ye come and fynde the mater no more towards you then ye dyd afortyme, ye wold no more put my fader and my lady my moder to no cost ner besenesse, for that cause, a good wyle aftur, weche causyth myne herte to be full hevy ; and yf that ye come, and the mater take to none effecte, then schuld I be meche mor sory and full of hevynesse.

And as for my selfe, I hafe done and undyrstond in the mater that I can or may, as Good knowyth ; and I let yowe pleynly undyrstond that my fader wyll no mor money parte with all in that behalfe but an £100 and 50 marke, which is ryght far fro the acomplyshment of yowr desyre.

Wherfore, yf that ye cowde be content with that good, and my por persone, I wold be the meryest mayden on grounde ; and yf ye thynke not yowr selffe so satysfyed, or that ye myght hafe mech mor good, as I hafe undyrstonde be yowe afor ; good, trewe, and lovyng volentyne, that ye take no such labur uppon yowe, as to come more for that mater, but let is (*it*?) passe, and never more to be spokyn of, as I may be yowr trewe lover and bedewoman [1] duryng my lyfe.

No more un to yowe at thys tyme, but Almighty Jesus preserve yowe, bothe body and sowle, &c.

Be your Voluntyne,
MARGERY BREWS.

VI

[John Paston to Margaret Paston. ' P.L.' No. 787]

8 March, 1477

To my ryght worchepfull modyr, Margaret Paston.

RYGHT worschepfull modyr, aftyr all dwtes [2] of recommendacyon, in as humble wyse as I can, I beseche yow of your dayly blyssyng. . . .

Modyr, I beseche yow for dyvers causys, that my syster

---

[1] prayer-woman.   [2] duties.

Anne may come with yow to Norwyche. Modyr, the mater
is in a resonable good wey, and I trust with Gods mercy,
and with your good help, that it shall take effect bettyr
to myn avauntage than I told yow of at Mawtby ; for I
trow ther is not a kynder woman leveing then I shall have
to my modyr in lawe, if the mater take, nor yet a kynder
fadyr in lawe then I shall have, though he be hard to me
as yett. All the cyrcumstancys of the mater, whyche I
trust to tell yow at your comyng to Norwyche, cowd not
be wretyn in iij. levys of paper, and ye know my lewd [1]
hed well i nough, I may not wryght longe, wherffor I ffery
over [2] all thyngs tyll I may awayte on yow myselff. . . .
Wretyn at Topcroft, the viij. day of Marche.

Your sone and humbyll servaunt,

J. P.

V. ANOTHER LOVE LETTER

After the Paston Letters *the most extensive private correspondence
of the fifteenth century is the* Stonor Letters and Papers. *Over three
hundred and thirty documents of this collection are still extant, and they
have recently been edited by C. L. Kingsford (Camden Society, Third
Series, vols. XXIX and XXX, 1919, and* Camden Miscellany).

*Katherine Riche, the daughter of Elizabeth Stonor by her first husband,
was a girl of some thirteen or fourteen years of age when she received
this letter from her suitor and future husband Thomas Betson, whom
she married in 1478. Betson became a partner of William Stonor in
the wool trade in 1475. Mr. C. L. Kingsford has said with justice that
this letter is ' one of the most charming of all private letters of the time
that have survived '.*

[*Thomas Betson to Katherine Ryche.* ' *S.L.*' *No.* 166]

1 June, 1476

My nowne hartely belovid Cossen Kateryn, I recomande
me unto yow withe all the inwardnesse of myn hart. And
now lately ye shall understond that I resseyvid a token
ffrom you, the which was and is to me right hartely welcom,
and with glad will I resseyvid it ; and over that I had a

<hr>

[1] unlearned.   [2] leave in abeyance.

letter ffrom Holake, youre gentyll Sqwyer, by the which
I understond right well that ye be in good helth off body,
and mery at hart. And I pray God hartely to his plesour
to contenew the same : ffor it is to me veray grete comfforth
that ye so be, so helpe me Jhesu. And yff ye wold be a
good etter off your mete allwaye, that ye myght waxe and
grow ffast to be a woman, ye shuld make me the gladdest
man off the world, be my trouth : ffor whanne I remembre
your ffavour and your sadde [1] loffynge delynge [2] to me
wardes, ffor south ye make me evene veray glade and
joyus in my hart : and on the tothersyde agayn, whanne I
remembre your yonge youthe, and seeth well that ye be
none eteter off youre mete, the which shuld helpe you
greately in waxynge, ffor south than ye make me veray
hevy agayn. And therffore I praye you, myn nown swete
Cossen, evene as you loffe me, to be mery and to eate your
mete lyke a woman. And yff ye so will do ffor my loveff,
looke what ye will desyre off me, whatsomever it be, and
be my trouth I promesse you by the helpe of our Lord to
perfforme it to my power. I can (no) more say now, but at
my comyng home I will tell you mych more betwene you
and me and God beffore. And where as ye, ffull womanly
and lyke a loffer, remembre me with manyffolde recomendacion in dyversse maners, remyttynge the same to my
discresscion to depart them ther as I loveff best, ffor south,
myn nown swete Cossen, ye shall understond that with
good hart and good will I resseyve and take to my self the
one halff off them, and them will I kepe by me ; and the
tother halff, with hartely loveff and ffavour I send hem to
you, myn nown swete Cossen, agayn, ffor to kepe by you :
and over that I send you the blissynge that our Lady
gaveffe hir dere sonne, and ever well to ffare. I pray you
grete well my horsse, and praye hym to gyffe yow iiij off
his yeres to helpe you with all : and I will at my comynge
home gyff hym iiij off my yeres and iiij horsse lofes till
amendes. Tell hym that I prayed hym so. And Cossen
Kateryn I thannke you ffor hym, and my wiff shall thanke

[1] discreet.   [2] dealing.

you ffor hym hereafter ; ffor ye do grete cost apon hym as it is told me. Myn nown swete Cossen, it was told me but late that ye were at Cales to seeke me, but ye cowde not se me nor ffynde me : ffor south ye myght have comen to my counter, and ther ye shuld bothe ffynde me and see me, and not have ffawtid off [1] me : but ye sought me in a wronge Cales, and that ye shuld well know yff ye were here and saw this Cales, as wold God ye were and som off them with you that were with you at your gentill Cales. I praye you, gentill Cossen, comaunde me to the Cloke, and pray hym to amend his unthryffte maners : ffor he strykes ever in undew tyme, and he will be ever affore, and that is a shrewde condiscion.   Tell hym with owte he amend his condiscion that he will cause strangers to advoide and come no more there.   I trust to you that he shall amend agaynest myn commynge, the which shalbe shortely with all hanndes and all ffeete with Godes grace. My veray ffeigtheffull Cossen, I trust to you that thowe all I have not remembred my right worshipfull maystres your modyr affore in this letter that ye will off your gentilnesse recomaunde me to her maystresshipe as many tymes as it shall ples you : and ye may say, yff it plese you, that in Wytson Weke next I intend to the marte ward.[2] And I trust you will praye ffor me : ffor I shall praye ffor you, and, so it may be, none so well.   And Almyghty Jhesu make you a good woman, and send you many good yeres and longe to lyveffe in helth and vertu to his plesour.   At greate Cales on this syde on the see, the ffyrst day off June, whanne every man was gone to his Dener, and the Cloke smote noynne, and all oure howsold cryed after me and badde me come down ; ' Come down to dener at ones ! ' : and what answer I gaveffe hem ye know it off old.

Be your ffeigtheffull Cossen and loffer Thomas Betson. I sent you this rynge ffor a token.

To my ffeigthefull and hartely belovid Cossen Kateryn Ryche at Stonor this letter be delyvered in hast.

---

[1] failed to find.   [2] To go to the mart or fair.

VI. 'A MARRIAGE HAS BEEN ARRANGED'

Medieval match-making was not altogether the charming affair the romancers would have us believe. The following letter from the Paston correspondence affords a very good example of the business-like way parents and suitors conducted the preliminary negotiations, and it also shows the harsher side of parental control. Stephen Scrope at this time was a widower of nearly fifty, and, according to his own account, he had 'suffered from a sickness that kept me a 13 or 14 years ensuing; whereby I am disfigured in my person and shall be whilst I live'. Elizabeth was only about 20 years of age when these proposals were made.

I

[Elizabeth Clere to John Paston. 'P.L.' No. 71]

About 1449

To my Cosyn, John Paston, be thys letter delyvered.

TRUSTY and weel be loved cosyn, I comannde me to yow, desyryng to here of yowre weelfare and good spede in youre matere, the qwech I prey God send yow to his plesaunce and to youre hertys ease.

Cosyn, I lete you wete [1] that Scrope hath be in this cuntre to se my cosyn youre sustyr, and he hath spoken with my cosyn youre moder, and sche desyreth of hym that he schuld schewe yow the endentures mad be twen the knyght that hath his dowter and hym, whethir that Skrop, if he were maried and fortuned to have children, if the children schuld enheryte his lond, or his dowter, the wheche is maried.

Cosyn, for this cause take gode hede to his endentures, for he is glad to schewe yow hem, or whom ye wol a-sygne with yow; and he seith to me he is the last in the tayle of his lyflode,[2] the qweche is three hundred and fifty marke [3] and better, as Watkyn Shipdam seith, for he hath take a compt [4] of his liflode dyvers tymes; and Scrop seith to

---

[1] know.   [2] lands or rents from which an income was derived.
[3] a mark was worth 13s. 4d.   [4] an inventory.

me if he be maried, and have a sone an eyre, his dowter
that is maried schal have of his liflode fifty marke and no
more ; and therfore, cosyn, me semeth he were good for
my cosyn yowre sustyr, with (out) that [1] ye myght gete her
a bettyr. And if ye can gete a better, I wold avyse yow
to labour it in as schort tyme as ye may goodly, for sche
was never in so gret sorow as sche is now a dayes, for sche
may not speke with no man, ho so ever come, ne not may
se ne speke with my man, ne with servauntes of hir moderys
but that sche bereth hire an hand otherwyse than she
menyth.[2] And sche hath sen [3] Esterne the most part be
betyn onys in the weke or twyes, and som tyme twyes
on o day, and hir hed broken in to or thre places. Wherfor,
cosyn, sche hath sent to me by Frere Newton in gret
counsell, and preyeth me that I wold send to yow a letter
of hir hevynes, and prey yow to be hir good brothyr, as
hir trost is in yow ; and sche seith, if ye may se be his
evydences that his children and hire may enheryten, and
sche to have resonable joynture, sche hath herd so mech
of his birth and his condicions, that and ye will sche will
have hym, whethyr that hir moder wil or wil not, not
withstandyng it is tolde hir his persone is symple, for sche
seyth men shull have the more deyute of hire if sche rewle
hire to hym as sche awte to do.

Cosyn, it is told me ther is a goodly man in yowre Inne,[4]
of the qweche the fadyr deyed litte,[5] and if ye thynk that
he were better for hir than Scroop, it wold be laboured,
and yif [6] Scroop a goodly answere that he be not put of
tyl ye be sure of a bettyr ; for he seid whan he was with
me, but if [7] he have som counfortable answer of yow, he
wil no more laboure in this mater, be cause he myght not
see my cosyn youre sustyr, and he seyth he myght a see
hire and sche had be bettyr than she is ; and that causeth
hym to demyr that hir moder was not weel willyng, and
so have I sent my cosyn yowre moder word. Wherfore,

---

[1] unless. [2] misconstrues her intentions. [3] since.
[4] i.e. a fellow-lawyer in London. [5] whose father died lately.
[6] give. [7] unless.

cosyn, thynk on this mateer, for sorow oftyn time causeth women to beset [1] hem otherwyse than thei schuld do, and if sche where in that case, I wot weel ye wold be sory. Cosyn, I prey yow brenne [2] this letter, that youre men ne non other man se it ; for and [3] my cosyn yowre moder knew that I had sent yow this letter, sche shuld never love me. No more I wrighte to yow at this tyme, but Holy Gost have yow in kepyng. Wretyn in hast, on Seynt Peterys day, be candel lyght.

Be youre Cosyn,
ELIZABETH CLERE.

VII. AN ETONIAN'S ROMANCE

This letter was written when William was a boy of nineteen, and well illustrates the mixture of sentiment and business-sense which characterized many medieval marriages.

[*William Paston, Junior, to John Paston. ' P.L.' No.* 827]

23 *February*, 1479.

To his worchepfull broder, John Paston, be thys delyvered in hast.

RYGHT reverent and worchepfull broder, after all dewtes [4] of recomendacion, I recomaunde me to yow, desyryng to here of your prosperite and welfare, whych I pray God long to contynew to Hys plesore, and to your herts desyr ; letyng yow wete that I receyved a letter from yow, in the whyche letter was viijd. with the whyche I schuld bye a peyer of slyppers. . . .

And as for the yong jentylwoman, I wol certyfye yow how I fryste felle in qweyntaince with hyr. Hir ffader is dede ; ther be ij. systers of them ; the elder is just weddyd ; at the whych weddyng I was with myn hostes,[5] and also desyryd by the jentylman hym selfe, cawlyd Wylliam Swanne, whos dwyllynge is in Eton.

---

[1] behave.   [2] burn.   [3] if.   [4] duties.   [5] i.e. his dame at Eton, with whom he resided outside the College.

So it fortuned that myne hostes reportyd on me odyrwyse than I was wordy, so that hyr moder comaundyd hyr to make me good chere, and soo in good feythe sche ded. Sche is not a bydynge ther sche is now ; hyr dwellyng is in London ; but hyr moder and sch come to a place of hyrs v. myle from Eton, were the weddyng was, for because it was nye to the jentylman whych weddyd hyr dowtyr. And on Monday next comynge, that is to sey, the fyrst Monday of Clene Lente, hyr moder and sche wyl goo to the pardon at Schene, and soo forthe to London, and ther to abyde in a place of hyrs in Bowe Chyrche Yerde ; and if it plese yow to inquere of hyr, hyr modyrs name is Mestres Alborow. The name of the dowtyr is Margarete Alborow, the age of hyr is be all lykelyod xviij. or xix. yere at the fertheste. And as for the mony and plate, it is redy when soo ever sche were weddyd ; but as for the lyvelod, I trow not tyll after hyr modyrs desese, but I can not telle yow for very certeyn, but yow may know by inqueryng. And as for hyr bewte, juge yow that when ye see hyr, yf so be that ye take the laubore ; and specialy beolde hyr handys, for and if it be as it is tolde me, sche is dysposyd to be thyke.[1]

And as for my comynge from Eton, I lake no thynge but wersyfyynge, whyche I troste to have with a lytyll contynuance.

> Quare, Quomodo non valet hora, valet mora,
>   Unde di' (*dictum, vel deductum ?*)
> Arbore jam videas exemplum. Non die possunt,
>   Omnia suppleri ; sed tamen illa mora.

And thes too verse afore seyde be of myn own makyng.
No more to yow at thys tyme, but God have yow in Hys kepyng.

Wretyn at Eton the Even of Seynt Matthy the Apostyll in haste, with the hande of your broder.

WYLL'M PASTON, JUN^B.

---

[1] is likely to grow stout.

VIII. MARITAL AMENITIES

' Love wol not been constreyned by maistrye' writes Chaucer, but nevertheless it was on a theory of ' such lordship as men have over their wives' that most medieval marriages were based. The complete submission of the wife to the husband, such as we see at the end of The Taming of the Shrew, *had nothing in it repugnant to medieval thought.*

The two following anecdotes are taken from the Book of the Knight of La Tour Landry *(ed. T. Wright, E.E.T.S. (O.S.) 1868 and revised in 1906). This volume was compiled about 1440 by the Knight for the instruction of his two daughters, and is a storehouse of medieval ideas. Here we get interesting sidelights on married life and the relation between husband and wife.*

I

(*p.* 94.) There was a lady that wolde not come ete with her husbond whanne he was atte mete, for no thyng that he coude saie her nor comaunde her. And he saw that ; and whanne he had etin, he sent for his swyneherde, and made fette [1] the kichin clothe that his disshes were wiped with, and spred it on a borde, and sette mete theron, and made the swyne-herthe sitte doun theratte. And thanne he called his lady his wyff, and saide her, ' Sethe ye wol not ete in my companie with me, ye shall sitte downe and ete here with the swyne-herthe, for there shal none other man holde you compani at youre mete.' And whedir she ware wrothe or gladde, he made her sitte doun. And she wepte and made moche sorugh that her husbonde wolde chastise her so, to make her be seryed in so ungoodly wise. And, therfor, all women aught to be humble, and to fulfell her husbondes comaundement.

II

(*p.* 25.) A woman aught not to strive with her husbonde afore straungers, as dide onis a woman that dide ansuere her husbonde afore straungeres like a rampe,[2] with gret velonis [3] wordes, dispraising hym and setting hym atte not ;[4] of the whiche he was ofte ashamed, and badde her holde

---

[1] fetch.　　[2] a virago.　　[3] villainous.　　[4] naught.

her pees for shame, but the more faire he spake, the worse
she dide.   And he, that was angri of her governaunce,
smote her with his fiste downe to the erthe.   And thanne
with hys fote he stroke her in the visage and brake her nose,
and all her lyff after she had her nose croked, the whiche
shent [1] and dysfigured her visage after, that she might not
for shame shewe her visage, it was so foule blemisshed.   And
this she had for her evell and gret langage, that she was
wont to saie to her husbonde.   And therfor the wiff aught
to suffre and lete the husbonde have the wordes, and to be
maister, for that is her worshippe ; for it is shame to here
striff betwene hem, and in especial before folke.   But I
saie not but whanne thei be allone, but she may tell hym
with goodly wordes, and counsaile hym to amende yef
he do amys.   And yef he canne [2] ani good, thanne he will
cunne [3] her moche thanke, and say she dothe as she aught
to do.

IX.   THE BACHELOR

*We must not forget, however, those who like Troilus, at the feast of
the Palladium, mocked at love and rejoiced in their freedom.   Perhaps
the best known example is Chaucer's own triple roundel with its trium-
phant close :*

> ' Sin I fro Love escaped am so fat
> I never thenk to ben in his prison lene ;
> Sin I am free, I counte him not a bene '.

*Two other songs may serve sufficiently for further illustration of this
attitude.*

I

THE BACHELOR'S SONG

This song was first printed by T. Wright for the Percy Society in his
Songs and Carols.   *It was probably written between* 1460–1490.

A, a, a, o,[4]
Yet I love wherso I go.

[1] spoilt.   [2] knows.
[3] acknowledge her service with much thanks.   [4] MS. a.

In all this warld nis [1] a meryar life
Than is a yong man withoutyn a wyfe;
For he may lyven withoughten stryfe,
  In every place wherso he go.

In every place he is loved over all
Among maydyns gret and small,
In dauncing, in pypyng, and rennyng at the ball,
  In every place wherso he go.   10

Thei lat lyght be husbondmen, [2]
Whan thei at the balle ren;
They cast hyr love to yonge men
  In every place wherso he go.

Than sey maydens: ' Farwell, Jake.'
Thi love is pressyd al in thi pake;
Thou beryst thi love behynd thi back,
  In every place wherso he go.

II

SOUR GRAPES

This travesty of the conventional ballade *is attributed to Hoccleve
and is printed in his* Minor Poems II, *ed. Sir I. Gollancz, E.E.T.S.
(E.S.), LXXIII, 1925.*

Of my lady, wel me rejoise I may;
  Hir golden forhead is ful narw [3] and smal;
  Hir browes been lyk to dym reed coral;
  And as the jeet hir yen [4] glistren ay.

Hir bowgy cheekes been as softe as clay,
  With large jowes and substancial.
Of my lady, (&c.

Hir nose a pentice [5] is, that it ne shal
  Reyne in hir mowth thogh shee vp-rightes lay.
Of (my lady &c.   10

---

[1] [there] is not.   [2] they that are readily married.   [3] narrow.
                 [4] eyes.   [5] pent-house.

Hir mowth is nothyng scant with lippes gray
  Hir chin unnethe [1] may be seen at al ;
  Hir comly body shape as a foot-bal :
  And shee syngith ful lyk a pape-Jay.
Of (my Lady &c.

X. ADVICE TO THE YOUNG

*The absolute domination of children by their parents, especially by
the father, was even more absolute in the Middle Ages than was the theory
and practice of supremacy of husband over wife. All contemporary
accounts insist on this and admonish children to be meek and obedient.
Many tracts or instructional treatises were written to explain to the
would-be aspirant to gentility how he should behave.*

*It has been suggested that they illustrate the proposed change that was
being effected in the social structure about this time; and that the*
nouveaux riches, *wishing to adopt the manners and customs of the
society to which they had attained, found it useful to have a book of
etiquette at their side. Many of these were collected and published in a
most interesting volume by F. J. Furnivall, entitled* Manners and Meals
in Olden Times, E.E.T.S. (O.S.), 1868. *The extracts here printed
are to be found on pp. 26 and 399 of that work. Following them will
be found further extracts from the* Paston Letters *to illustrate the
relation between parents and children.*

I

My dere childe, first thiself enable
With all thin herte to vertuous disciplyne
Afor thi soverayne standing at the table,
Dispose thi youth aftir my doctryne
To all norture thi corage [2] to enclyne.
First when thu spekist be not rekles,
Kepe feete and fingeris and handes still in pese.

Be symple of chiere, cast nat thyn eye aside,
Agenst the post lete nat thy bak abyde ;
Gaase nat aboute, tournyng overalle ;   10
Make nat thy myrrour also of the walle,
Pyke nat thy nose, and in especialle
Be right wele ware, and sette hieron thi thought,
By-fore thy soverayne cracche [3] ne rubbe nought.

    [1] scarcely.   [2] heart.   [3] scratch.

Who spekithe to the in any maner place,
Rudely cast nat thyn eye adowne,
But with a sadde [1] chiere loke hym in the face;
Walke demurely by strete in the towne,
Advertise thee withe Wisdom and Reasoune.
Withe dissolute laughters do thow non offence   20
To-fore thy soverayn, whiles he is in presence.

Pare clene thy nailes, thyn handes wasshe also
To-fore mete, and whan thow dooest arise;
Sitte in that place thow art assigned to;
Prease [2] nat to hye in no maner wise;
And til thow se afore thee thy service.
Be nat to hasty on brede for to byte,
Of gredynesse lest men wolde the endwyte.

Grennyng and mowes [3] at the table eschowe;
Cry nat to lowde; kepe honestly silence;   30
To enboce [4] thy jowis [5] withe mete is nat diewe;
Withe ful mowthe speke nat, lest thow do offence;
Drynke nat bretheles for hast ne necligence;
Kepe clene thy lippes from fat of flesshe or fisshe;
Wype clene thi spone, leve it nat in thy disshe

Of brede I-byten no soppis that thow make;
In ale nor wyne withe hande leve no fattenes;
Withe mowthe enbrewed [6] thy cuppe thow nat take;
Enbrewe no napery for no rekelesnes;
For to souppe loude is agenst gentiles;   40
Never at mete begynne thow nat stryf;
Thi tethe also thow pike nat withe no knyf.

Of honest myrthe late [7] be thy daliaunce; [8]
Swere none othes, speke no ribawdrye;
The best morsel, have in remembraunce,
Hole to thyself alwey do nat applie;
. Part [9] withe thy felaw, for that is curtesie:
Laade nat thy trenchour withe many remyssailes; [10]
And from blaknes alwey kepe thy nayles.

[1] steadfast.   [2] press.   [3] grimaces.   [4] bulge out.   [5] jaws.
      [6] wet.   [7] let.   [8] sport.   [9] share.   [10] remnants.

Of curtesye also agenst the lawe,   50
Withe sowne [1] dishonest for to do offence ;
Of old surfaytes [2] abrayde [3] nat thy felawe ;
Toward thy soverayne alwey thyn advertence ;
Play withe no knyf, take heede to my sentence ;
At mete and soupper kepe thee stille and soft ;
Eke to and fro meve [4] nat thy foote to oft.

Droppe nat thy brest withe sawce ne withe potage ;
Brynge no knyves unskoured to the table ;
Fil nat thy spone, lest in the cariage
It went beside, whiche were nat comendable ;   60
Be quyke and redy, meke and servisable,
Wele awaityng to fulfille anone
What that thy soverayne comaundithe the to be done.

And whereso ever that thow dyne or soupe,
Of gentilesse take salt withe thy knyf ;
And be wele ware thow blow nat in the cuppe.
Reverence thy felawe, gynne withe hym no stryf ;
By thy powere kepe pees al thy lyf.
Interrupt nat, where so thow wende,
None other mans tale, til he have made an ende ; 70

Withe thy fyngres make thow nat thy tale ;
Be wele avised, namly [5] in tendre age,
To drynk by mesure [6] bothe wyne and ale ;
Be nat copious also of langage ;
As tyme requyrithe, shewe (not) thy visage,
To gladde ne to sory, but kepe atwene tweyne,
For losse or lucre or any case sodayne.

Be meke in mesure, nat hasti, but tretable ; [7]
Over moche is nat worthe in no maner thyng ;
To children it longithe nat to be vengeable,   80
Sone meeved and sone forgyvyng ;
And as it is remembrid bi writyng,
Wrathe of children is sone overgone,
With an apple the parties be made atone.

[1] sounds.   [2] excesses.   [3] upbraid.   [4] move.   [5] especially.
[6] moderately.   [7] tractable.

In children werre [1] now myrthe and now debate,
In theyr quarel no grete violence ;
Now pley, now wepyng, (selde) in one estate ;
To theyr playntes gyve no credence ;
A rodde refourmythe al theyr insolence ;
In theyr corage no rancour dothe abyde ;   90
Who sparithe the yerd, [2] al vertu set aside.

Go, litel bille, bareyn of eloquence,
Pray yonge children that the shal see or reede,
Thoughe thow be compendious of sentence,
Of thi clauses for to taken heede,
Whiche to al vertu shal theyr yowthe leede.
Of the writyng, thoughe ther be no date,
If ought be (a)mysse—worde, sillable, or dede,—
Put al the defaute upon John Lydegate.

II

All maner chyldryn, ye lysten and lere
A lesson of wysedome that ys wryte here !
My chyld, I rede [3] the be wys, and take hede of this ryme !
Old men yn proverbe sayde by old tyme
' A chyld were beter to be unbore
Than to be untaught, and so be lore.'
The chyld that hath hys wyll alway
Shal thryve late, I thei [4] wel say,
And ther-for every gode mannys chyld
That is to wanton and to wyld,   10
Lerne wel this lesson for sertayn,
That thou may be the beter man.
Chyld, I warne thee yn all wyse
That thu tel trowth and make no lyes.
Chyld, be not froward, be not prowde,
But hold up thy hedde and speke a-lowde ;
And when eny man spekyth to the,
Do of thy hode [5] and bow thy kne,

[1] contend.   [2] rod.   [3] advise.   [4] thee.   [5] Doff thy hood.

And waysch thy handes and thy face,
And be curteys yn every place. 20
And where thou comyst, with gode chere
In halle or bowre, bydde 'God be here!'
Loke thou cast to no mannes dogge,
With staff ne stone at hors ne hogge;
Loke that thou not scorne ne jape
Nother with man, maydyn, ne ape;
Lete no man of thee make playnt;
Swere thou not by God, nother by saynt.
Loke thou be curteys stondyng at mete;
And that men gevyth thee, thou take and ete; 30
And loke that thou nother crye ne crave,
And say, 'that and that wold ye have;'
But stond thou stylle be-fore the borde,
And loke thou speke no lowde worde.
And, chyld, wyrshep thy fader and thy moder,
And loke that thou greve nother on ne other,
But ever among thou shalt knele adowne,
And aske here blessyng and here benesowne.
And, chyld, kepe thy clothes fayre and clene,
And lete no fowle fylth on hem be sene. 40
Chyld, clem thou not over hows ne walle
For no frute, bryddes, ne balle;
And, chyld, cast no stonys over men hows,
Ne cast no stonys at no glas wyndowys;
Ne make no crying, yapis,[1] ne playes,
In holy chyrche on holy dayes.
And, chyld, I warne thee of another thynge,
Kepe thee fro many wordes and yangelyng.[2]
And, chyld, whan thou gost to play,
Loke thou come home by lyght of day. 50
And, chyld, I warne the of a-nother mater,
Loke thou kepe thee wel fro fyre and water;
And be ware and wyse how that thou lokys
Over any brynk, welle, or brokys;
And when thou stondyst at any schate,[3]

[1] jests.   [2] quarrels.   [3] ? fence.

4

By ware and wyse that thou cacche no stake,
For meny chyld with-out drede
Ys dede or dysseyvyd throw ywell hede.
Chyld, kepe thy boke, cappe, and glovys,
And al thyng that thee behovys ;   60
And but thou do, thou shat fare the wors,

.   .   .   .

Chyld, be thou lyer nother no theffe ;
Be thou no mecher for myscheffe.
Chyld, make thou no mowys [1] ne knakkes
Be-fore no men, ne by-hynd here bakkes,
But be of fayre semelaunt and contenaunce,
For by fayre manerys men may thee a-vaunce.
Chyld whan thou gost yn eny strete,
Iff thou eny gode man or woman mete,
Avale [2] thy hode to hym or to here,   70
And bydde, ' God spede dame or sere ! '
And be they smalle or grete,
This lesson that thou not for-gete,—
For hyt is semely to every mannys chylde,—
And namely to clerkes to be meke and mylde.
And, chyld, rise by tyme and go to scole,
And fare not as wanton fole,
And lerne as fast as thou may and can,
For owre byschop is an old man,
And ther-for thou most lerne fast   80
Iff thou wolt be bysshop when he is past.
Chyld, I bydde the on my blessyng
That thou for-gete nat this for no thyng,
But thou loke, hold hyt wel on thy mynde
For the best thu shalt hyt fynde ;
For, as the wyse man sayth and prevyth,
A leve [3] chyld, lore he be-hovyth ; [4]
And as men sayth that ben leryd, [5]
He hatyth the chyld that sparyth the rodde ;
And as the wyse man sayth yn his boke   90
Off proverbis and wysedomes, ho wol loke,

[1] faces.   [2] Lower.   [3] good.   [4] needeth learning.   [5] learned.

'As a sharppe spore makyth an hors to renne
Under a man that shold werre wynne,
Ryght so a gerde [1] may make a chyld
To lerne welle hys lesson, and to be myld.'
Lo, chyldryn, here may ye al here and se
How al chyldryn chastyd shold be ;
And therfor, chyldere, loke that ye do well,
And no harde betyng shall ye be-falle :
Thys may ye al be ryght gode men.   100
God graunt yow grace so to preserve yow.
                                        Amen !

XI. A REFRACTORY SON

*John Paston had fallen foul of his father for some unknown reason,
and was in disgrace.   Despite the fact that, at this time, he was a grown
man, the following extracts will show how strong was the convention
which insisted on the father's right to implicit obedience from his children whatever their standing might be.*

I

[John Paston, the Elder Son, to his Father.   ' P.L.' No. 323]

5 *March,* 1459

To my ryght wyrschypful fadre, John Paston, Esquyer,
    be thys letter delyveryd in hasty wyse.

RYGHT worschypful Syr, in the most lowly wyse, I comaund
me to yowr good faderhod, besechyng yow of yowre
blyssyng.   Mut it plese yowr faderhod to remembre and
concydre the peyn and hevynesse that it hath ben to me
syn yowr departyng owt of thys contre, here abydyng tyl
the tyme it please yow to schewe me grace, and tyl the
tyme that by reporte my demenyng be to yowr plesyng ;
besechyng yow to concydre that I may not, ner have noo
mene to seke to yow as I awght to do, and savyng under
thys forme, whych I besech yow be not take to no dysplesur,

¹ rod.

ner am not of power to do any thynge in thys contre for
worschyp or profyht of yow, ner ease of yowr tenantys
whych myght and scholde be to yowr pleasyng.   Wherfor
I besech yow of yowr faderly pyte to tendre the more thys
symple wryghtyng, as I schal owt of dowght her after doo
that schal please yow to the uttermest of my power and
labor ; and if ther be any servyce that I may do if it please
yow to comaund me, of if y maye understonde it, I wyl
be as glad to do it as any thyng erthely, if it wer any thyng
that myght be to yowr pleasyng. And no mor, but
Allmyghty God have yow in kepyng.

Wretyn the v. day of Marche.

By your older sone,

JOHN PASTON.

II

[Margaret Paston to John Paston. ' P.L.' No. 325]

29 April, 1459

Tho my ryth worschopffull hossebond, John Paston, in hast.

RYTHE worchepfwl hosbond, I recommawnd me onto yow
. . . I prey yow that ye vowchesaf to send word in hast
how ye wyl that yor sone be demenyd herin.   Men thynk
her, that ben yowr wel wyllerys,[1] that ye may no lesse do
than to send hym forthe.   As for hys demenyng, swn [2] ye
departyd, in god feythe, it hath ben ryth good, and lowly,
and delygent inn ovyr sythe [3] of yowre servawntys, and
odyr thinggys, the whiche I hope ye wold abe plesyd wyth,
and ye had be at hom.   I hope he wyl be well demenyd
to plese yow heraftyrward. He desyryd Alblaster to
bemene [4] to yow for hym, and was ryte hevy of hys
demenyng to yow, as I sent yow word also be Alblaster,
how I dede to hym aftyr that ye wer go ; and I beseche
yow hartyly that ye wocheshaf to be hys god fadyr, for I
hope he is schastysyd, and wil be the worher [5] heraftyr. . . .

_____

[1] well-willers.   [2] since.   [3] over-sight.   [4] plead.   [5] worthier.

Wretyn in hast at Norwece, on the Sonday next before
the Assencyon Day. Ser, I wold be ryte glad to he[ar]
somme gode tydynggs fro yow.

Be yorys,

M. P.

XII. AN UNWANTED DAUGHTER

*The practice of boarding out children in the houses of powerful lords
or rich patrons was a common one at this time and was noticed with
surprise by the Venetian author of* The Italian Relation of England
(Camden Society 1847). *He tells us that he was told that people did it
' in order that their children might learn better manners '. However
true this may have been in a few instances, there can be little doubt that
many people did it, as did the writer of this letter, hoping that material
advantages of worldly advancement or a profitable marriage might
ensue.*

[*Margaret Paston to John Paston the Younger.* ' P.L.'
No. LXV]

Before 1466.

I GRETE you wele, letyng you wete that as for your sustrys
beyng with my Lady, if your fader wull aggrey therto I
hold me right wele pleasyd ; for I wuld be right glad that
she shuld do her servyse be for any other, if she cowde do
that shuld pleas my ladyes good grace. Wherfor I wuld
that ye shuld speke to your fader therof and lete hym wete
that I am pleasid that she shuld be ther if he wuld, for I
wuld be right glad and she myght be preferrid by mariage
or be servyce, so that it myght be to her wurchep and
profight in dischargyng of her frendis ; and I pray you do
your parte therin for your owyn wurchep and herys.[1] And
assone as ye may with ought daunger, purvey that I may
have ageyn the vj. marks that ye wote of, for I wuld not
that your fader wust [2] it. Item, if ye pas London, send
me ageyn my chene and the litill chene that I lent you
be for, be sum trusty person ; and if ye wull have my good
wille, eschewe such thyngis as I spake to you of last in owr

[1] hers. [2] knew.

parisch chirch. I pray God make you as good a man as ever was any of your kynne, and Goddis blissyng mote ye have and myn, so that ye do wele, &c. Wretyn the Sonday next after your departyng.

And I pray you, send me sum tydyngis as sone as ye may after that ye be comyn to London, how your fader spedyth and your brother in here materes. Be your moder.

XIII. A FIFTEENTH-CENTURY SCHOOLBOY

Besides the education which was to be gained from being thrown into life in other people's houses, etc., there was a more formal type of learning provided. Many families made use of a private tutor, while others sent their sons to schools ; one of the Pastons was at Eton (see above, p. 18), while others were at Cambridge and London at various times. Here is a letter concerning one of them, which is followed first by Lydgate's account of his own early school-days, and then by a cri de cœur which has a curiously modern ring about it.

Erands to London of Augnes Paston, the xxviij. day of Jenure, the yer of Kyng Henry the Sext, xxxvj. (28 Jan. 1458). 'P.L.' No. 311.

To prey Grenefeld to send me feythfully word, by wrytyn, who [1] Clement Paston hath do his dever [2] in lernyng. And if he hathe nought do well, nor wyll nought amend, prey hym that he wyll trewly belassch hym, tyl he wyll amend ; and so ded the last maystr, and the best that ever he had, att Caumbrege. And sey Grenefeld that if he wyll take up on hym to brynge hym in to good rewyll and lernyng, that I may verily know he doth hys dever, I wyll geve hym x. marcs [3] for hys labor, for I had lever he wer fayr beryed than lost for defaute.

Item, to se who many gownys Clement hathe ; and the that be bar, late hem be reysyd.[4] He hathe achort [5] grene gowne, and achort musterdevelers [6] gowne, [which] wer never reysyd ; and achort blew gowne that was reysyd, and mad of a syde gowne, whan I was last at London ; and asyde russet gowne, furryd with bevyr,

---

[1] how. [2] duty. [3] £6 13s. 4d. [4] i.e. let them have a new nap set upon them. [5] a short. [6] a mixed grey woollen cloth.

was mad this tyme ij. year ; and asyde murry [1] gowne was mad this tyme twelmonth.

Item, to do make me [2] vj. sponys, of viij. ounce of troy wyght, well facyond and dubbyl gylt.

And sey Elyzabet Paston that she must use hyr selfe to werke redyly, as other jentylwomen done, and sumwhat to helpe hyr selfe ther with.

Item, to pay the Lady Pole . . . xxvjs. viijd. for hyr bord.[3]

And if Grenefeld have do wel hys dever to Clement, or wyll do hys dever, geffe hym the nobyll.[4]

AGNES PASTON.

XIV. JOHN LYDGATE'S YOUTH

John Lydgate, who ultimately became a monk at Bury St. Edmunds, has left the following account of his schoolboy life. Perhaps he is a little tempted here to imagine himself more undisciplined than was actually the case, but the whole forms an interesting picture of a medieval boy's life. It is reprinted with a few emendations from Minor Poems *of Lydgate, E.E.T.S. (E.S.) 1910, p. 351.*

Du᾽yng the tyme of this sesoun ver,
    (I mene, the sesoun of my yeres grene,)
Gynnyng fro chyldhode strecched up so fer
    To the yeres accounted ffull fyftene,
    B' experyence, as it was weel sene,
The geryssh [5] sesoun, straunge of condiciouns,
Disposed me to unbrydeled passiouns.

Voyd of resoon, given to wilfulnesse,
    Froward to vertu, of thryfte take litel hede,
Loth to lerne, I loved no besynesse,   10
    Save pley or merth ; was straunge to spelle or rede,
    Folowyng alle appetytes longyng to childhede,
Lyghtly turnyng, wylde and selden [6] sad,
Wepyng for nowght, and anone after glad.

---

[1] purple-red. [2] get made for me. [3] see above, p. 41. [4] 6s. 8d.
[5] garish. [6] seldom.

For litel wroth to stryve with my felawe,
  As my passiouns did my brydell lede,
Of the yerd [1] sumtyme I stood in awe,
  To be skowr(g)ed, that was al my drede ;
  Loth toward skole, I lost my tyme in dede,
Lyke a yong colt that ran without brydell,   20
Made I my frendes ther good to spend in ydell.

I had in custome to come to skole late,
  Nat for to lerne, but for a contenaunce,[2]
With my felawes was redy to debate,
  To Jangle or Jape was sett all my pleasaunce ;
  Wherof rebuked, this was my chevesaunce,[3]
To forge a lesyng, and therupon to muse,
Whanne I trespaced, my-selven to excuse.

To my better I did no reverence,
  Of my sovereynes gaf no force [4] at all,   30
Wex obstinat by Inobedience
  Ran in-to gardeynes, apples ther I stall ;
  To gadre frutes spared nedir hegge nor wall,
To plukke grapes in other mennes vynes
Was I more redy, than for to sey matynes.

My lust was all to skorne folke and jape,
  Shrewed turnes ever among them to use ;
To skoffe and mowen like a wantoun ape ;
  Whan I dyd evele, other I koude accuse ;
  My wyttes fyve in waste I did all use,   40
Redier cheri-stones for to telle
Than gon to chirche, or here the sacryng belle.

Loth to ryse, lother to bedde at eve,
  With unwasshe hondes redy to dyner,
My pater noster, my crede, or my beleve,
  Cast atte cok, lo, this was my maner !
  Waved with eche wynd, as doth a reedspere,

[1] rod.   [2] appearance.   [3] trick.   [4] heed.

Snybbed of my frendes, sucche teeches [1] t'amende,
Made a deef ere, list not to them attende.

A chyld resemblyng which was not lyke to thryve,   50
  Froward to God, rekles in his servyce,
Loth to correccioun, slow my-selve to shryve.
  All good themes redy to despise,
  Chief bel-wether of (feynyd) truandice,
This is to mene, myself I coude feyne,
Sicke like a truant, and felt no maner peyne.

My port, my pas, my foot allwey unstable,
  My loke, myn eyen, unsure and vagabound,
In alle my werkes sodeynly chaungeable,
  To all good themes contrarye I was founde,   60
  Now oversadd, now mornyng, now jocunde,
Wilfull, rekles, made stertyng as a hare,
To folowe my lust for no man wold I spare.

XV. THE SCHOOLBOY'S SONG

This poem is dated about 1500 *by F. J. Furnivall, who prints
it in his* Manners and Meals in Olden Time, *E.E.T.S. (O.S.)* 1868,
p. 403.

  HAY! hay! by this day!
  What avayleth it me thowgh I say nay?

  I wold ffayn be a clarke;
  But yet hit is a strange werke;
  The byrchyn twyggis be so sharpe,
  Hit makith me have a faynt harte.
    What avaylith it me thowgh I say nay!

  On Monday in the mornyng whan I shall rise
  At six of the clok, hyt is the gise
  To go to skole without a-vise   10
  I had lever go twenti myle twyse!
    What avaylith it me thowgh I say nay?

        [1] faults.

My master lokith as he were madde :
' Wher hast thou be, thow sory ladde ? '
' Milked dukkis, my moder badde ' :
Hit was no mervayle, thow I were sadde.
   What vaylith it me thowgh I say nay ?

  .   .   .   .

I wold my master were a watt [1]
And my boke a wyld Catt,
And a brase of grehowndis in his toppe :   20
I wold be glade for to se that !
   What vayleth it me thowgh I say nay ?

I wold my master were an hare,
And all his bokis howndis were,
And I myself a joly hontere :
To blowe my horn I wold not spare !
Ffor if he were dede I wold not care.
   What vaylith me thowgh I say nay ?

XVI. A TRADESMAN'S LETTER

*This letter from Thomas Bradbury, a London mercer, has a modern
touch about it, with its suave reasoning as to the ultimate economy of
taking the best.*

[*Thomas Bradbury to Dame Elizabeth Stonor.* ' S.L.' No.
252]

15 *Oct.*, 1479.

AFTER due ffourme I recommaunde me unto your ladyship
lyke it you to wytte that I have R (eceived) a letter fro
you by Master Makeney, and accordyng to your letter I
send you : that is :—
vj. elles holland at ij s. an ell, Summa,   xij. s.
Itm. ij elles holland at ij s. viij d., Summa,   v. s. iiij. d.
Itm. xij elles holland at xvj d. Summa,   xvj. s.
Itm. xxxviij yerdes grene sarcenet [2] at v s. the yerd,
                         Summa, ix. li. x. s

     [1] a hare.   [2] a fine and soft cloth.

Itm. j. p. greene bokame [1] to lyne it with, pris, vj s. viij. d. Totalis, xj. li. x. s.

Madame, the sarcenet is verry ffyne. I thynke most profytable and most worshipfull for you, and shall (last) you your lyff and your chyldes after you, wher as harlatry [2] of xl. d. or xliiij. d. a yerd wold nat indure too sesons with you : Therfor for a lytill more cost, me thinketh most wysdom to take of the best. In certen I have bought the most part of the sarcenet, for I had nat I-now to perfourme yt. I wynne never a peny in that [3] &c. I shall see your ladyship hastly by Goddes grace, who preserve you to his plesour &c. Wret at London the xv daye of Octobr., A⁰ lxxix.

Be your servaunt, Thomas Bradbury.

To my right worshipful Dame Elizabeth Stonore be this delivered.

XVII. A ROYAL FEAST

Eating and drinking played a considerable part in medieval home life. The poor dwellers in cots had to make the best of what meagre victuals came their way (see pp. 49 and 68 ff.), and Extract XVIII confirms this ; but we may see from the anonymous fourteenth-century poem Winner and Waster *how elaborate and profuse a royal meal could be. Our extract is taken from Sir Israel Gollancz's edition, ll. 325 ff.*

Bot than this wrechede wynnere full wrothely [4] he lukes,
Sayse, ' This es spedles speche to speken thies wordes !
Loo, th(ou) w(eryed) [5] wastoure, that wyde-whare es knawenn,
Ne es nothir kaysser, ne kynge, ne knyghte that the folowes,
Barone, ne bachelere, ne beryn [6] that thou loveste,
Bot foure felawes or fyve, that the fayth ow(es) ;
And (thou) schall dighte thaym to dyne with dayntethes so many
That iche a wy [7] in this werlde may wepyn for sorowe.

---

[1] buckram.   [2] inferior stuff.   [3] i.e. you have it at cost price.
[4] wrathfully.   [5] accursed.   [6] burgess.   [7] man.

The bores hede schall be broghte with (bayes) appon lofte,
Buk-tayles full brode in brothes there be-syde, 10
Venyson with the frumentes,[1] and fesanttes full riche,
Baken mete ther-by one the burde [2] sett,
Chewettes of choppede flesche, charbiande fewlis,[3]
And iche a segge [4] that I see has sexe mens doke.[5]
If this were nedles note, anothir comes aftir,—
Roste with the riche sewes,[6] and the ryalle spyces,
Kiddes cleven by the rigge, quarter(e)d swannes,
Tartes of ten ynche. That tenys myn hert [7]
To see the borde over-brade [8] with blasande disches,
Als it were a rayled rode [9] with rynges and stones. 20
The thirde mese to me were meruelle to rekken,
For alle es Martynmesse mete that I with moste dele,
Noghte bot worttes [10] with the flesche, with-owt wilde
      fowle,
Save ane hene to hym that the howse owethe ; [11]
And (y)e will hafe birdes bownn [12] one a broche riche,
Barnakes [13] and buturs [14] and many billed snyppes,
Larkes and lyngwhittes,[15] lapped in sogoure,
Wodcokkes and wodwales,[16] full wellande [17] hote,
Teeles and titmoyses, to take what (yowe) lykes ;
(Caudel)s of conynges,[18] & custadis swete, 30
(Daryo)ls [19] & dische-metis, that ful dere coste,
(Mawme) ne that men clepen, your mawes to fill,
(Twelve) mese at a merke,[20] by-twen twa men,
(Thog)he bot brynneth [21] for bale your bowells with-in.
(Me ten)yth [22] at your trompers, thay tounen [23] so heghe
(That iche) a gome in the gate goullyng may here :[24]
(Than) wil thay say to tham-selfe, as thay samen [25] ryden,
Ye hafe no myster [26] of the helpe of the heven kyng.

---

[1] dish of wheat boiled in milk. [2] board. [3] grilled chickens.
[4] every man. [5] shares. [6] sauces. [7] It pains my heart.
[8] covered. [9] rood adorned. [10] vegetables. [11] owns.
[12] prepared. [13] barnack-geese. [14] bitterns. [15] linnets.
[16] wood-peckers. [17] boiling. [18] hot broths of rabbits. [19] pasties.
[20] dishes at a time. [21] burneth. [22] vex. [23] blow. [24] that every
man on the way may hear their howling. [25] together. [26] need.

Thus are ye scorned by skyll, & scathed theraftir,
That rechen [1] for a repaste a rawnsom of silver.   40
Bot one(s) I herd in a haule [2] of a herdmans tong,—
' Better were meles many than a mery nyghte.'

XVIII. SHEPHERD'S FARE

[Chester Plays, ed. H. Deimling, E.E.T.S. (E.S.) LXII,
1893, *p.* 137]

HERE is bread this day was baken,
Onyons, garlik, and lyckes,[3]
Butter that bought was in Blacon,
And greene [4] cheese that will grease your cheekes.

And here ale of Halton I have,
And what meat I had to my hyre !
A pudding maye no man deprave ;
And a Janock [5] of Lancashyre.

Lo ! here a sheepes head souced in ale,
And a groyne to lay on the grene,   10
And soure mylke my wife had on sale :
A noble supper as well is seene.

.   .   .   .

Nowe will I cast of my Cloake,
And pull out parte of my livery,
Pull out that I have in my poke,
And a pigges foote from pudding purie

.   .   .   .

And that is in my sachell to shake out,
To shepheardes am I not ashamed :
This Ox tongue, pared round about,
For your tooth it shall be attamed.[6]   20

[1] give.   [2] hall.   [3] leeks.   [4] fresh.   [5] oat-cake.   [6] begun.

XIX. FINE FEATHERS

The excessive display of costume was much complained of by many
fifteenth-century writers. Dresses became fantastic and quite unsuited
for everyday use. The following passage is from Hoccleve's Regement
of Princes, *E.E.T.S. (E.S.) 1897, pp. 16 ff.*

BUT this me thinkith an abusioun,
To se on [1] walke in gownes of scarlet,
Twelve yerdes wyd, with pendant sleves downe
On the grounde, and the furrour therin set
Amountyng unto twenty pound or bet; [2]
And if he for it payde have, he no good
Hath lefte him where-with for to bye an hood.

For thogh he jette [3] forth among the prees,
And overloke everey pore wight,
His cofre and eke his purs ben penylees,   10
He hath no more than he goth in ryght.
For lond, rent, or catel, he may go light;
The weght of hem schal not so moche peyse [4]
As doth his gowne. Is swiche array to preyse?

Nay sothely, sone, it is al amys me thinkyth;
So pore a wight his lord to counterfete
In his array, in my conceyit it stynkith.
Certes to blame ben the lordes grete,
If that I durste seyn, that hir men lete
Usurpe swiche a lordly apparaille,   20
Is not worth, my childe, withouten fayle.

Som tyme, afer [5] men myghten lordes knowe
By there array, from other folke; but now
A man schal stody and musen a long throwe [6]
Whiche is whiche: O lordes, it sit [7] to yowe
Amende this, for it is for youre prowe. [8]
If twixt yow and youre men no difference
Be in array, lesse is youre reverence.

[1] one.   [2] better.   [3] strut.   [4] weigh.   [5] from afar.   [6] time.
[7] belongs.   [8] profit.

Also ther is another newe get,[1]
A foul wast of cloth and an excessyf ;   30
Ther goth no lesse in a mannes tipet
Than of brood cloth a yerde, by my lif ;
Me thynkyth this a verray inductif
Unto stelthe : ware hem of Hempen Lane !
For stelthe is medid with a chekelew bane.[2]

Let evere lord, his owne men deffende [3]
Swiche gret array, and than, on my peryl,
This land within a while schal amende.
In Goddys name, putte it in exyl !
It is synne outragious and vyl ;   40
Lordes, if ye your estat and honour
Loven, fleemyth [4] this vicius errour !

What is a lord withouten his meynee ? [5]
I putte cas that his foos hym assaile
Sodenly in the stret. What help schale he,
Wos sleeves encombrous so syde [6] traille,
Do to his lord ? He may hym nat availle ;
In swych a cas he nys but a womman ;
He may nat stand hym in steed of a man.

His armys two han ryght ynow to done,   50
And sumwhat more, his sleeves up to holde ;
The taillours, trow I, moot heerafter soone
Shape in the feeld ; thay shal nat sprede and folde
On hir bord, thogh thei never so fayn wolde,
The cloth that shal ben in a gowne wroght ;
Take an hool cloth is best, for lesse is noght.

The skynner unto the feeld moot also,
His hous in London is to streyt and scars
To doon his craft ; sum tyme it was nat so.
O lordes, yeve unto your men hir pars [7]   60

[1] fashion.   [2] Stealing is rewarded with a choking death.
[3] forbid.   [4] banish.   [5] retinue.   [6] wide.   [7] portions.

That so doon, and aqwente hem bet with Mars,
God of bataile ; he loveth non array
That hurtyth manhode at preef [1] or assay.

Who now moost may bere on his bak at ones
Of cloth and furrour, hath a fressch renoun ;
He is ' a lusty man ' clept for the nones ;
But drapers and eek skynners in the toun,
For swich folk han a special orisoun
That troppid [2] is with curses heere and there,
And ay schal, til thei paid be for hir gere.   70

In dayes olde, whan smal apparaille
Suffisid unto hy estat or mene,
Was gret houshold wel stuffid of victaille ;
But now housholdes ben ful sclender and lene.
For al the good that men may repe or glene,
Wasted is in outrageous array,
So that housholdes man nat holde may.

Pryde hath wel lever [3] bere an hungry mawe
To bedde, than lakke of array outrage ;
He no prys settith be mesures lawe,   80
Ne takith of hym clothe, mete, ne wage :
Mesure is out of londe on pylgrymage ;
But I suppose he schal resorte as blyve, [4]
For verray neede wol us therto dryve.

Ther may no lord tak up no newe gyse
But that a knave shal the same up take.
If lordes wolden in this wyse,
For to do [5] swiche gownes to hem make
As men did in old tyme, I undertake
The same jet [6] sholde up be take and usid,   90
And al'this costelew outrage [7] refusid.

. . . .

---

[1] proof.   [2] sprinkled.   [3] rather.   [4] quickly.   [5] order.
   [6] fashion.   [7] extravagant outlay.

Now hath thise lordes but litil neede of broomes
To swepe away the filthe out of the street,
Syn syde sleves of penylees gmroes
Wile it up likke, be it drye or weet.
O Engelond ! stand upryght on thy feet !
So foul a wast in so symple degree
Bannysshe ! or sore it schal repente the.

XX. A WARDROBE REPLENISHED

This letter will serve as an example of the constant ordering and renewing of clothing that occurs throughout the Paston Letters. *Any member of the family residing in London or Norwich was liable to be worried in this way. For other examples see* P.L. *Nos.* 67, 260, 472, 528, *etc.*

[*Edmund Paston to John Paston.* ' *P.L.' No. LXXXV*]

18 *Nov.*, 1471

Tho my rytgh wurshepfull brother John Paston in hast.

RYGH wurshipful brother, I recumawnd me to zow, prayeng zow hartely that ze wyl remembyr soche maters as I wryth to zow. I send zow now be the brynggar her of mony, wycche mony I pray zow that (ye) be stowe yt as I wryth to zow. I wend a don yt [1] my sylf but consyderyng costis and other dyvers thyngis I may not bryng yt abowthe. Wher for I pray zow hartely to take the labour up on zow, and I trust to deservyt, I pray zow be stow thys mony thus : to Christofyr Hanyngton vs. : to the prynspall of Stapylin [2] vs. in parte of payment. Also I pray zow to bye me iij. zerddis of porpyl schamlet, [3] price the zerd iiijs., a bonet of depe murry, [4] pryce ijs. iiijd., an hose clothe of zelow carsey [5] of an ellyn, I trow yt wyl cost ijs. ; a gyrdyl of plunkket [6] ryban, price vjd. ; iiij. lacis of sylke ij. of one color and ij. of ane other, price viijd. ; iij. doseyn poynttis [7] wythe red and zelow, price vjd. ; iij. peyer of

---

[1] I thought to have done it.   [2] Staple Inn.   [3] a cost'₄' fabric of wool.   [4] purple-red.   [5] a coarse cloth, usually ribbed.   [6] a blue tint.   [7] tagged points or laces.

5

pateyns.[1] I pray zow late Wylliam Mylsant purvey for them.   I was wonte to pay but ijd. ob. for a payer, but I pray zow late them not be lefte behyng thow I pay mor ; they must be lowe pateyns ; late them be long inow and brode up on the hele. . . .   Also I pray zow that the welvet that levyt of my typet may be send hom a geyn, for I woold strype a dobelet ther with. . . .

EDMOND PASTON.

[1] wooden shoes, clogs, or perhaps thick-soled shoes.

SECTION TWO

VILLAGE LIFE

Medieval England was a land of few towns and many villages; it was still a rural community with its wealth of small villages and hamlets hidden away in valleys and among the uplands. Here and there was some market town which formed a convenient centre for trade and for the exchange of the produce of the country-side, Here the villagers flocked at the time of fair or weekly market. But it was in the village itself, and in the fields which they cultivated around their homes, that most of their lives were spent. They lived as a self-contained community with the Lord of the Manor controlling and dominating their earthly lives, and with the village church, towering above their insignificant cottages, reminding them of the authority which controlled and dominated their spiritual lives. Thus their outlook and activities were very circumscribed : superstition and credulity marred their thinking and the heavy daily drudgery they endured left them but little time for sports and lighter amusements. The extracts which follow attempt to illustrate the various phases of such an existence, which was the lot of a very large proportion of English men and women in Chaucer's day, and for some time afterwards.

I. THE LORD AND HIS SERVANTS

Piers Plowman gives us an admirable picture of the power of feudal custom. Piers thinks nothing of labouring to keep the ' lovely ladyes with longe fyngers ', and to support the knight so that he may hunt and go abroad with his hawks, while in return Piers and Holy Church are protected against harm and wrong-doers. Our extract comes from the B text, passus VI, ll. 1–58.

QUATH Perkyn the plouman, ' by seynt Peter of Rome,
I have an half acre to erye [1] by the heighe way ;

[1] plough.

Hadde I eried this half acre and sowen it after,
I wolde wende with yow and the way teche.'
' This were a longe lettynge ' [1] quod a lady in a sklayre,[2]
' What sholde we wommen worche there whiles ? '
' Somme shal sowe the sakke', quod Piers, ' for shedyng
of the whete ; [3]
And ye, lovely ladyes with youre longe fyngres,
That ye han silke and sendal [4] to sowe, whan tyme is,
Chesibles [5] for chapelleynes, cherches to honoure.   10
 Wyves and wydwes wolle & flex spynneth,
Maketh cloth, I conseille yow, and kenneth so yowre
doughtres ;
The nedy and the naked nymmeth [6] hede how hii [7] liggeth,
And casteth hem clothes for so comaundeth treuthe.
For I shal lene hem lyflode [8] but gif the londe faille,
Flesshe and bred bothe, to riche and to pore,
As longe as I lyve for the lordes love of hevene.
 And alle manere of men that thorw mete and drynke
lybbeth,
Helpith hym to worche wightliche [9] that wynneth yowre
fode.'
 ' Bi Crist ', quod a knyghte tho, ' he kenneth us the
best ;   20
Ac on the teme trewly taughte was I nevere.
Ac kenne [10] me,' quod the knyghte ' and, by Cryst, I will
assaye ! '[11]
 ' Bi seynt Poule,' quod Perkyn ' ye profre yow so faire,
That I shal swynke and swete and sowe for us bothe,
And other laboures do for thi love al my lyf tyme,
In covenaunt that thow kepe holikirke and my-selve
Fro wastoures and fro wykked men that this worlde
strvyeth.
 And go hunte hardiliche to hares and to foxes,
To bores and to brockes [12] that breketh adown myne
hegges,

[1] hindrance.   [2] veil.   [3] to prevent the wheat spilling.   [4] silken stuff.
[5] chasubles.   [6] take.   [7] they.   [8] give them sustenance.   [9] sturdily.
          [10] teach.   [11] try.   [12] For boars and badgers.

And go affaite [1] the faucones wilde foules to kille ;   30
For suche cometh to my croft and croppeth my whete.'
  Curteislich the knyghte thanne comsed [2] thise wordes,
' By my power, Pieres,' quod he, ' I plighte the my
    treuthe
To fulfille this forward thowgh I fighte sholde ;
Als longe as I lyve I shal the mayntene.'
  ' Ye, and yit a poynt,' quod Pieres ' I preye yow of
   ·more ;
Loke ye tene [3] no tenaunt but treuthe wil assent.
And thowgh ye mowe amercy [4] hem, late mercy be taxoure,
And mekenesse thy mayster maugre medes chekes,
And thowgh pore men profre yow presentis and giftis, 40
Nym it naughte, an aventure ye mowe it naughte deserve ; [5]
For thow shalt yelde it agein at one yeres ende,
In a ful perillous place, purgatorie it hatte.[6]
  And mysbede [7] noughte thi bonde-men the better may
    thow spede ;
Thowgh he be thyn underlynge here, wel may happe in
    hevene,
That he worth worthier sette and with more blisse,
Than thow, bot thou do bette, and lyve as thow shulde ;
    Amice, ascende superius.
For in charnel atte chirche cherles ben yvel to knowe,
Or a knighte fram a knave there. Knowe this in thin
    herte,   50
And that thow be trewe of thi tonge, and tales that thow
    hatie,[8]
But if thei ben of wisdome, or of witte thi werkmen to
    chaste.
Holde with none harlotes,[9] ne here noughte her tales,
And nameliche atte mete suche men eschue ;
For it ben the develes disoures, I do the to vnderstande.'
  ' I assente, bi seynt Jame ', seyde the knighte thanne,
' Forto worche bit thi wordes the while my lyf dureth.'

---

[1] tame.   [2] began (to say).   [3] vex.   [4] amerce.
[5] take it not, peradventure you may not deserve it.
[6] is called.   [7] misgovern.   [8] hate.   [9] loose talkers, ribalds.

II. A NIGHT PIECE

The next extracts illustrate one side of medieval village life very clearly. Constant uncertainty and constant turmoil seem to have been omnipresent, although often no doubt in a much milder degree than the total effect of these passages might suggest to the unwary. But force was constantly invoked, whether for so desperate a deed as murder or merely for the wrongful seizure of a neighbour's crop. Both the Paston Letters and many other contemporary sources are full of instances, of which the following may serve as examples.

[*James Gresham to John Paston. ' P.L.' No.* 257]

28 *Oct.*, 1455

To my right worshipfull maister, John Paston, at Norwiche, be this delyvred.

PLEASE it your maistership to wete . . . there is gret varyance bytwene the Erll of Devenshire and the Lord Bonvyle, as hath be many day, and meche debat is like to growe therby ; for on Thursday at nyght last passed, the Erll of Denshyres sone and heir come with lx. men of armes to Radford's place in Devenshire,[1] whiche was of counseil with my Lord Bonvyle ; and they sette an hous on fyer at Radfords gate, and cryed and mad an noyse as though they had be sory for the fyer ; and by that cause Radfords men set opyn the gats and yede owt to se the fyer ; and for with th'erll sone forseid entred into the place and intreted Radford to come doun of his chambre to sp(e)ke with them, promyttyng hym that he shuld no bodyly harm have ; up on whiche promysse he come doun, and spak with the seid Erll sone.

In the mene tyme his menye robbe his chambre, and ryfled his huches,[2] and trussed suyche as they coude gete to gydder, and caryed it awey on his own hors. Thanne th'erll sone seid, ' Radford, thou must come to my lord my fadir.' He seid he wold, and bad oon of his men make

---

[1] ' Nicolas Radford was a lawyer who lived at Poghill, near Kyrton, co. Devon.'—Fenn.
[2] chests containing clothes, deeds, etc.

redy his hors to ride with hem, whiche answerd hym that alle his hors wern take awey. Thanne he seid to th'erll sone, ' Sir, your men have robbed my chambre, and thei have myn hors, that I may not ride with you to my lord your fadir ; wherfor, I pray you, lete me ride, for I am old, and may not go.'

It was answerid hym ageyn, that he shuld walke forth with them on his feete ; and so he dede till he was a flyte shote or more from his place, and thanne he was [1] . . . softly, for cawse he myght not go fast. And whanne thei were thus departed, he turned . . . oon ; forwith come ix. men ageyn up on hym, and smot hym in the hed, and fellid . . . of them kyt his throte. . . .

Yowr poer,

J. GR.

III. A LANDLORD'S ' TRIALS '

This letter, also from the Paston Correspondence, gives us a picture of manorial affairs as seen from the landowner's point of view.

[James Gloys to John Paston. ' P.L.' No. 146]

1 *March*, 1451

To my right reverente and wurchepfull Mayster, John Paston, Esquyer, be this delivered in hast.

RIGHT reverent and wurchepfull Sir, I recomand me to you, besechyng you to wete that Wharles . . . told my mayster, John of Berney, at the court,[2] that he repented hym that he payd you any peny till he had be [3] distreyned ; and he seid than pleynly that he wull nomore pay till he were distreyned. I have be there divers tymes for to distreyn hym, and I cowde never do it but if [4] I wuld a [5] distreyned hym in his moders hous, and there I durst not for her cursyng. The baly of the hundred told me that Wharles spake to hym in cas he had be distreyned that

---

[1] From this point the MS. is decayed.   [2] Manor Court.
[3] been.   [4] unless.   [5] have.

he wold have gete hym a replevy;[1] and the baly bad hym kete a replevy of his mayster and he wold serve it.

Item, the maner lonibs at Gresham, with othre tenaunts londs that be fallyn in your hands ben letyn to ferme.[2] I can gete no tenaunte to dwell in the maner hous. And if the rede shuld be caryed thens, the tenaunts shuld thynk that ye fered sum new entre, and it shuld sore discomfort hem, for thei whisshed whan it was caried to the maner that it had be leyd ther thus pesibly ij. yer afore. Asfor the obligacyon that ye shuld have of the parson of Cressyngham, he seth he cam never at Cressyngham syth he spake with you, and that he be heste it you not till Fastyngong.[3] His hors ben stolyn, and therfore he may not ryde.

Item, Gonnore kept a court at Routon the Thursday next after Seynt Mathy [4] the Appostell, and it was told me that Bettes was ther with hym; wherefore I rode theder. And be cause that it was a fraunchised town and within the Duchye,[5] and also that Gonnor had gret rewle in the seid town, I toke with me the baly of the hundred and set hym with me in my Lord of Norffolks warant, and than yede [6] in to the court ther as Gonnor and Bettes wern. The seid baly told Gonnor of this warant, and Gonnor rebuked hym so that he durst not a rest the seid Bettes. Than I toke it up on me and arested hym myself as he sate be Gonnor. Gonnor desired than to se my warant, and I shewed it hym, and he seid he wold obey it as the lawe wold. And he proferyd me suerte,[7] men of the seid town of Routon. Than I told hym, and [8] he wold be bownd hym self with othre I would agre ther to, but I wuld have no shipmen that had nought, ner such men that rought [9] never, and thei were onys on the see, wheder thei come ageyn or noght. Than Bettes toke Gonnor a *supersedias* [10] that he had of Wychyngham twelmoneth

---

[1] a writ ordering the return of the distrained goods until the case has been tried.   [2] at a fixed rental.   [3] Shrove Tuesday: the 9th March in 1451.   [4] St. Matthew.   [5] Duchy of Lancaster.   [6] went.   [7] surety.   [8] if.   [9] cared.   [10] a writ staying proceedings, on good cause shown, which otherwise ought to proceed.

ago for anothre man that asked suerte of the seid Bettes.
I wold have had it, and he wold not lete me have it, ner
shewe it me but in his hands. Than I told hym that it
was noght, and he seid it was gode i nowe. I bad hym
take it me for my discharge, and he seid pleynly I
shuld not have it. Than I told hym I wold have my
prisoner. The seid Gonnor seid I shuld not have hym,
and dede set alle the tenaunts up on me and made a gret
noyse, and seydyn alle pleynly I shuld not have hym yf
he wold abyde with hem. Than I told Gonnor that I
shuld certifie a *rescuse*,[1] and prayd the baly of the hundred
that he wold record the same. Item, the seid Gonnor
seid I myght have favoryd the seid Bettes the more be
cause the seid Bettes was my mayster Stapylton man,
and that his men shuld not be bownd and I shuld go lose.
He seid I shuld be tyed or aght longe and alle my feleshep
bothyn ;[2] but, God yeld hym, he hath yovyn me iiij.
days respyte. Than I told hym it shuld never ly in his
power to bynde me, ner non of my feleshep so fast but
that it shuld be in your power to make hym to losyn
us, and if that he abode in Norffolk he shuld be made to
seke the skyrts of his sadill or Esterne.[3] And if he had
kept his wey that nyght I shuld have kept hym trewe
covenaunte, for I lay on wayte up on hym on the heth
as he shuld have comen humward, and if I myght have
met with hym I shuld have had Bettes from hym ; but he
had leyd such wetche that he had aspied us or [4] he cam
fully at us ; and he remembered Wyndhams manhood,
that iiij. swyft fete were better than ij. hands, and he toke
his hors with the spores and rode to Felbrygge Hall as fast
as he myght rydyn, and I suppose he lay ther all that
nyght.

Item, the seid Gonnor manased [5] and thret John of Beston
for he wuld not warn hym her of ; and he dede sease alle his
lond in Routon, and warned hym that he shuld not occupy

[1] a taking away and setting at liberty of a distress formerly seized.
[2] tied ere long, both me and all my fellowship.
[3] before Easter.   [4] ere.   [5] menaced.

his lyme kyll [1] ner no lond that he had in Routon ; and he mad his avaunte [2] whan I was gon, if that I had not brought the baly of the hundred with me I shuld never have go thens ; and yet, not withstandyng that I brought the baly with me, and thei had wust [3] where myn hors had stond I shuld have be wele betyn. All this language had thei whan that I was gon.

Item, the seid Gonnor seid after that I was gon to the tenaunts of the seid town, that his *supersedias* [4] was noght, and as for the *rescuse*,[4] he shuld purvey a mene [5] to excuse it. Where fore and it pleasyd you to send my mastres word how that I shuld be demened with the seid Bettes, and wheder that ye wuld I shuld a rest hym ageyn or nought, and to purvey such a mene for Gonnor that he myght ley [6] his bost, it shuld be gret comfort to all yowr frendes and tenauntes ther abowtyn.

IV. AGRICULTURAL AMENITIES

[*John Paston to Sir John Paston. ' P.L.' No. LXX*]

27 *Jan.*, 1467

To my mastyr, Sir John Paston, logyng in Fletstret, be thys delyveryd.

Syr, lyekyth it yow to wet that thys day my modyr sent me your lettyrs, wer by I undystand, blessyd be God, all thyng standyth in good wey. Also I undystand by your lettyr sent to my modyr and me that ye wold have your lyvelod gadyrd as hastyly as we myght do it. Syr, as to that, and [7] othyr folk do no wers ther dever [8] in gaderyng of othyr manerys [9] then we have don in Caster, I tryst to God that ye schall not be long unpayid ; for thys day we had in the last comb of barly that eny man had owyth in Caster towne, not with standyng Hew Awstyn and hys men hathe crakyd many a gret woord in the tym

---

[1] lime-kiln.   [2] boast.   [3] if they had known.   [4] see above.
[5] means.   [6] and to make such arrangements as to Gonnor as to render his boasting null.   [7] if.   [8] devoir.   [9] manors.

that it hathe ben in gaderyng. And twenty comb Hew Awstyns man had doun cartyd redy for to have led it to Yarmowth. And when I herd ther of, I let slype a sertyn of whelpys [1] that gave the cart and the barly syche a torn that it was fayn to tak covert in your bakhous systern at Caster halle, and it was wet within an owyr aftyr that it cam hom, and is nye redy to mak of good malt all, ho ho! William Yelverton hathe ben at Gwton and hathe set in a new bayly ther and hathe dystreynyd the tenauntis, and hathe geve hem day till Candyllmas to pay syche mony as he axyth of hem. Also the seyd Yelverton hathe ben at Saxthorpe, and hathe dystreynyd the fermour ther and takyn of hym swerte [2] to paye hym. And thys day the seyd Yelverton and viij. men with hym, with jakys [3] and trossyng dobletis [4] all the felawshep of hem, wer redy to ryd; and one of the same felawschep told to a man that sye hem all redy that they shuld ryd to tak a dystres in sertayn maners that wer Syr John Fastolffys; wherfor I suppose veryly that they be to Gwton and Saxthorp. Wher for, to morrow I purpose to send Dawbeney thedyr to wet [5] what they do, and to comand the tenauntis and fermors that they pay no mony to nobody bot to yow. John Grey, othyrwyse callyd John Delesbay, and John Burgeys they be Yelvertons kapteyns, and they ryd and go dayly, as well in Norwych as in othyr plasys of yours and othyr menys, in the contre in ther trossyng dowblettis with bombardys and kanonys and chafeveleyns, [6] and do what so ever they wyll in the contre; ther dar no pore man dysplese theym, for what so evyr they do with ther swordys they make it lawe; and they tak dystressys out of mens howsys, hors or catell, or what they wyll, thow it be not on that for that they ask the dwte for. Wher for, me thynkys with esy menys ye myth get a prevy seall of the Kyng to be dyrectyd to the meyer of Norwyche, as for the towne of Norwyche, and for the countre a nothyr prive seall, dyrect to me and to som othyr good felaw, Syr

---

[1] certain whelps.   [2] surety.   [3] cuirasses.
[4] padded doublets.   [5] know.   [6] javelins.

William Calthorp, for he hatyth Grey, for to arest the seyd felaws for syche ryot and to bryng hem to the next prison, ther to abyed with out bayle tyll syche tym as the Kyng sendyth othyrwyse woord, and they that the prive sale shall be dyrect to, to be chargyd vpon peyne of ther alegeans [1] to execut the Kyngis comandment ; and, this done, I warant your lyvelod that my lord delys [2] not with shall be gadyrd pesybylly. As to that lyvelod that my lord clemys [3] I shall do my dever,[4] our logyng kep, to tak as myche profyt of it as I may by the grase of God, Whom I pray send you the acomplyshement of your hertys desyir, and other por folys [5] thers. All my felawshep ar mery and well at ease, blyssyd be God, and recomandyth hem all on to yow.   Wretyn the Twesday next befor Kandylmas. Your brodyr,

J. P.

V. THE MANOR COURT

The normal affairs of the manors were regulated by the Manor Courts which were held at intervals by the Lord of the Manor, or by his representative. At these courts all kinds of manorial affairs were transacted : men were fined for not working ; exchanges or new grants of land were authorized ; rents and dues were collected, etc. The holding of the Court was an outward sign of a man's right to a manor, and it was this that led to the dramatic incidents described in the extracts (a) and (b) which follow. Extract (c) shows us how the drab existence of the serf was at times unconsciously brightened by his betters.

I

[Thomas Howes to (John Paston ?) 'P.L.' No. 219]

Oct. or Nov., 1454

PLEASE your maistership to wete, for as mych as the wryt directed to the exchetor cam not tyl in the Vigil of Symond and Jude, [6] at viij. of the clocke at evyn, whiche coude in no wyse profit us that day ; notwithstondynge we had a yoman of my Lords chamber, and were at Cowhaw, havyng

---

[1] allegiance.   [2] deals.   [3] claims.   [4] devoir, duty.   [5] fools.
[6] The Vigil of SS. Simon and Jude falls on 27 October.

Bertylmeu Elys with us, and ther was Long Bernard sytting to kepe a court. And we at the furst Noy [1] come in the court, and Bertylmeu havynge this termys to Bernard, seying, ' Sir, forasmych as the Kyng hathe grauntyd be hese lettres patent the wardship with the profites of the londes of T. Fastolf duryng hese nun age [2] to you [3] and T. H.,[4] wherfor I am comyn as ther styward, be ther comaundement, upon ther pocession to kep court and lete, whiche is of old custum usyd [5] upon thys day ; wherfor I charge you, be the vertu herof, to seas [6] and kepe nouthir court nor lete, for ye have non autoryte.' Quod Bernard, ' I wyll kepe bothe court and lete, and ye shal non kepe here ; for there is no man hath so gret autoryte.' Than quod Bertylmeu, ' I shal sytte by you, and take a reconysaunce as ye do '. ' Nay ', quod Bernard, ' I wyl suffre you to sytte, but not to wryte.' ' Well,' quod Bertylmeu, ' thanne forsybly ye put us from our pocession, whiche I doute not but shalbe remembryd you anothir day,' &c. ' But, Seres,' quod he, ' ye that be tenaunts to this manoyr, we charge you that ye do nowthir seute nor servise, no(r) paye ony rents or fermys but to the use of John Paston and T. [7] ; fo(r) and ye do, ye shal paye it ageyn ; and as for on yeer past, we have sewyrte [8] of Skylly, whiche hath resevid it of you to ther use.' And thus we departid, and Bernard kept court and lete.

II

[John Paston to Sir John Paston. ' P.L.' No. 688]

23 *Jan.*, 1472

(*b*)

ITEM, yestyrday W. Gornay entryd in to Saxthorp and ther was he kepyng of a coort, and had the tenaunts attou(r)nyd to him, but er the coort was all doon, I cam thedyr with a man with me and no more, and ther, befor

---

[1] opening formula. [2] nonage. [3] i.e. J. Paston.
[4] (Sir) Thomas Howes. [5] held. [6] cease.
[7] Probably T. Fastolf, the ward. [8] surety.

hym and all hys felluwschep, Gayne, Bomsted, &c., I chargyd the tenaunts that they shold proced no ferther in ther coort upon peyn that myght folle [1] of it, and they lettyd for a seasen.[2] But they sye [3] that I was not abyll to make my partye good, and so they procedyd ferther ; and I sye that, and set me downe by the stward and blottyd hys book wyth my fyngyr as he wrot, so that all tenaunts afermyd that the coort was enterupte by me as in yowr ryght, and I reqwered them to record that ther was no pesybyll coort kept, and so they seyd they wold.

III

[J. Whetley to Sir John Paston.   'P.L.' No. 817]

20 *May*, 1478

(c)

AND as for Haylysdon, my Lord of Suffolk was ther on Wedensday in Whytson Weke, and ther dined, and drew a stew [4] and toke gret plente of fych ; yet hath he left you a pyke or ij., agayn ye come,[5] the wych wold be gret comford to all your frendes, and dyscomford to your enmys ; for at hys beyng ther that daye ther was never no man that playd Herrod in Corpus Crysty [6] play better and more agreable to hys pageaunt then he dud.   But ye schall understond that it was after none, and the weder hot, and he so feble for sekenes that hys legges wold not bere hyme, but ther was ij. men had gret payn to kepe hym on hys fete ; and ther ye were juged.   Som sayd ' Sley ' ; some sayd ' Put hym in preson '.   And forth com my lord, and he wold met you with a spere, and have none other mendes for the troble at ye have put hym to but your hart blod, and that will he gayt with hys owen handes ; for and ye have Haylesdon and Dreton, ye schall have hys lyff with it. . . .

---

[1] follow.   [2] stopped for a time   [3] saw.   [4] fish-pond.
[5] for your arrival.   [6] Herod was the traditional ranter in the religious dramas, which were usually performed on Corpus Christi Day.

VI. VILLAGE NEIGHBOURS

*This and the five following extracts, with one exception (p. 69), are
all taken from the pages of* Piers Plowman *and give us an extraordinary
series of vignettes of medieval village life. Langland presents life as
he saw it with no attempt to palliate its horror or its more unpleasant
aspects; and, side by side with the more gracious pictures of Chaucer,
we must place these portraits of the poor dwellers in cots. This extract
is from* Piers Plowman, *B text.V.* 94–119.

I HAVE a neighbore neyghe me I have ennvyed [1] hym
    ofte,
And lowen on [2] hym to lordes to don [3] hym lese his silver,
And made his frendes ben his foon thorw my false tonge ;
His grace and his good happes greveth me ful sore.
Bitwene many and many I make debate ofte,
That bothe lyf and lyme is lost thorw my speche.
And whan I mete him in market that I moste hate,
I hailse hym hendeliche [4] as I his frende were ;
For he is doughtier than I, I dar do non other.
Ac hadde I maystrye and myghte : God wote my wille ! 10
And whan I come to the kirke and sholde knele to the
    Rode,
And preye for the pople as the prest techeth,
For pilgrimes and for palmers for alle the poeple after,
Thanne I crye on my knees that Cryste gif hem sorwe
That baren awey my bolle and my broke schete.[5]
Awey fro the auter thanne turne I myn eyghen,[6]
And biholde how Eleyne hath a newe cote ;
I wisshe thanne it were myne and al the webbe after.[7]
And of mennes lesynge [8] I laughe that liketh myn herte ;
And for her wynnynge I wepe and waille the tyme, 20
And deme that hii don ille there I do wel worse ; [9]
Who-so undernymeth me here-of [10] I hate hym dedly
    after.

[1] annoyed.   [2] lied against.   [3] make.   [4] I greet him courteously.
[5] broken (ragged, torn) sheet.   [6] eyes.   [7] and the whole piece
(from which it was cut) was mine too.   [8] At men's lyings.
[9] And I judge that they do ill, where I do much worse.
          [10] whoever reproves me for it.

I wolde that uche a [1] wyght were my knave,
For who-so hath more than I that angreth me sore.
And thus I lyve loveless luke a luther [2] dogge,
That al my body bolneth [3] for bitter [4] of my galle.

VII. THE POOR PEASANTS

[*Piers Plowman, C text. X.* 71–97]

THE most needy aren oure neighebores and we nyme [5]
   good hede,
As prisones in puttes,[6] and poure folke in Cotes,[7]
Charged with children and chef lordes rente,
That thei with spynnynge may spare spenen hit in hous-
   hyre,
Bothe in mylk and in mele to make with papelotes,[8]
To a-glotye with here gurles [9] that greden [10] after fode.
Also hem-selve suffren muche hunger,
And wo in winter-tyme with wakynge a nyghtes
To ryse to the·ruel [11] to rocke the cradel,
Bothe to karde and to kembe, to clouten and to wasche, 10
To rubbe and to rely,[12] russhes to pilie,[13]
That reuthe is to rede othere [14] in ryme shewe
The wo of these women that wonyeth in Cotes;
And of meny other men that muche wo suffren,
Bothe a-fyngrede and a-furst [15] to turne the fayre out-
   warde,[16]
And beth abasshed for to begge and wolle nat be aknowe
What hem needeth at here neihebores at non and at
   even.
This ich wot witerly [17] as the worlde techeth,
What other by-hoveth that hath meny children,

---

[1] every.   [2] ill-tempered.   [3] swells.   [4] bitterness.   [5] take.
[6] pits, i.e. dungeons.   [7] cottages.   [8] porridge.   [9] children.
[10] cry.   [11] the space between the bed and the wall.
[12] to wind the yarn from the spindle on to a reel.   [13] peel.
[14] or.   [15] hungry and thirsty.   [16] to keep up appearances.
[17] clearly.

And hath no catel bote hus crafte to clothy hem and to
    fede,   20
And fele to fonge ther-to, and fewe pans taketh.[1]
Ther is payn [2] and peny-ale as for a pytaunce y-take,
Colde flessh and cold fyssh for veneson ybake ;
Frydayes and fastyng-dayes a ferthyng-worth of muscles
Were a feste for suche folke other so fele Cockes.[3]
These were almes, to helpe that han suche charges,
And to comfortie suche cotyers and crokede men and
    blynde.

VIII. THE PLOUGHMAN

This most vivid picture comes from Pierce the Ploughman's Crede.
*Although no early MS. of it exists, Dr. Bradley has stated that parts of
it at least would seem to be of the fourteenth century.   Our extract is
taken from Skeat's edition of 1906, p. 17, ll. 420 ff.*

AND as I wente be the waie wepynge for sorowe,
(I) seigh a sely man me by opon the plow hongen.
His cote was of a cloute that cary was y-called,
His hod was full of holes and his heer oute,
With his knopped schon clouted full thykke ;
His ton toteden out as he the londe treddede,
His hosen overhongen his hokschynes on everiche a side,
Al beslombred in fen as he the plow folwede ;
Twey myteynes, as mete maad all of cloutes ;
The fyngers weren for-werd and ful of fen honged.   10
This wight waselede in the fen almost to the ancle,
Foure rotheren hym by-forn that feble were worthen ;
Men myghte reknen ich a ryb so reufull they weren.
His wiif walked him with with a longe gode,
In a cutted cote cutted full heyghe,
Wrapped in a wynwe-schete to weren hire fro weders,
Barfote on the bare iis that the blod folwede.
And at the londes ende lay a litell crom-bolle,
And theron lay a litell childe lapped in cloutes,

[1] anfd many to grasp thereat, and he receives but few pence.
[2] bread.   [3] A farthing's worth of mussels, or as many cockles
were a feast for such folk.

And tweyne of tweie yeres olde opon a-nother syde, 20
And alle they songen o songe that sorwe was to heren ;
They crieden alle o cry,—a carefull note.
The sely man sighede sore, and seide : ' children, beth
    stille ! '

As I went by the way, weeping for sorrow, I saw a poor man
hanging on to the plough. His coat was of a coarse stuff which was
called cary ; his hood was full of holes and his hair stuck out of it.
As he trod the soil his toes peered out of his worn shoes with their
thick soles ; his hose hung about his hocks on all sides, and he was
all bedaubed with mud as he followed the plough. He had two
mittens, made scantily of rough stuff, with worn-out fingers and
thick with muck. This man bemired himself in the mud almost to
the ancle, and drove four heifers before him that had become feeble,
so that men might count their every rib so ' sorry looking they were '.

His wife walked beside him with a long goad in a shortened cote-
hardy looped up full high, and wrapped in a winnowing-sheet to
protect her from the weather. She went barefoot on the ice so that
the blood flowed. And at the end of the row lay a little crumb-
bowl, and therein a little child covered with rags, and two two-year
olds were on the other side, and they all sang one song that was
pitiful to hear : they all cried the same cry—a careful note. The
poor man sighed sorely, and said ' Children be still ! '.

IX. PEASANTS AND LABOURERS

[*Piers Plowman, B text. VI.* 282–332]

' I HAVE no peny,' quod Peres ' poletes forto bigge,[1]
Ne neyther gees ne grys [2] but two grene [3] cheses,
A fewe cruddes and creem and an hauer [4] cake,
And two loves of benes and bran y-bake for my fauntis.[5]
And yet I sey, by my soule I have no salt bacoun,
Ne no kokeney,[6] bi Cryst coloppes [7] forto maken.
Ac I have percil,[8] and porettes,[9] and many kole-plantes,[10]
And eke a cow, and a kalf, and a cart-mare
To drawe a-felde my donge the while the drought lasteth.
And bi this lyflode we mot lyve til lammasse tyme ; 10

---

[1] to buy pullets.   [2] young pigs.   [3] new.   [4] oat.   [5] children.
[6] eggs.   [7] eggs and bacon.   [8] parsley.   [9] leeks.   [10] cabbages.

And bi that, I hope to have hervest in my croft ;
And thanne may I dighte thi dyner as me dere liketh.'
Alle the pore peple tho pesecoddes fetten,[1]
Benes and baken apples thei broughte in her lappes
Chibolles,[2] and chervelles,[3] and ripe chiries manye,
And profred Peres this present to plese with hunger.
　Al hunger eet in hast and axed after more.
Thanne pore folke for fere fedde hunger yerne [4]
With grene poret and pesen to poysoun hunger thei
　　thoughte.
By that [5] it neighed nere hervest newe corne cam to
　　chepynge ; [6]　　　　　　　　　　　　　　　　20
Thanne was folke fayne and fedde hunger with the best,
With good ale, as glotoun taughte and gerte hunger go
　　slepe.
　And tho [7] wolde wastour nought werche but wandren
　　aboute,
Ne no begger ete bred that benes inne were,
But of coket or clerematyn [8] or elles of clene whete ;
Ne none halpeny ale [9] in none wise drynke,
But of the best and of the brounest that in borghe is to
　　selle.
　Laboreres that have no lande to lyve on but her handes,
Deyned nought to dyne a-day nyght-olde wortes.[10]
May no peny ale hem paye, ne no pece of bakoun,　30
But if it be fresch flesch other [11] fische fryed other bake,
And that *chaude* or *plus chaud* for chillyng of here mawe.[12]
　And but if he be heighlich huyred ellis wil he chyde,
And that he was werkman wrought waille the tyme,[13]
Ageines Catones conseille comseth he to jangle : [14]—

　　　Paupertatis onus pacienter ferre memento.

　He greveth hym ageines God and gruccheth ageines
　　resoun,

---

[1] fetched.　[2] chibolles (a small onion).　[3] chevrils.　[4] eagerly.
[5] until.　[6] market.　[7] then.　[8] coket and clere martyr were
varieties of white bread.　[9] thin ale.　[10] Deigned not to dine to-day
on last night's vegetables.　[11] or.　[12] stomach.　[13] bewail the
time that he was born a workman.　[14] grumble.

And thanne curseth he the Kynge and al his conseille
    after,
Suche lawes to loke laboreres to greve.[1]
Ac whiles hunger was her maister there wolde none of
    hem chyde,   40
Ne stryve ageines his statut so sterneliche he loked.
    Ac I warne yow, werkemen, wynneth while ye mowe,
For hunger hider ward hasteth hym faste,
He shal awake with water wastoures to chaste.
Ar fyve yere be fulfilled suche famyn shal aryse,
Thorwgh flodes and thourgh foule wederes frutes shul faille,
And so sayde saturne and sent yow to warne :
Whan ye se the sonne amys and two monkes hedes,
And a mayde have the maistrie and multiplie bi eight,[2]
Thanne shal deth [3] withdrawe and derthe be justice, 50
And Dawe the dyker deye for hunger,
But if God of his goodnesse graunt us a trewe.[4]

X. THE PEASANT'S HOUSE

[Piers Plowman, B text. XVII. 315–326]

THRE thinges there ben that doth [5] a man by strengthe
Forto fleen his owne hous as holywryt sheweth.
That one is a wikked wyf that wil nought be chasted,[6]
Her fiere [7] fleeth fro hyr, for fere of her tonge.
And if his hous be vnhiled and reyne on his bedde,[8]
He seketh [9] and seketh til he slepe drye.
And whan smoke & smolder smyt in his syghte,
It doth hym worse than his wyf or wete to slepe.

---

[1] the famous Statute of Labourers.   [2] These lines are inexplic-
able: perhaps Langland's comment on much of the meaningless
prophecy of his time.   [3] the great Death, i.e. the pestilence, cf.
Chaucer, C.T. Prologue, 605.   [4] truce.   [5] make.   [6] corrected.
[7] companion.   [8] And if his house has a leaky roof, and the rain
falls on his bed.   [9] searches.

For smoke & smolder smyteth in his eyen,
Til he be blere-nyed, or blynde, and hors in the throte, 10
Cougheth, and curseth that Cryst gyf hem sorwe
That sholde brynge in better wode, or blowe it til it brende.

XI. THE WIDOW'S COTTAGE

[Chaucer. *Canterbury Tales*, B. 4011 ff.]

A POVRE widwe, somdel stope [1] in age,
Was whylom dwelling in a narwe cotage,
Bisyde a grove, stonding in a dale.
This widwe, of which I telle yow my tale,
Sin thilke day that she was last a wyf,
In pacience ladde a ful simple lyf,
For litel was hir catel [2] and hir rente.
By housbondrye of such as God hir sente
  She fond [3] hir-self, and eek hir doghtren two.
Three large sowes hadde she, and namo ;   10
Three kyn, and eek a sheep, that highte Malle.
Ful sooty was hir bour, and eek hir halle,
In which she eet ful many a sclendre meel ;
Of poynaunt sauce hir neded never a deel.
No deyntee morsel passed thurgh hir throte ;
Hir dyete was accordant to hir cote.
Repleccioun ne made hir never syk ;
  Attempree [4] dyete was al her phisyk,
And exercyse, and hertes suffisaunce.
The goute lette hir no-thing for to daunce,   20
N'apoplexye shente [5] nat hir heed ;
No wyn ne drank she, neither whyt ne reed ;
Hir bord was served most with whyt and blak,—
Milk and broun breed,—in which she fond no lak ;
Seynd [6] bacoun, and somtyme an ey [7] or tweye,
For she was as it were a maner deye.[8]

---

[1] somewhat advanced.   [2] chattels.   [3] provided.   [4] a temperate.
[5] hurt.   [6] singed.   [7] egg.   [8] a dairy-woman.

A yerd she hadde, enclosed al aboute
With stikkes, and a drye dich with-oute,
In which she hadde a cok, hight Chauntecleer.
In al the land of crowing nas his peer.   30

XII. THE VILLAGE ALE-HOUSE

[Piers Plowman B text. V. 304-369]

Now bigynneth Gloutoun for to go to schrifte,
And kaires [1] hym to kirkeward, his coupe [2] to schewe ;
Ac [3] Beton the brewestere bad hym good morwe,
And axed of hym with that whiderward he wolde.
' To Holi Cherche ', quod he, ' for to here masse,
And sithen [4] I wil be shryven, and synne na more.'
' I have gode ale, gossib ', quod she ; ' Glotown, wiltow
    assaye ? '
' Hastow aughte in thi purs ?—any hote spices ? '
    ' I have peper and piones ',[5] quod she, ' and a pounde
    of garlike,
A ferthyngworth of fenel-seed for fastyng-dayes.'   10
    Thanne goth Glotoun in, and grete othes after ;
Cesse the souteresse [6] sat on the benche,
Watte the warner [7] and hys wyf bothe,
Tymme the tynkere, and tweyne of his prentis,
Hikke the hakeneyman, and Hughe the nedeler,[8]
Clarice of Cokkeslane, and the clerke of the cherche,
Dawe the dykere, and a dozeine other ;
Sire Piers of Pridie, and Peronelle of Flaundres,
A ribibour,[9] a ratonere,[10] a rakyer of Chepe,[11]
A ropere,[12] a redyngkyng,[13] and Rose the dissheres,[14] 20
Godfrey of Garlekehithe, and Gryfin the Walshe,
And upholderes [15] an hepe erly bi the morwe
Geven Glotoun with glad chere good ale to hansel.[16]

[1] gets.   [2] guilt.   [3] but.   [4] afterwards.   [5] peony-seeds.   [6] shoemaker.
[7] game-keeper.   [8] needle-seller.   [9] rebeck-player.   [10] rat-catcher.
[11] scavenger.   [12] rope maker.   [13] laquey.   [14] dish-seller.
[15] furniture-brokers.   [16] to propriate him.

Clement the cobelere cast of his cloke,
And atte new faire [1] he nempned [2] it to selle ;
Hikke the hakeneyman hitte [3] his hood after,
And badde Bette the bochere ben on his side.
There were chapmen ychose this chaffare to preise ;
Whoso haveth the hood shuld have amendes of the cloke.
Two risen up in rape,[4] and rouned [5] togideres,   30
And preised these penyworthes apart bi hemselve ;
Thei couth noughte bi her conscience acorden in treuthe,
Tyl Robyn the ropere arose bi the southe,
And nempned hym for a noumpere [6]—that no debate
    nere—
For to trye this chaffare bitwixen hem thre.
Hikke the hostellere hadde the cloke,
In covenaunte that Clement shulde the cuppe fille,
And have Hikkes hode hostellere,[7] and holde hym yserved ;[8]
And whoso repented rathest [9] shulde arise after,
And grete Sire Glotoun with a galoun ale.   40
    There was laughyng and louryng, and ' Let go the
    cuppe ! '
And seten so til evensonge, and songen umwhile,[10]
Tyl Glotoun had yglobbed a galoun an a jille.
    He myghte neither steppe ne stonde er he his staffe
    hadde ;
And thanne gan he go liche a glewmannes bicche.[11]
Somme tyme aside, and somme tyme arrere,
As whoso leyth lynes for to lacche foules.[12]
And whan he drowgh to the dore, thanne dymmed his
    eighen ;
He stumbled on the thresshewolde, an threwe to the erthe.
Clement the cobelere caughte hym bi the myddel,   50
For to lifte hym alofte, and leyde him on his knowes.[13]
    With al the wo of this worlde, his wyf and his wenche
Baren hym home to his bedde, and broughte hym therinne ;

---

[1] to chaffer at the new fair, to exchange.   [2] named.   [3] threw
down.   [4] haste.   [5] whispered.   [6] umpire.   [7] the hood of Hikke
the innkeeper.   [8] contented.   [9] soonest.   [10] at intervals.
[11] a (blind) minstrel's dog.   [12] catch birds.   [13] knees.

And after al this excesse, he had an accidie,[1]
That he slepe Saterday and Sonday til sonne gede to
reste.
Thanne waked he of his wynkyng, and wiped his eyghen;
The fyrste worde that he warpe [2] was : ' Where is the
bolle ? '

XIII. A VILLAGE RECTORY

*No picture of medieval village life could omit the village church.
It stood for much in the life of every villager : the priest entered into
his life at the most poignant and decisive moments ; its services and
sacraments were something far aloof from the toil and squalor of his
everyday surroundings ; its teaching influenced many of his daily
actions and thoughts. The extracts which follow illustrate these points,
but Section Four dealing with the Church and clergy should also be
consulted to complete the picture.*

*The following document was drawn up at a time when Margaret
Paston was urgently seeking for a new incumbent for the family living
of Oxnede in Norfolk. It gives us a clear picture of a typical country
rectory with its comfortable house and farmyard, its gardens, arable and
pasturage.*

[*Oxnead Parsonage. ' P.L.' No.* 819]

31 *July*, 1478

The comodytys off the parsonage and the valew off the
benyfyce off Oxned.

My new parson off Oxned, whan he is instute and inducte,
at the first entre in to the chyrch and benefyce off Oxned,
must off awncyent custom long contynued with in the
dyosesse off Norwyche, pay to the byschopp off Norwych,
for the first frutes off the seyd benefyce, xiiij. marke ; [3]
for wyche xiiij. marke, iff the new parson be wytty and
have favour a bowt the Byschops offycers, he schall have
days off paiment to pay the seid xiiij. marke in xiiij.
yere, that is, a marke a yere, till it be payd ; so that he
can fynd suffycyent mene to be bownd to the Bischopp
be obligacion to kepe his days off payment.

---

[1] bout of slothfulness.   [2] uttered.   [3] a mark was worth 13s. 4d.

And the chyrch is but litill, and is resonable plesaunt, and reparyd. (And the) dwellyng place of the parsonage is a yoynyng to the . . . . d[1] well howsyd and reparyd, hall, chamberes, barn, doffhowse.[2] and all howsys off offyce.

And it hath a doffhowse worth a yere, xiiijs.iiijd.

And it hath ij. large gardens with frute, and is yonynge [3] to the place and chyrch yard, wher off the frute is worth yerly, xxvjs. viijd.

And ther longith to the seid parsonage in fre lond, arable, pasture and medowe ayonyng to the seid parsonage, xxij[tl] acre or more, wher off every acre is worth ijs. ; to latyn [4] iij li.iiijd.

And William Paston, Justice, qwan he cam fyrst to dwell in the maner of Oxned, paid to the parson that was than for the corne growyng on the parsonage londys and for the tythynges, ondely but in corne whan it was inned in to the barn, xxiiij li.

And the same yere the parson had all the awterage [5] and oder profytes be syde the seyd xxiiij li.

It is yerly worth, as the world goth now, xli.

And it is butt an esy cure to kepe, ffor ther ar natt past xx[tl] persons to be yerly howselyd.[6]

The parsonage stant be a fresh ryver syde.

And ther is a good markett town callyd Alysham, within ij. myle off the parsonage.

And the cyte of Norwych is within vj. myle off the parsonage.

And the see is within x. myle off the parsonage.

And if a parson cam now, and warr presentyd, institute, and inducte, he shuld have by the lawe all the cropp that is now growyng, that was eryd [7] and sowyn off the old parsons cost, growyng on the parsonage landes now, as his own good, and all the tyth off all maner grayngs off the maner, londes, and tenantes londes, towardes his

---

[1] The original is torn here (probably churchyard is the word missing). [2] dove-house. [3] adjacent. [4] to let. [5] altarage. [6] communicated. This was usually only done once a year, generally at Easter. [7] ploughed.

charges off the fyrst frutes. And if it ware innyd it war (the crop now growyng) worth his first frutes.

He that hath this benefice, and he were a pore man, myght have lycens to have service be side.

The Beshop ought not to have the valew of this cropp for the arrerages of the fyrst fruttes that Sir Thomas Everard, last parson of Oxned, oght [1] to the Bysshop whan he died, for the said Sir Thomas Everard was bond to the Bisshop in an obligacion for the said frutes, and the said Sir Thomas Everard, for to defraude the Bysshop and oder men that he owid mony to, gaff a way his gooddes to serten persons, qwech persons toke a way the said goodes, and also durres and wyndow of the said parsonage ; and it is though [2] that both the Bysshop and the patron myght take accions a gayns the said persons.

XIV. IN CHURCH

Medieval moralists were fond of inveighing against the two faults illustrated by this extract (e.g. La Tour Landry, p. 40, or Myroure of Oure Ladye, p. 54, both published by the E.E.T.S.) In choir the offices were frequently gabbled with indecent haste, while in the nave the congregation chattered among themselves. Jacob's Well, *from which this exemplum on p.* 114 *is taken, is one of those ' bokes and tretees of vyces and vertues, and of dyverse doctrynes ' which appeared in such profusion in the fifteenth century. Jacob's Well represents the sinful body of man which has to be cleansed until it becomes a fit receptacle for the water of Grace. It has been edited in part for the E.E.T.S. in 1900 by A. Brandeis, and the concluding part is now being prepared by Dr. G. R. Owst.*

SLOWTHE makyth the the restyng place of the devyl, for thou art the feendys pylwe.[3] Slowthe makyth the as a cyte unwallyd, redy and esy for alle synnes and for alle feendys to entryn in-to thi soule. Slouthe makyth the as a schetyng [4] hyll, redy to be schett wyth the arwe [5] of every temptacyoun.

Jacobus de Vitriaco tellyth that an holy man stood in cherch in a qwere,[6] and seygh a feend beryng a gret sacchett full of thyng. The feend, as the man askyd the feend

[1] owed. [2] thought. [3] pillow. [4] shooting. [5] arrow. [6] choir.

what he bare, the feend seyde : ' I bere in my sacche sylablys and woordys, overskyppyd and synkopyd,[1] and verse and psalmys the whiche these clerkys han stolyn in the qweere, and have fayled in here servyse.'

Fforsothe, thanne I trowe the feend hath a gret sacche full of youre ydell woordys, that ye jangelyn [2] in cherche in slowthe. Ffor this same clerk seyth that the devyl in a cherche wrote the woordys of the peple, whiche thei jangledyn and rownedyn [3] in cherch, and whan his scrowe was to lytel, he drewe it out, wyth his teeth, broddere ; and in his drawyng he smote his hevyd agens the walle. An holy man seygh this, and askyd the feend why he dyde so. The feend seyde : ' I wryte thise talys of the peple in this cherche, to recordyn hem a-fore God at the doom for here dampnacyoun, and my book is to narwe to wryten on alle here talys ; thei say so manye. Therfore I drawe it out braddere, that none of here talys schulde be unwretyn.'

I drede me thanne, the feend hath a gret book agens you, wretyn of youre janglynges in cherch, and yit ye excusyn yow there-in, and seyn : ' me muste speke to hym that spekyth to me.' Beth ware, and levyth suche talys for dreed of God and for rewthe of youre soule ! Forsakyth youre slowthe, and takyth the ground of gostly strengthe, to travaylen myghtely in prayerys, to duryn myghtely in goodnes, to wythstonden myghtily temptacyoun, to sufferyn myghtyly adversite and tribulacyoun. For this stengthe overcomyth slowthe, and savyth youre soule.

XV. HOW THE PLOUGHMAN LEARNED HIS PATERNOSTER

This interesting fifteenth-century poem gives us both an excellent picture of a good labourer of the times, and also enables us to see something of the relation existing between the clergy and their simple parishioners. The poem is reprinted from Reliquiæ Antiquæ, *ed. T. Wright and J. O. Halliwell,* 1841, *Vol. I, p.* 43.

SOM tyme in Fraunce dwelled a plowman,
Whiche was myghty bolde and stronge ;

[1] cut short.   [2] chatter.   [3] whispering.

Goode skyll he cowde in husbondry,
And gate his lyvynge full merely.[1]
He cowde eke sowe and holde a plowe,
Bothe dyke, hedge, and mylke a cowe,
Thresshe, fane,[2] and gelde a swyne,
In every season and in tyme ;
To mowe and repe both grasse and corne
A better labourer was never borne ; 10
He coude go to plowe with oxe and hors.
With whiche it were, he dyde for fors ;
Of shepe the wolle of for to shere,
His better was founde no where ;
Strype hempe he coude to cloute[3] his shone,
And set gese abrode in reason of the mone.
Of fruytte he graffed many a tre,
Fell wode, and make it as it sholde be.
He coude theche a hous, and daube a wall ;
With all thinge that to husbondry dyde fall. 20
By these to ryches he was brought.
That golde ne sylver he lacked nought ;
His hall rofe was full of bakon flytches,
The chambre charged was with wyches[4]
Full of egges, butter, and chese,
Men that were hungry for to ease ;
To make good ale, malte had he plentye ;
And Martylmas befe to hym was not deyntye ;
Onyons and garlyke had he inowe ;
And good creme, and mylke of the cowe. 30
Thus by his labour ryche was he in dede ;
Now to the mater wyll I procede.
Grete good he gate and lyved yeres fourty,
Yet coude[5] he neyther *pater noster* nor *ave.*
In Lenten tyme the parsone dyde hym shryve ;
He sayd, ' Syr, canst thou thy byleve ? '
The plowman sayd unto the preste,
' Syr, I byleve in Jhesu Cryste,

---

[1] merrily. [2] winnow. [3] patch.
[4] wicker baskets. [5] knew.

Whiche suffred dethe and harowed hell,
As I have herde myne olders tell.'   40
The parsone sayd, ' Man, late me here
The saye devotely thy *pater noster*,
That thou in hit no worde do lacke.'
Then sayd the plowman, ' What thynge is that,
Whiche ye desyre to here so sore ?
I herde never therof before.'
The preest sayd, ' To lerne it thou arte bounde,
Or elles thou lyvest as an hounde :
Without it, saved canst thou not be,
Nor never have syght of the Deyte ;   50
From chyrche to be banysshed aye,
All they that can not theyr *pater noster* saye.
Therfore I mervayll ryght gretly,
That thy byleve was never taught the.
I charge the, upon payne of deedly synne,
Lerne it, heven yf thou wylte wynne.'
' I wolde thresshe,' sayd the plowman, ' yeres ten,
Rather than I it wolde leren.
I praye the, syr persone, my counseyll kepe ;
Ten wethers wyll I gyve the of my best shepe,   60
And thou shalte have in the same stounde [1]
Fourty shelynges in grotes [2] rounde,
So ye me shewe how I may heven reche.'
' Wele ! ' sayd the preest, ' I shall the teche ;
Yf thou do by my counsell,
To heven shalte thou come ryght well.'
The husbonde sayd, ' Yf ye wyll so,
What ever ye bydde me, it shall be do.
' Well ! ' sayd the persone, ' syth thou haste graunt
Truly to kepe this covenaunt,   70
To do as I shalle warne the shortly,
Marke well the wordes that I saye to the :
Thou knowest that of corne is grete skarsnesse,
Wherby many for hungre dye, doubtlesse,

[1] time.   [2] groats.

Bycause they lacke theyr dayly brede ;
Hondredes this yere I have sene dede ;
And thou haste grete plentye of whete,
Whiche men for moneye now can not gete.
And yf thou wilte do after me,
Fourty poore men I shall sende the,   80
And to eche of them gyve more or lasse
Or they awaye fro the passe.
I shall the double for thy whete paye,
Se thou bere truly theyr names awaye,
And yf thou shewe them all and some
Ryght in ordre as they do come,
Who is served fyrste and who laste of all.'
' In fayth ! ' sayd the plowman, ' so I shall ;
Go when ye wyll and sende them hyder,
Fayne wold I se that company togyder.'   90
The parsone wente to fetche the route,
And gadred poore people all aboute ;
To the plowmans hous forthe he wente ;
The husbondeman was well contente
Bycause the parsone was theyr surety.
That made his herte moche more mery.
The preest sayd, ' Se here thy men echone,
Serve them lyghtly that they were gone.'
The husbondeman sayd to hym agayne,
' The lenger they tary, the more is my payne.' 100
Fyrst wente *pater*, feble, lene, and olde ;
All his clothes for hungre had he solde ;
Two busshelles of whete gate he there
Unethe ¹ for age myght he it bere.
Then came *noster* ragged in araye ;
He had his backe burden, and so wente his waye.
Two peckes were gyven to *Qui est in celis* ;
No wonder yf he halted, for kybed were his helys.²
Then came *sanctificetur*, and *nomen tuum* ;
Of whete amonge them they gate an hole tunne ; 110

¹ Scarcely.   ² for his heels had chilblains.

How moche was therin I can not saye;
They two laded a carte, and wente theyr waye.
In ordre folowed them other thre,
Adveniat, regnum, tuum, that was deed nye:
They thought to longe that they abode,
Yet eche of them had an hors-lode.
The plowman cryed, 'Sirs, come awaye!'
Than wente *fiat, voluntas, tua, sicut, in celo, et, in terra,*
Some blere eyed, and some lame, with botell and bagge,
To cover their [backs] they had not an hole ragge; 120
Aboute ten busshelles they had them amonge,
And in the waye homewarde full merely [1] they songe.
Then came *Panem, nostrum, cotidianum, da nobis, hodie,*
Amonge them five they had but one peny;
That was gyven them for Goddes sake;
They sayde therwith that they wolde mery make:
Eche had two busshelles of whete that was gode,
They songe goyne home-warde a Gest of Robyn Hode.[2]
Et dimitte, nobis, debita, nostra, came than;
The one sonburned, another black as a pan; 130
They preased in the hepe of corne to fynde;
No wonder if they fell, for they were all blynde;
Eche of them an hole quartre they had,
And streyght to the ale-hous they it lad.
Sicut, et nos, dimittimus, debitoribus, nostris,
Came in anone, and dyde not mys;
They had ten busshelles, withouten fayle,
And layde fyve to pledge for a kylderkyn of ale.
Than came *et, ne, nos, inducas, in temptationem:*
Amonge them all they had quarters ten; 140
Theyr brede was baken in a tankarde,
And the resydue they played at the hazarde.
By and by came *sed libera nos a malo;*
He was so wery he myght not go.
Also *Amen* came rennynge anone;
He cryed out 'spede me, that I were gone';

[1] merrily.   [2] Story of Robin Hood. See below, p. 173.

He was patched, torne, and all to-rente ;
It semed by his langage that he was borne in Kente.
The plowman served them everychone,
And was full gladde whan they were gone.   150
But whan he sawe of corne he had no more,
He wyshed them at the devyll therfore.
So longe had he meten [1] his corne and whete,
That all his body was in a swete.
Than unto his hous dyde he go ;
His herte was full of payne and wo,
To kepe theyr names and shewe them ryght,
That he rested but lytell that nyght.
Ever he patred [2] on theyr names faste ;
Than he had them in ordre at the laste.   160
Than on the morowe he wente to the parsone,
And sayd, ' Syr, for moneye am I come ;
My corne I delyvered by the counseyll of the,
Remember the promes, thou arte theyr suretye.'
The preest sayd, ' Theyr names thou must me shewe.'
The plowman rehersed them on a rewe ;
How they were called he kepte in mynde,
He sayd that *Amen* came all behynde.
The parsone sayde, ' Man, be gladde this daye,
Thy paternoster now canst thou saye.'   170
The plowman sayde, ' Gyve me my moneye !
The preest sayd, ' I owe none to the to paye ;
Thoughe thou dyde thy corne to poore men gyve,
Thou mayst me blysse whyle thou doost lyve ;
For by these maye ye paye Cryste his rente,
And serve the Lorde omnipotente.'
' Is this the answere ', he sayd, ' that I have shall ?
I shall sommon the afore the offycyal.' [3]
So to the courte wente they bothe indede ;
Not beste of all dyde the plowman spede.   180
Unto the offycyall the parsone tolde all,
How it bytwene them two dyde fall,

---

[1] measured out.   [2] said over (pattered).
[3] The official was one of the Bishop's disciplinary officers.

And of this *pater noster* lernynge.
They laughed, and made sporte inowe.
The plowman for angre bended his browe,
And sayd, ' This poor men have a-way all my corne,
And for my labour the parsone dothe me skorne.'
The offycyall praysed gretly the parsone,
And sayd ryght well that he had done ;
He sayd, ' Plowman, it is shame to the,   190
To accuse this gentylman before me.'
He badde him go home, fole as he was,
And aske God mercy for his trespas.
The plowman thought ever on his shete,
And sayd, ' Agayne I shall it never gete.'
Than he wente, and to his wyfe sayd,
How that the parsone had hym betrayde,
And sayd, ' Whyle that I lyve certayne,
Preest shall I never trust agayne.'
Thus for his corne that he gave there,   200
His *pater noster* dyde he lere ; [1]
And after longe he lyved withouten stryfe.
Tyll he went from his mortall lyfe.
The persone disceased after also ;
Theyr soules I truste to heven dyde go.
Unto the whiche he us brynge,
That in heven reygneth eternall kynge.

XVI. THE RELIC MONGER

From the wonders and miracles of the Church to the charms and superstitions of the country-side was but a step. The credulous were easily enough deceived, as Chaucer shows us well enough, and as is further illustrated by our next extract. Witch-craft, magic, superstition flourished : only a very few aspects of this immense subject can be indicated in the following extracts, but it must always be remembered in considering the day-to-day life of medieval England.

This extract comes from p. 484, ll. 18,111 ff. of an English version of Deguilleville's fourteenth-century work : La Pèlerinage de la Vie Humaine, *which was made by John Lydgate in 1426. It has been edited by F. J. Furnivall, and published by the E.E.T.S., Vols. 77, 83, 92.*

---

[1] learn.

7

To abbeys eke I can wel gon,
Stell [1] ymagis of tre and stone,
Thowghe they ben old & paynt them newe,
And make them semë freshe of hewe,
With colours bothë whit and redd ;
And at theyr brestis and at ther hedd
I set berryls and crystall.
Undar, I make an hole full smale,
I put in oylë, wyne, and blood,
And melke also, to getten good ;   10
Make the lycour round about,
At small holes to rennyn out,
As it were done by myracle.
That ther nis [2] balme nor triacle
In this world, so ryche of prys,
Of foltyshe [3] people that ben nat wys.
  I set eke out swyche ymagis,
In stretis and at hermytagis,
And in subbarbys at many a towne,
With bullis fret full of pardon. [4]   20
Byshops seles be nat behynd :
And thus I makë folkës blynd,
By my sleyght and by my guyle.

XVII. A ROYAL NIGROMANCER

Lydgate's Troy Book *was written between* 1412-20, *and contains the
following interesting description of the powers of a nigromancer. It
may serve as a good example of the credulity of our ancestors, and of the
way in which this was played upon by hordes of unscrupulous knaves.
This extract comes from the* E.E.T.S. (E.S.) *edition of H. Bergen,
published in* 1906, *p.* 60.

AND sche knewe of the firmament
The trewe cours, and of the sterris alle,
And by her mevyng what that schulde falle,
So expert sche was in astronomye.
But most sche wrought by nygromauncye,

---

[1] steal.   [2] is not.   [3] foolish.
[4] with papal bulls fully loaded with pardon.

With exorghismes and conjurisons;
And used also to make illusions
With hir charmys seide in sondri wyse:
And with rytis of diverse sacrifice,
Encens and rikelis cast in-to the fire,   10
To schewe thinges liche to hir desyre—
With gotis hornys and with mylke and blod,
Whan the mone was equat and stood
In the fifthe or the seventhe hous,
And was fortuned with lokyng gracious,
To chese an hour that were convenient
And fortunat, by enchauntement,
To make and werke sondry apparences:
So wel sche knewe the hevenly influences
And aspectis, bothe wrothe and glade;   20
For sche by hem alle her thingis made
That appartene to swyche experimentis.
For whan hir list, by hir enchauntementis,
Sche koude make the wyndes for to blowe,
To thondre and lighte and to hayle and snowe,
And frese also, to greve men with peyne;
And sodeinly sche coude make it rayne,
Schewe what wedir that hir liste to have,
And gasten [1] men with sodein erthe-quave,
And turne the day unwarly un-to nyght;   30
And thanne anoon make the sonne bright
Schewe his bemys, ful persyng and ful schene,[2]
With goldene hornys, to voyde nyghtes tene;
And reyse floodis, with many dredful wowe;
And whan hir list sche koude hem eft with-drawe.
Eke yonge trees to sere, rote and rinde,
And afterward make hem, ageines kynde,
With lusty braunchis blosme and budde newe;
Also in wynter with flouris fresche of hewe
Araye the erthe and tapite [3] hym in grene,   40
That to beholde a Joye it was to sene;

---

[1] frighten.   [2] most piercing and bright.   [3] clothe.

With many colour schewyng ful diverse,
Of white and rede, grene, ynde, and pers,[1]
The dayesye with hir riche croune,
And other floures, that wynter made froune,
Up-on her stalke freschely for tapere.
And sodeinly, with a dedly chere,
Sche koude somer in-to wynter torne,
Causyng the day with mystes for to morne ;
And olde men sche koude make yong,   50
And eft ageyn, or [2] any her was sprong,
Sche koude hem schew bothe in hed and berd
Ful hor and grey, in craft sche was so lered.
And trees with frute sche koude make bare
Of rynde and lef, to do men on hem stare ;
Clipse the mone and the brighte sonne,
Or [2] naturally thei hadde her cours y-ronne
To hem approprid,[3] whiche thei may not passe ;

XVIII. THE VILLAGE WITCH

Robert Mannyng of Brunne wrote the poem called Handlyng Synne
from which this extract is taken, in 1303. *The poem is a translation
of a French work, the* Manual des Pechiez *of William Waddington,
but Mannyng adds many touches and some stories of his own. The
whole work is full of information concerning medieval life and manners.
Our extract is taken from p.* 19, *line* 501, *of the E.E.T.S. edition of*
1901-3, *edited by F. J. Furnivall.*

THERE was a wycche, and made a bagge,
A bely [4] of lethyr, a gretë swagge,[5]
She sygaldryd [6] so thys bagge bely
That hyt gede [7] and soke [8] mennys ky,[9]
At evene, and at morw tyde,
Yn here pasture, other ellys be syde.
Long hyt gede aboute fast,
Tyl hyt was parceyved at the last ;
Than all the godemen of the toune,
Before the bysshop dyden here somoune ;   10

---

[1] blue.   [2] ere.   [3] allotted.   [4] bellows.   [5] bulky mass.
[6] charmed.   [7] went.   [8] sucked.   [9] kine.

They dyden the baggë with here bere,
To wete [1] what she shuld answere.
Hyt was shewyd before the bysshop,
That she dyde [2] to goo swych a melk slop, [3]
Thurgh wycchecraft and mysaventure,
To sugke here keyn yn here pasture.
The bysshop merveyled, and other mo, [4]
How that she myght do hyt go.
'Dame', seyd the bysshop, 'do thy quentyse, [5]
And late [6] us se how hyt shal ryse.'   20
Thys wycche here charme began to sey,
The slop ros up, and gede the weye.
The bysshop seyd, 'thys have we seyn ;
Do hyt now to lygge [7] ageyn ',
The wycchë dede al at hys wylle :
She made the slop agen lygge stylle.
The bysshop made a clerk than wryte
Al that she seyd, mochel and lyte, [8]
And alle how she did and ment ;
The bysshop tharto gaf gode entent.   30
'Than ', seyde the bysshop, ' now shal y,
As thou hast do, do thy maystry.' [9]
The bysshop began the charme to rede,
And as she dyde, he dyde yn dede ;
He seyd and dede every deyl, [10]
Ryght as she dede, he dede as weyl.
The sloppe lay stylle, as hyt ded wore,
For hym ne ros hyt never the more.
'Why ', seyd he, ' wyl hyt nat ryse,
And y have do the same wyse,   40
And seyd the wurdys, lesse ne mo, [11]
And for my seyyng wyl hyt nat go ? '
'Nay ', she seyd, ' why shuld hyt so ?
Ye beleve nat as y do :

---

[1] know: [2] caused. [3] bag. [4] others too. [5] enchantment.
[6] let. [7] lie down. [8] much and little. [9] trick. [10] part.
[11] neither more nor less.

Wulde ye beleve my wurdys as y,
Hyt shulde a go, and sokun ky.'
He seyd, 'Than faleth [1] noght but belevyng ? '
She seyd, ' That helpeth al my thyng ;
And so hyt ys for oure lawe,
Beleve ys more than the sawe ; [2]   50
For thou mayst sey what thou wylt,
But [3] thou beleve hyt, ellys ys alle spylt ;
Alle that y seyd, ye beleve hyt weyl,
My beleve hath do the dede every deyl.'
The bysshop comaundyd that she shuld noght
Beleve ne wurche [4] as she had wroght.

XIX. IN HOLIDAY MOOD

*Amusements probably did not figure largely in the villager's day.
His scanty leisure left him little time for such games as we find detailed
in the extract which follows ; but Manor Court rolls, with their ' John
Herberd is at mercy for trespassing in the Lord's wood ', etc., are the prose
equivalent of the magnificent poaching scene which opens* The Parlement
of the Thre Ages. *And to it, we may add the other familiar occupation
of the country-side, whether openly or furtively pursued—the art of
fishing, whose claims are so persuasively put forth in the last extract
of this Section.*

*The following compendious account of medieval sports comes from the
Englished version of the* Pilgrimage of the Life of Man, *by John Lydgate, which has already been referred to (see above, p. 85). Our extracts
are from p. 366, ll. 11, 181 ff., and p. 317, ll. 11,610 ff..*

AND my name ys ek fful kouthe, [5]
Ffor I am ycallyd ' youthe ' ;

.   .   .   .   .   .

Pleye at the cloos, [6] among, I shal,
And somwhyle rennyn at the bal
Wyth a staff mad lyk an hook ;
And I wyl han a kampyng crook ; [7]
Ffor I desyre, in my depos, [8]
Ffor to hav noon other croos.

---

[1] lacketh.   [2] saying.   [3] Unless.   [4] work.
[5] And my name is also well-known.   [6] a game much like ninepins.   [7] Possibly a staff used in athletic contests.   [8] death.

And among,[1] I wyl not spare
To hunte for hert, ffor buk & hare ;   10
Somtyme ffysshe, & cachche ffowlys,
And sometyme pleyen at the bowlys ;
Among, shetyn at bessellys,[2]
And affter pleyn at the merellys.[3]
Now at the dees, in my yong age,
Bothe at hassard & passage ; [4]
Now at the ches, now at the tablys,[5]
Rede no storyes but on ffablys,
On thyng that ys nat worth a lek,
Pleye at the keyles [6] & the quek.[7]   20
Somewhyle my wyttys I applye
To here song & menstralcye,
And pleye on dyvers Instrumentys :
And the ffyn [8] of myn entent ys
To folwe the lust of my corage, [9]
And to spende my yonge age
In merthe only, & in solace,
    Ffolwe my lustys in ech place ;
Ther-to hooly I me enclyne,
Rather than to han doctryne   30
Off ffader, moder, thogh they be wyse.
Al ther techyng I despyse,
And in no thyng ys set my cure,[10]
But my lustys to procure.

. . . .

    I (Idleness) teche hem daunce,
And also, ffor ther lady sake,
Endyte lettyrs, & songys make
Up-on the glade somerys dayes,
Balladys, Roundelays, vyrelayes.
I teche hem ek, (lyk ther ententys,)   40
To pleye on sondry Instrumentys,

---

[1] at times.   [2] archer's butt.   [3] nine-men's morrice.
[4] games played with dice.   [5] backgammon.   [6] ninepins.
[7] quickboard.   [8] end.   [9] the desires of my heart.   [10] care.

On harpe, lut, & on gyterne,
And to revelle at taverne,
Wyth al merthe & mellodye,
On rebube [1] and on symphonye ;
To spende al the day in ffablys,
Pleye at the ches, pley at the tablys,
At treygobet [2] & tregetrye, [3]
In karyyng & in Joglorye ;
And to al swych maner play,   50
Thys the verray ryghte way.

XX. IN THE WOODS

*This extract forms the Prologue to the fourteenth-century alliterative
poem* The Parlement of the Thre Ages. *It displays the same close
observation of nature and the same detailed knowledge of the chase that
is to be found in other alliterative poems of the time such as* Sir Gawaine
and the Grene Knight. *Here we have a magnificent picture of the
medieval villager, stealing into the Lord's wood at dawn and his adventures there. The poem has recently been admirably edited by Sir I.
Gollancz, to whose edition of* 1915 *I am indebted for much help in the
rough translation I append.*

In the monethe of Maye when mirthes bene fele,
And the sesone of somere when softe bene the wedres,
Als I went to the wodde my werdes to dreghe,
In-to the schawes my-selfe a schotte me to gete
At ane hert or ane hynde, happen as it myghte :
And as Dryghtyn the day droue frome the heuen,
Als I habade one a banke be a bryme syde,
There the gryse was grene growen with floures—
The primrose, the pervynke, and piliole the riche—
The dewe appon dayses donkede full faire,   10

In May, when there are many pleasures, and in the summer season
when airs are soft, I went to the wood to take my luck, and in among
the shaws to get a shot at hart or hind, as it might happen. And,
as the Lord drove the day through the heavens, I stayed on a bank
beside a brook where the grass was green and starred with flowers—
primroses, periwinkles and the rich penny-royal. The dew dappled
the daisies most beautifully, as well as the buds, blossoms and branches

---

[1] violin.   [2] a dice game.   [3] juggling, mumming, conjuring, cf,
Chaucer's *Franklin's Tale*, ll. 413–20,

Burgons & blossoms & braunches full swete,
And the mery mystes full myldely gane falle :
The cukkowe, the cowschote, kene were thay bothen,
And the throstills full throly threpen in the bankes,
And iche foule in that frythe faynere than other
That the derke was done & the daye lightenede :
Hertys and hyndes one hillys thay gouen,
The foxe and the filmarte thay flede to the erthe,
The hare hurkles by hawes, & harde thedir dryves,
And ferkes faste to hir fourme & fatills hir to sitt.   20
Als I stode in that stede one stalkynge I thoghte ;
Bothe my body and my bowe I buskede with leues ;
And turnede to-wardes a tree & tariede there a while ;
And als I lokede to a launde a littill me be-syde,
I seghe ane hert with ane hede, ane heghe for the nones ;
Alle vnburneschede was the beme, full borely the mydle,
With iche feetur as thi fote, for-frayed in the greues,
With auntlers one aythere syde egheliche longe ;
The ryalls full richely raughten frome the myddes,
With surryals full semely appon sydes twayne ;   30
And he assommet and sett of vi. and of fyve,
And ther-to borely and brode and of body grete,
And a coloppe for a kynge, cache hym who myghte.

while the soft mists began to subside. Both the cuckoo and
cushat were singing loudly, and the throstles in the bank-sides
eagerly poured out their songs, and every bird in the wood was
more delighted than his neighbour that darkness was done and the
day-light come.

Harts and hinds betake themselves to the hills ; the fox and pole-
cat seek their earths ; the hare squats by the hedges, hurries and
hastens thither to her forme, and prepares to lurk there. As I
stood in that place the idea of stalking, came to me ; so I covered both
bow and body with leaves, turned in by a tree and waited there a
while. And as I gazed in the glade near by me I saw a hart with
tall antlers : the main beme was unburnished, and the middle
very strong. Like thy foot was each antler frayed in the thicket
with exceedingly long antlers on each side. The royal antlers rose
proudly from the centre, while the crown-antlers on both sides full
seemly were set. He was full grown and set of six and of five,
large and broad and big of body : whoever might catch him, he
was a dish for a king.

Bot there sewet hym a sowre that seruet hym full gerne
That woke & warned hym when the wynde faylede,
That none so sleghe in his slepe with sleghte scholde hym
    dere,
And went the wayes hym by-fore when any wothe tyde,
My lyame than full lightly lete I doun falle,
And to the bole of a birche my berselett I cowchide ;
I waitted wiesly the wynde by waggynge of leues,   40
Stalkede full stilly no stikkes to breke,
And crepite to a crabtre and couerede me ther-vndere :
Then I bende vp my bowe and bownede me to schote,
Tighte vp my tylere and taysede at the hert :
Bot the sowre that hym sewet sett vp the nese,
And wayttede wittyly abowte & wyndide full gerne.
Then I moste stonde als I stode, and stirre no fote ferrere,
For had I my(n)tid or mouede or made any synys,
Alle my layke hade bene loste that I hade longe wayttede.
Bot gnattes gretely me greuede and gnewen myn
    eghne ;   50
And he stotayde and stelkett and starede full brode,
Bot at the laste he loutted doun & laughte till his mete,
And I hallede to the hokes and the hert smote,
And happenyd that I hitt hym by-hynde the lefte scholdire,

But there followed him a fourth-year buck that most eagerly
attended him and aroused and warned him when the wind failed
so that no one should be sly enough by stealth to harm him in his
sleep. He went in front of him when any danger was feared. I
let the leash fall to the ground quietly, and couched my hound by
the bole of a birch-tree and took heed of the wind by the waving of
the leaves. I stalked on very quietly so as to break no twigs and
crept to a crab-tree and hid underneath it. Then I wound up my
bow and prepared to shoot, drew up the tiller and aimed at the hart,
but the buck who attended the hart lifted up his nose, looked
cautiously around, and eagerly snuffled about. Then, perforce, I had
to stand without moving and stir no foot, although gnats grievously
troubled me and bit my eyes ; for if I had tried to move, or made
any sign, all my sport, that I had so long awaited, would have been
lost. The hart paused, went on cautiously, staring here and there,
but at last he bent down and began on his feed. Then I hauled to
the hook and smote him. It so happened that I hit him behind the
left shoulder and the blood streamed out on both sides. He stopped ;

That the blode braste owte appon bothe the sydes :
And he balkede and brayed and bruschede thurgh the
greues,
As alle had hurlede one ane hepe that in the holte
longede ;
And sone the sowre that hym sewet resorte to his feris,
And thay, forfrayede of his fare, to the fellys thay hyen ;
And I hyede to my hounde and hent hym vp sone, 60
And louset my lyame and lete hym vmbycaste ;
The breris and the brakans were blody by-ronnen ;
And he assentis to that sewte and seches hym aftire,
There he was crepyde in-to a krage and crouschede to
the erthe ;
Dede als a dore-nayle doun was he fallen ;
And I hym hent by the hede and heryett hym vttire,
Turned his troches & tachede thaym in-to the erthe,
Kest vp that keuduart and kutt of his tonge,
Brayde (out) his bowells my berselett to fede,
And I s(clis)te hym at the assaye to see how me
semyde, 70
And he was floreschede full faire of two fyngere brode.
I chese to the chawylls chefe to be-gynn,
And ritte doun at a rase reghte to the tayle,
And than the herbere anone aftir I makede,
I raughte the righte legge by-fore, ritt it ther-aftir,

brayed and then brushed through the thickets as if everything in the
wood had crashed together. And soon the attendant buck returned
to his fellows who were terrified by his behaviour and took to the
fells. I went to my hound, and soon seized him and loosed the
leash and let him cast about. The briars and bracken were smeared
with blood, and the hound fell upon the scent and pursued the
hart. There he had crept into a cave ; and, crouched to the earth,
had fallen dead as a door-nail.

I took him by the head and dragged him out ; pushed back his
tynes and fastened them into the ground, and turned the rogue
over and cut out his tongue. I pulled out his bowels to feed my
hound and then slit him open to see how fat he was, and found he
was overlaid with fat full two fingers in breadth. I chose to begin
at his jowls, and at a stroke I slit him up right to the tail. Then
after that I tied up his first stomach, and pulled the right leg in front

And so fro legge to legge I lepe thaym aboute,
And the felle fro the fete fayre I departede,
And flewe it doun with my fiste faste to the rigge ;
I tighte owte my trenchore and toke of the scholdirs,
Cuttede corbyns bone and kest it a-waye ;   80
I slitte hym full sleghely, and slyppede in my fyngere,
Lesse the poynte scholde perche the pawnche or the
      guttys :
I soughte owte my sewet and semblete it to-gedre,
And pullede oute the paw(n)che and putt it in an hole :
I grippede owte the guttes and graythede thaym be-syde,
And than the nombles anone name I there-aftire,
Rent vp fro the rygge reghte to the myddis ;
And than the fourches full fayre I fonge fro the sydes,
And chynede hym chefely, and choppede of the nekke,
And the hede and the haulse homelyde in sondree ;   90
The fete of the fourche I feste thurgh the sydis,
And heuede alle in-to ane hole and hidde it with ferne,
With hethe and with hore mosse hilde it about,
That no fostere of the fee scholde fynde it ther-aftir ;
Hid the hornes and the hede in ane hologhe oke,
That no hunte scholde it hent ne haue it in sighte.
I foundede faste there-fro for ferde to be wryghede,
And sett me oute one a syde to see how it cheuede,

and removed the flesh afterwards, and so ran my knife around each
leg and pulled off the skin from each leg, and flayed him right down
to his back.   I drew my hunting-knife and cut off the shoulder, then
cut out the raven's bone and threw it away.   I cleverly slit him up
and put in my fingers lest the point should pierce the paunch or
guts.   I groped for the suet and got it all together ;   pulled out the
paunch and put it in a hole ;   next beside them I put the guts ;   and
then after that I took the entrails.   I cut him up right from the back
to his middle, pulled back his forks from the sides, cut along the
backbone and chopped off the neck, and cut the head and neck into
parts.   The feet of the haunch I fastened through the sides and
heaved the lot into a hole, hid it with fern, and covered it over with
heather and hoar moss, so that no forrester of the fee should find it
afterwards.   The horns and the head I hid in a hollow oak so that
no hunter should get sight of it or seize it.   Then I hastened quickly
away for fear of being discovered and sat down on one side of the

To wayte it frome wylde swyne that wyse bene of nesse ;
And als I satte in my sette the sone was so warme, 100
And I for slepeless was slome and slomerde a while.

wood to see what happened, and to guard it from wild swine that
are cunning of scent.   As I sat in my retreat the sun was so warm
and I was heavy with sleep and slumbered awhile.

XXI. FIELD SPORTS

*The following passage is taken from the fifteenth-century pamphlet
which gives us an older form of the* Treatise of Fysshynge wyth an
Angle, *attributed to Dame Juliana Barnes (ed. T. Satchell, London,
1883).*

(p. 1) SALOMAN in hys paraboles seith that a glad spirit
maketh a flowryng age, that is to sey, a fair age and a
long ; and sith hyt ys so I aske this questyon, ' Wyche
bynne the menys and cause to reduce a man to a mery
spryte ' ?   Truly, into my symple discrescion, it semyth
me good and honest dysportes and games in wyche a man's
hert joythe withowt any repentans. . . .   Therfor now
will I cheys of four good disportes and honest gamys—
that is to sey of huntyng, haukyng, fowlyng and fyschyng,
namely anglyng with a rod or a yarde, a line and a hook,
and therof to treyt as my sympulnes may suffice, both
for the seyde reson of Saloman and also for the reson of
physyke mayd in this wyse :

> Si tibi deficiant medici medici tibi fiant
> Hec tria mens leta labor et moderata dieta.

That ys to sey, yf a man lak leches or medicens he schall
make 3 thinges hys medicens or leches and he shall never
neyd mo.   The fyrst of them ys mery thowght.   The
second is labour mesurably, the third ys good dyet of
cleyn metes and drynkes seasonable.   Fyrst then yf a man
wyl be mery and have a glad, spry spiryt, he must eschew
all contraryus companye, and all places of debates and
stryves, where he myght have occasyon of malencoly, and
yf he wyl have a labur not outrage[ou]s he must orden

hym to hys hertes plesens withowt stody pensefulnes, or travel a mery occupacion wyche may rejoyce hys hert and hys spryit in honest maner, and yf he wyl dyet hymselfe mesurably he must eschew all places of ryot wiche is cause of surfettes and seknes, and he must draw hym to a place of sweyt eyr and hungre and ete norysching metes and defyabul.[1]

I wyl now dyscryve the seyd four disportes and gamys to fend the best of them as wyll as I can.   All-be-it that the ryght nobul Duke of Yorke, late calde ' Master of the Game ', hath dyscryved the myrths of huntyng, lyke as I thynké to scryve of it, and all the grevys.[2]

Huntyng as to myne content is too gret labur.   The hunter must all day renne and folow hys houndes, travelyng and swetyng full soyr.   He blowythe tyl hys lyppes blyster ; and wen he wenyt [3] hyt be a hare, ful often hit is a hey-ghoge.   Thus he chaset, and when he cummet home at even,—reyn-beton, seyr prykud with thornes and hys clothes torne, wet-shod, fulwy,[4] some of hys howndes lost, some surbatted,[5]—suche grevys and meny other to the hunter hapeth, whiche for displesour of them that lovyth hyt I dare not report all.   Trewly me semythe that this is not the best disport and game of the seid four.

Hawkynge.

Thys disporte and game of hawkynge is laborous and ryght noyous [6] also, as me semyth. . . .   The fawkner often tymes leseth hys hawkes, the hunter hys howndes,—then all hys disporte ben gon and don.   Full often he cryethe and wystel tyl he be sore athryst, hys hawke taketh a bowe and list not onys to hym reward [7] when he wolde have her for to fle. . . .

Fowlyng.

The disporte and game of fowlyng me seemyth most symplest for yn the season of somer the fowler spedyth not.

---

[1] Digestible.   [2] griefs, pains.   [3] thinks.
[4] miry.   [5] foot-sore.   [6] troublesome.
[7] His hawk makes a random circuit and does not once listen to the fowler.

But in the most herde and colde wedyre he is soyr greved,
for he wolde go to hys gynnes ¹ [but] he may not for
colde. Many a gyn and many a snayr he maketh and
many he leseth. In the mernyng he walketh in the dew ;
he goyth also wetschode, and sor a-colde to dyner by the
morow, and sum-tyme to bed or he have wyl sowpud for
anythynge that he may geyt by fowlyng. Many other
sych I can rehers, but my magre ² or angre maketh me to
leyf. Thus me seemyth that huntyng, haukyng and fowlyng
be so laborous and grevous that none of them may performe to enduce a man to a mery spyryt, the wyche ys
cause of longe lyfe, according to the seyd parabul of Salo-
mon.

Fischynge.

Dowtles then folowyth it that it must nedys be the disporte
and game of fyschyng with an angul rode, for all other
maner of fyschyng is also ryght labure and grevous, often
causyng men to be ryght weyth and colde, wyche mony
tymes hath be seyn the cheyf cause of infyrmyte and sum
tyme deythe. But the angleer may have no colde ne no
disese ne angur, but ³ he be causer hymselfe, for he may
not gretly lose but a lyne or an hoke, of wyche he may hayf
plente of hys owyne makyng, or of other mens, as thys
sympul tretes schall teche hym . . . and other grevous
may he have none. . . . For yf he fayl of one [fish] he
may not faylle of another, yf he do as thys tretes schall
ynfo me hym, but yf ⁴ ther ben non in the watur wer he
schall angul.

Yet at the leste ⁵ he schall have hys holsom walke and
mery at hys own ease, and also many a swete ayr of dyvers
erbis and flowres that schall make hyt ryght hongre ⁶ and
well disposud in hys body. He shall heyr the melodyes
melodious of the Ermony of bryde, he schall see also the
youn swannys and signetes, followyng ther Eyrowrs,⁷
ducks, cootes, herons and many other fowlys with the
brodys, wyche we semyt better than all the noyse of

---

¹ traps.   ² ill-will. *Fr.* mal grè.   ³ unless.
⁴ unless.   ⁵ least.   ⁶ hungry.   ⁷ a brood of swans.

houndes, and blastes of hornes, and other games that fawkners and hunters can make. . . .

(p. 37) And for by cause that this present treatyse sholde not come to the hondys of eche ydle persone whyche wolde desire yt, yf it were emprynted allone by itself and put in a lytyll plaunflet, therfore I have compylyd it in a greter volume of dyverse bokys concernynge to gentyll and noble men to the entent that the forseyd ydle persones whyche sholde have but lytyll mesure in the sayd dysports of fysshyng sholde not by this means utterly dystroye it.

SECTION THREE

T O W N   L I F E

Any series of extracts must fail to do justice to the highly organized, varied and picturesque microcosm that was the big town of the fifteenth century. It might include all ranks from king to scullion, as it might harbour within its walls a dozen highly organized and important industries which sustained the majority of its population. The master of the gild jostled shoulders with the runaway serf who had sought shelter and eventual freedom within its protecting walls ; the trader from the far-off Hanse towns or from Guienne chaffered with its citizens in the market place ; the town-walls gave ocular demonstration that under their shadow men might dwell secure from raids and warlike marauders, and also reminded the citizens that they were a self-governing community and that these privileges had been won at a great price, and were to be protected and retained by every means in their power. The story of all this may be read in Mrs. J. R. Green's excellent work, *Town Life in the Fifteenth Century*, 2 vols., 1894 ; while Miss M. Bateson's *Borough Customs*, the two volumes of *British Borough Charters* edited by A. Ballard and J. Tait, and *The Gild Merchant* by C. Gross, contain many original documents and are indispensable to a thorough understanding of Town life. The subject is so vast that a handful of extracts can no more than indicate its wealth.

I. THE MEDIEVAL TOWN

No better description of the ordinary town of the fifteenth century could be desired than the following, which purports to describe the planning and building of New Troy. It is taken from Lydgate's Troy Book, written between 1412–20. It will recall the building of the '. new-towns ' and the ' bastides ' of the time of Edward I, and must have reminded many contemporary readers of such places as Winchel-

sea, Hull or Libourne, which they may have seen and at which their fathers and grandfathers may have worked. Our extract is from the edition of H. Bergen for the E.E.T.S. (E.S.) 1906, Vol. I, p. 158.

(a) THE BUILDERS

(l. 481) THIS worthi kyng, callyd Priamus,
Is in his herte nowe so desyrous,
Up-on the pleyn, that was so waste and wylde,
So strong a toun of newe for to bilde,
At his devyse a cite edefye,
That schal thassautys outterly defye
Of alle enmyes, and his mortal foon,
With riche tourys and wallys of hard stoon.
And al aboute the contres enviroun,
He made seke in every regioun   10
For swiche werkemen as were corious,[1]
Of wyt inventyf, of castyng[2] merveilous;
Or swyche as coude crafte of gemetrye,
Or wer sotyle in her fantasye;
And for everyche that was good devysour,
Mason, hewer, or crafty quareour,
For every wright and passyng carpenter,
That may be founde, owther fer or nere;
For swyche as koude grave, grope,[3] or kerve,
Or swiche as werne able for to serve   20
With lym or stoon, for to reise a wal,
With bataillyng and crestis marcial;
Or swiche as had konyng in her hed,
Alabastre, owther white or redde,
Or marbil graye for to pulsche[4] it pleyn,
To make it smothe of veynes and of greyn.
He sent also for every ymagour,
Bothe in entaille,[5] and every purtreyour
That coude drawe, or with colour peynt
With hewes fresche, that the werke nat feynt;[6] 30

---

[1] highly skilled.   [2] reckoning.   [3] groove.   [4] polish.
[5] engraving.   [6] would not fade.

And swiche as coude with countenaunces glade
Make an ymage that wil nevere fade :
To counterfet in metal, tre, or stoon
The sotil werke of Pigmaleoun,
Or of Appollo, the whiche as bokis telle,
In ymagerye alle other dide excelle ;
For by his crafty werkyng corious,
The towmbe he made of kyng Daryus,
Whiche Alysaundre dide on heyghte reise,
Only for men schuld his fame preise,   40
In his conquest by Perce whan he went.
And thus Priam for every maister sent,
For eche kerver and passynge joignour,
To make knottis with many corious flour,
To sette on crestis with-inne and with-oute
Up-on the wal the cite rounde aboute ;
Or who that were excellyng in practik
Of any art callyd mekanyk,
Or hadde a name flouryng or famus,
Was after sent to come to Priamus.   50
For he purposeth, this noble worthi kyng,
To make a cite most royal in byldyng,
Brod, large, and wyde, and lest it were assailed,
For werre proudly abouten enbatailled.
And first the grounde he made to be sought,
Ful depe and lowe, that it faille nought
To make sure the fundacioun ;
In the place where the olde toun
Was first ybilt, he the wallis sette ;
And he of lond many myle out mette,[1]   60
Aboute in compas, for to make it large,
As the maysters that toke on hem the charge
Devysed han the settyng and the syyt,
For holsom [2] eyr to be more of delyt.
And whan the soille, defouled with ruyne
Of walles old, was made pleyn as lyne,

---

[1] measured.   [2] wholesome.

The werkmen gan this cite for to founde,
Ful myghtely with stonys square and rounde,
That in this world was to it noon lyche
Of werkmanschip, nor of bildyng riche,   70
Nor of crafte of coryous masounry.
I can no termys to speke of gemetrye,
Wherfore as now I muste hem sette a-syde ;
For douteles I radde never Euclide,
That the maister and the foundour was
Of alle that werkyn by squyre or compas,
Or kepe her mesour by level or by lyne ;
I am to rude clerly to diffyne
Or to discrive this werk in every parte,
For lak of termys longyng to that arte.   80

. . . .

(b) THE CITY

The lenthe was, schortly to conclude,
Thre day(es) journe, lyche the latitude,
That never I herd make mencioun
Of swiche another of fundacioun,
So huge in compas nor of swiche larges,
Nor to counte so passyng of fayrnes,
So edyfied or lusty to the syght.
And, as I rede, the walles wern on highte
Two hundrid cubites, al of marbil gray,
Maskowed [1] with-oute for sautis [2] and assay ;   90
And it to make more plesaunt of delyt,
A-mong the marbil was alabaster white
Meynt [3] in the walles, rounde the toun aboute,
To make it schewe with-inne and with-oute
So fresche, so riche, and so delitable,
That it alone was incomperable
Of alle cites that any mortal man
Sawe ever yit, sithe the world began.
And at the corner of every wal was set
A crowne of golde with riche stonys fret,[4]   100

[1] Machicolated.   [2] assaults.   [3] Mingled.   [4] ornamented.

That schone ful bright ageyn the sonne schene :
And every tour bretexed[1] was so clene
Of chose stoon, that wer nat fer a-sondre,
That to beholde it was a verray wonder.
Ther-to this cite compassed enviroun,
Hadde sexe gatis to entre in-to the toun :

.   .   .   .

With square toures set on every syde.
At whos corners, of verray pompe and pride,
The werkman han, with sterne and fel visages,
Of riche entaille, set vp gret ymages,   110
Wrought out of ston, that never ar like to fayle,
Ful coriously enarmed for batayle.
And thorugh the wal, her fomen for to lette.[2]
At every tour wer grete gunnys sette,
For assaut and sodeyn aventurys ;
And on tourettis wer reysed up figurys
Of wylde bestis, as beris and lyouns,
Of tigers, bores, of serpentis and dragouns
And hertis eke, with her brode hornes,
Olyfauntes and large unicornes,   120
Buglis,[3] bolys, and many grete grifoun,
Forged of brasse, of copur and latoun.
That cruelly by sygnes of her facys
Up-on her foon[4] made fel manacys.
Barbykans and bolewerkys huge,
A-fore the toun made for highe refuge,
Giffe nede were, erly and eke late ;
And portecolys stronge at every gate,
That hem thar nat noon assailyng charge ;
And the lowkis thikke, brode, and large,   130
Of the gatys al of goten bras.
And with-inne the myghty schittyng[5] was
Of strong yrne barres square and rounde,
And gret barrerys picched[6] in the grounde,

---

[1] battlemented.   [2] hinder.   [3] Buffaloes.   [4] foes.
       [5] fastening.   [6] set.

With huge cheynes forged for diffence,
Whiche nolde [1] breke for no violence,
That hard it was thorugh hem for to wynne.
And every hous, that was bilt with-inne,
Every paleys and every mancioun,
Of marbil werne thorugh-out al the toun,　　　140
Of crafty bildyng and werkyng most roial.
And the heght was of every wal
Sixty cubites from the grounde acountid;
And ther was non that other hath surmountid
In the cite, but of on heght alyche,
In verray sothe, bothe of pore and riche,
That it was harde of highe estat or lowe
Hous or palys asounder for to knowe,
So egaly of tymbre and of stoon
Her housis wern reysed everychon.　　　150

．　　．　　．　　．　　．　　．　　．

And of this toun the stretis large and wyde
Wer by crafte so prudently provided,
And by werkemen sette so and devided,
That holsom eyr amyddis myght enspire
Erly on morwe to hem that it desyre;
And zephirus, that is so comfortable
For to norysche thinges vegetable,
In tyme of yere, thorugh-oute every strete,
With sugred flavour, so lusty and so swete,
Most plesantly in the eyr gan smyte,　　　160
The cytegheyns only to delyte;
And with his brethe hem to recomfort,
Whan thei list walke hem silven to disport.
And thorugh the toun, by crafty purviaunce,
By gret avys and discret ordynaunce,
By compas cast, and squared out by squires.[2]
Of pulsched marbil vp-on strong pilleris,
Devised wern, longe, large, and wyde,
In the frountel of every stretis syde,

---

[1] would not　　　　　　　　[2] squares.

Fresche alures [1] with lusty highe pynacles,   170
And moustryng [2] outward riche tabernacles,
Vowted [3] a-bove like reclinatories, [4]
That called werne deambulatories,
Men to walke to-gydre tweine and tweyne,
To kepe hem drie whan it dide reyne,
Or hem to save from tempest, wynde, or thonder,
Gif that hem list schrowde hem silve ther-under.
And every hous cured [5] was with led ;
And many gargoyl and many hidous hed
With spoutis thorugh, and pipes as thei ought, 180
From the ston-werke to the canel raught, [6]
Voyding filthes low in-to the grounde,
Thorugh gratis percid of yren percid rounde ;
The stretis paved bothe in lengthe and brede,
In cheker wyse with stonys white and rede.
And every craft, that any maner man
In any lond devise or rekene can,
King Priamus, of highe discrecioun,
Ordeyned hath to dwellyn in the toun,
And in stretis, severyd her and yonder,   190
Everyche from other to be sette a-sonder,
That thei myght, for more comodite,
Eche be hym silfe werke at liberte :
Gold-smythes first, and riche jowellers,
And by hem silf crafty browdereris,
Wevers also of wolne and of lyne,
Of cloth of gold, damaske, and satyn,
Of welwet, cendel, and double samyt eke,
And every clothe that men list to seke ;
Smythes also, that koude forge wele   200
Swerdis, pollex, [7] and speris scharp of stele,
Dartis, daggeris, for to mayme and wounde,
And quarel [8] hedis scharp and square y-grounde.

---

[1] covered ways.   [2] showing.   [3] vaulted.
[4] couches.   [5] covered.   [6] gutter reached.   [7] pole axe.
[8] cross-bow shafts.

Ther wer also crafty armoureris,
Bowyers,[1] and fast(e) by fleccheris,[2]
And swyche as koude make schaftes pleyn,
And other eke that dide her besy peyn
For the werre to make also trappuris,[3]
Bete [4] baners and royal cote armuris,
And by devise, stondardis and penowns,   210
And for the felde fresche and gay gytouns.[5]
And every crafte that may rekned be,
To telle schortly, was in this cite.
And thorugh this toun, so riche and excellent,
In the myddes a large river went,
Causyng to hem ful gret commodite ;
The whiche on tweyne hath partid the cite,
Of cours ful swyft, with fresche stremys clere,
And highte Xanctus, as Guydo doth us lere.
And as I rede, that up-on this flood,   220
On eche-asyde many mylle stood,
Whan nede was her grayn and corn to grinde,
Hem to sustene, in story as I fynde.
This river eke, of fysche ful plenteuous,
Devided was by werkmen corious
So craftely, thorugh castyng sovereyne,[6]
That in his course the stremys myght atteyn
For to areche, as Guydo doth conjecte,
By archis strong his cours for to reflecte
Thorugh condut [7] pipis, large and wyde with-al, 230
By certeyn meatis [8] artificial,
That it made a ful purgacioun
Of al ordure and fylthes in the toun,
Waschyng the stretys as thei stod a rowe,
And the goteris in the erthe lowe,
That in the cite was no filthe sene ;
For the canel skoured was so clene,
And devoyded [9] in so secre wyse,
That no man myght espien nor devyse

[1] bow-makers.   [2] arrow-featherers.   [3] trappings.   [4] embroider.
[5] little flags.   [6] skilful devices.   [7] conduit.   [8] channels.   [9] emptied.

By what engyn the filthes, fer nor ner,   240
Wern born a-wey by cours of the ryver—
So covertly every thing was cured.[1]
Wher-by the toun was outterly assured
From engenderyng of al corrupcioun,
From wikked eyr and from infeccioun,
That causyn ofte by her violence
Mortalite and gret pestilence.
And by example of this flode ther was
Made Tibre at Rome, and wrought by Eneas,
The which also departeth Rome on two,   250
Myn auctor seith, I not wher [2] it be so.

II. LONDON

This panegyric of London by one of the greatest of Scottish poets—
William Dunbar—is an indication of the pride and admiration in which
the capital was held throughout the Middle Ages. *The poem is re-*
printed from The Poems of William Dunbar, *edited by H. B. Baildon,*
1907, *p.* 36.

LONDON, thou art of townes A per se.
  Soveraign of cities, semeliest in sight,
Of high renown, riches and royaltie ;
  Of lordis, barons, and many a goodly knyght ;
  Of most delectable lusty ladies bright ;
Of famous prelatis, in habitis clericall ;
  Of merchauntis full of substaunce and of myght :
London, th art the flouowr of Cities all.

Gladdith anon thou lusty Troy novaunt,[3]
  Citie that some tyme cleped was New Troy,   10
In all the erth, imperiall as thou stant,
  Pryncesse of townes, of pleasure and of joy,
  A richer restith under no Christen roy ; [4]
For manly power, with craftis naturall,
  Fourmeth none fairer sith the flode of Noy : [5]
London, thou art the flour of Cities all.

---

[1] covered.   [2] know not whether.
[3] According to legend, London was founded as a second Troy, by
Brutus, grandson of Æneas.   [4] king.   [5] Noah.

Genme of all joy, jasper of jocunditie,
  Most myghty carbuncle of vertue and valour ;
Strong Troy in vigour and in strenuytie ;
  Of royall cities rose and geraflour ;[1]   20
  Empresse of townes, exalt in honour ;
In beawtie beryng the crone imperiall ;
  Swete paradise precelling [2] in pleasure :
London, thow art the floure of Cities all.

Above all ryvers thy Ryver hath renowne,
  Whose beryall stremys, pleasaunt and preclare,[3]
Under thy lusty wallys renneth down,
  Where many a swanne doth swymme with wyngis fare ;
  Where many a barge doth saile, and row with are,[4]
Where many a ship doth rest with toppe-royall.   30
  O ! towne of townes, patrone and not compare :
London, thou art the floure of Cities all.

Upon thy lusty Brigge of pylers white
  Been merchauntis full royall to behold ;
Upon thy stretis goth many a semely knyght
  In velvet gownes and [in] cheynes of gold.
  By Julyus Cesar thy Tour founded of old
May be the hous of Mars victoryall,
  Whos artillary with tonge may not be told :
London, thou art the flour of Cities all.   40

Strong be thy wallis that about the standis ;
  Wise be the people that within the dwelles ;
Fresh is thy ryver with his lusty strandis ;
  Blith be thy chirches, wele sownyng be thy bellis ;
  Rich be thy merchauntis in substance that excellis ;
Fair be their wives, right lovesom, white and small ;
  Clere be thy virgyns, lusty under kellis : [5]
London, thou art the flour of Cities all.

[1] gilly-flower.   [2] excelling.   [3] famous.   [4] oar.
                [5] head-dress.

Thy famous Maire, by pryncely governaunce,
  With swerd of justice, the rulith prudently.   50
No Lord of Parys, Venyce, or Floraunce
  In dignytie or honoure goeth to hym nye.
  He is exampler, loode-ster, and guye ; [1]
Pryncipall patrone and roose orygynalle,
  Above all Maires as maister moost worthy ;
London, thou art the flour of Cities all.

III. 'MAD PRINCE HAL'

*The rejection of Falstaff and his followers is one of the most striking
scenes in* Henry IV. Part II. *The following extract from* The Brut
*(ed. F. W. Brie, E.E.T.S. 1908, p. 594) gives us an example of the
material Shakespeare had before him when he wrote that scene.*

AND in the same yer he was crownyd Kyng of Englond
at Westmenster on the nynthe day of Aprill ; and he was
a worthy kyng, and a gracious man, and a worthy con-
querour.   And before he was Kyng, what tyme he regnyd
Prince of Walyes, he fylle and yntendyd gretly to ryot,
and drew to wylde company ; and dyvers jentylmen and
jentylwommen folwyd his wylle and his desire at his commaundment ; and lykewyse all his meyne [2] of his housolde
was attendyng and plesyed with his gouernaunce, out-sept
iij. men of his howsolde, whiche were ful hevy and sory
of his governaunce ; and they counseylyd hym ever contrary, and fayne woolde an had hym to doon wele, and
forsake ryot. and therefor he hatyd them iij. most of al
men in his house, unto the tyme that his fadyr was dede.
And thanne he beganne to regne for Kyng, and he remembryd the gret charge and wourship that he shulde take
vpon him ; And anon he comaundyd al his peple that
were attendaunt to his mysgovernaunce afore tyme, and
al his housolde, to come before hym.   And whan they
herde that, they were ful glad, for they subposyd that he
woolde a [3] promotyd them in-to gret offices, and that they
shulde a stonde in gret favyr and truste with hym, and

---

[1] guide.   [2] retinue.   [3] have.

neerest of counsel, as they were afore tyme. And trustyng here-upon, they were the homlyer and bolder unto hym, and nothyng dred hym ; ynsomoche, that whan they were come before hym, some of them wynkyd on hym, and some smylyd, and thus they made nyse semblaunte [1] vnto hym, meny one of them. But for al that, the Prynce kept his countynaunce ful sadly unto them, And sayde to them : 'Syrys, ye are the peple that I have cherysyd and mayntynyd in Ryot and wylde governaunce ; and here I geve yow all in commaundment, and charge yow, that from this day forward that ye forsake al mysgovernaunce, and lyve aftyr the lawys of Almyhety God, and aftyr the lawys of oure londe. And who that doyth contrarye, I make feythful promys to God, that he shall be trewly ponisid [2] accordyng to the lawe, withoute eny favour or grace.' And chargyd them, (on) payn of deth, that they shulde never geve hym comforte nor counsel to falle to ryot no more ; for he had takyn a charge on hym, that alle his wittis and power were to lytyl, withoute the helpe of God and good governaunce. And so he rewardyd them richely with gold and sylver, and othyr juelys, and chargyd them alle to voyde his housolde, and lyve as good men, and never more to come in his presence, be-cause he woold haue noon occasioun nor remembraunce wherby he shulde falle to ryot ayen. And thus he voydyd al his housolde, savyng tho iij. personys that he hatyd most, whiche were ful sory of his governaunce ; and them he lovyd aftyrward best, for there good counsayle and good governaunce, and made them aftyrward gret lordys ; And thus was lefte in his housolde nomo but tho iij. men. And menyone of them that were eydyng [3] and consentyng to his wyldnes, fyl aftyrward to gret myschefe and sorw.

Than Kyng Herry sent to Dame Kateryn Swynfor, Countesse of Herforde, whiche was tho a wel-governed woman, and kept the most worshipful housolde, and the best rewlyd that was within the londe ; and to her he sent for men that were of good disposicyoun ; and she sent

---

[1] foolish grimaces.   [2] punished.   [3] aiding.

hym xij Ientylmen of sad [1] governaunce, and so this
gracious Kyng forsoke al wyldnes, and toke hym to good
governaunce, and kept streytly his lawys with ryghtwisness
and justise. For, in the first yere of his regne, ther were
ij knyhtis at gret debate ; the tone was of Lankestyr-shire,
and the tothyr of York-shire ; and they made them as
stronge of peeple as they cowde, and scarmyshid [2] togedyr ;
and men were slayne and hurte on bothe partyes. And
whán the Kyng herde therof, he sent for them : and they
came to the Kyng to Wyndelysore,[3] as he was goyng to
his dyneer. And whan the Kyng undirstode that they
were come, he commaundyd them to come before him.
And than he axyd them, whois men they were. And they
seyde, his lege men. ' And whois men be tho that ye have
a-reysyd up to fyghte for youre quarel ? ' ; and they seyde,
his men. ' And what awtoryte [4] or comaundement had
ye, to reyse up my men or my peeple, to fyght and sle
eche othyr for your quarel ? yn this ye ar worthy to dye.'
And they coude not askewse [5] them, but besowhte the
Kyng of his grace. And than the Kyng seyd, ' Be the
feith that he owte to God and to Seint George, but yf they
agreyd and accordyd, be that tyme that he had etyn his
owystrys, they shulde be hangyd bothe two or evyr he
sopyt.' [6] And than they yede [7] a-parte, and agreyd be
themselfe, and cam in ayen whan the Kyng had etyn his
owistris. And than the Kyng sayde : ' Syrys, how ston-dyth
yt with yow ? ' And than they knelyd downe, and seyde :
' Yf it plese your good grace, we be agreyd and accordyd.'
Anc than the Kyng seyde be the feythe that he owte to
God and to Seint George, that and evyr they made eny more
Insurreccioun or dethe of his lege peple, they, or ony othyr
lordys withynne his reawme, withowte his commaundment,
whatsomeeuer they were, they shulde dye, acordyng to
the lawe. And so, aftyr that, ther durst no lorde make
no party nor stryf ; and thus he beganne to kepe his
lawis and justise, and therfor he was belovyd and bedred.[8]

[1] wise, discreet. [2] scirmished. [3] Windsor. [4] authority.
[5] excuse. [6] before he supped. [7] went. [8] feared.

IV. AT THE COURT

Louis, sire de Gruthus or Gruthuyse, came on an embassy to Edward
IV in 1472 *from Charles, duke of Burgundy. Gruthus had showed*
kindness to Edward when he was an exile in Holland and Flanders,
and this extract recounts the reception of Gruthus in London by Edward.
The whole passage is taken from Bluemantle Pursuivant's contemporary
narrative and was first printed in Archælogia, *xxvi, pp.* 265 *ff, and later*
in a fuller and better form by C. L. Kingsford in his English Historical Literature of the Fifteenth Century, *p.* 386.

MEMORANDUM that the Kynge dyd to be impareled[1] on
the far syde of the quadrant ij chambres richeley hanged
with clothes of Arras, and with Beddes of astate ; and
when he had spoken with the Kinges good grace and the
Quene, he was accompanied to his chamber by me lorde
Chamberlein (and) Syr John A Parre, with dyvers moo,
which soopt with hym in his chamber : also there sopt
his servauntes. When they had sopt, my lord chamberleyn
had hym againe to ye Kinges chamber, and incontinent
the Kinge had hym to ye Quenes chamber, wher she sat
plainge with her ladyes at the morteaulx,[2] and some of
the ladyes and gentlewomen at the Closheys of yvery,[3]
and Daunsing. And some at dyvers other games accordinge. The whiche sight was full plesant to them. Also
ye Kinge daunsed with my lady Elizabethe, his eldest
doughter. That done, the night passed over, they wente
to his chamber. The lord Gruthuse toke leve, and my
lorde Chamberleyn with dyvers other nobles accompanied
hym to his chamber, where they departed for that night.
And in the morninge, when Matens was done, the Kinge
herde in his owne chappell our lady masse, which was
melodyousely songe, the lorde Grutehuse beinge there
presente. When the mas was done, the Kinge gave the
sayde lorde Grutehuse a cup of golde, garneshed with
perrye,[4] and in mydest of the cup is a grete pece of an
unicornes horne to my estimacyon vij ynches compasse.
And on the cover was a grete safyre.[5] Then he wente to

---

[1] apparelled.   [2] a game resembling bowls.   [3] Closh, or ninepins
[4] jewels.   [5] sapphire.

his chamber where he had his brekefaste. And when he had broken his faste, the Kynge come into ye quadrant. My lorde Prince also, borne by his Chamberleyn called Mr Vaghan, which bad ye foresaide lord Gruthuse welcome. Then the Kinge had hym and all his company into ye lytell Parke, where he made hym to have grete sport. And there ye Kinge made hym ryde on his owen horsse, a fayre hoby, the which the Kinge gave hym. Item, there in the Parke the Kinge gave hym a royall crosbowe, the strynges of sylke, the case covered with velvette of the Kinges colers, and his armes and bages thervpon. The heddes of ye quarrelles [1] were gilt. The Kynges dynner was ordeined [2] at the lodge. Before dynner they keld no game, saving a doo, ye which the Kinge gave to ye seruauntes of ye lorde Grutehuse. And when the Kinge had dyned, they wente a huntinge agayne. And by the castell were founden certein dere lyinge ; and what with greyhoundes and what were ren to dethe with bok [3] houndes, there were slayne halfe a dosen bokes, the which the Kinge gave to the sayde lorde Grutehuse. By yt tyme it was nere night, yet the Kinge shewed hym his garden and Vineyard of Plesyre, and so tourned into ye Castell agayne, where they herde evensonge in theire chambers.

The Quene dyd order a grete banket [4] in her owne chambre. At the which banket were the Kinge, the quene, my lady Elizabethe the Kinges eldest doughter, the Duches of Excester, my lady Ryvers, and the lorde Gruthuse, settinge at oone messe, and at the same table sat the Duke of Bokingham, My lady his wyff, with divers other Ladyes, whose names I have not, My Lorde Hastinges, Chamberleyn to the Kinge, My lorde Barnes, chamberleyn to the quene, John Gruthehuse son to ye forsaid lorde, Mr. George Bart, secretory to the Duc of Burgoine, Loys Stacy, usher to the Duke of Burgoine, and George Mytteney : also certeyn nobles of the kinges owne courte. Item, there was a syde table, atthe which sat a grete vewe of ladyes all on ye one

---

[1] a square-headed cross-bow bolt.   [2] ordered.
[3] buck-hounds.   [4] banquet.

syde. Also in the utter chamber sat the quenes gentle-women all on one syde. And at the other syde of the table agenest them sat as many of the lorde Gruthuse servauntes : as touchinge to ye abondant welfare, lyke as hyt ys accordinge to soche a banket. And when they had sopt, my lady Elizabeth, the Kinges eldest doughter, daunsed with the Duke of Bokingham : and dyvers other ladyes also. And aboute ix of the clocke the king and the quene with her ladies and gentlewomen brought ye sayde lorde Grutehuse to three chambers of Pleasance, all hanged and besyne with whyt sylke and lynnen-clothe, and all ye flowers[1] couered with carpettes. There was ordeined a bed for hym selff of as good downe as coulde be thought, the shetes of Raynes,[2] also fyne fustyan, the counterpoynt cloth[3] of gold furred with ermyne, ye tester and ye seler[4] also shyning clothe of gold, curtens of whyt sarsenette[5] : as for his bed shete and pelowes they were of the quenes owen ordinaunce. In ye second chamber was an other of a state, the which was alle whyt. Also in the same chamber was made a couche with fether beddes, hanged with a tent knit lyke a nett ; and there was ye coberd. Item, in the third chamber was ordeined a bayne[6] or ij, which were covered with tentes of whyt clothe. And when the Kinge and the quene, with all her ladyes and gentlewemen, had shewed hym these chambres, they turned againe to theire owne chambres, and lefte ye said lorde Grutehuse there, accompanied with my lorde chamberleyn, which dispoyled[7] hym and wente bothe to gether in the bane. Also there was Syr John a Parr, John Grutehuse, son to ye saide lorde, Mayster George Bartte, Secretory to the Duke of Burgoine, Loys, Jeys, Mytteney, and those servauntes that were longinge to theire chambres. And when they had been in theire baines as longe as was theire playsir, they had grene synger,[8] dyvers cyryppes,[9] comfyttes

---

[1] floors.　　[2] Rennes, a town famous for its cloth, cf. Chaucer, *Bk. of Duchesse*, l. 251 ff.　　[3] counterpane.　　[4] the head frame and canopy of the bed.　　[5] sarcenet : a very fine and soft silk.　　[6] bath.　　[7] undressed.　　[8] ginger.　　[9] various syrups.

and Ipocras,[1] and then they wente to bedde. And on ye morne he toke his conie or leve of the Kinge and the quene, and turned to Westmynster agayne, accompanied with certein knightes, esquiers and oder the Kinges servauntes, home to his loging.

And the Sonday next foloinge the King gave hym a gowne of cloth of golde furryd.

And on seynt Edwardes day opynly in ye parlement chamber he was commended to the Kinges good grace by ye speker of ye parlement : were opynly by the three estates of ye Realme, ye Kinge, beinge crowned, gyrd a sword about hym and creat hym Erle of Wynchester : Mr William Atclif, ye kinges secretory, red openly his patent that all folke might hear yt. Also he bare ye Kinges sworde that day tyll the Kyng went to dynner. Ye King kept that day his estate in ye Whyt Hall, where he dyned on the left of ye King at his owne table.

Larges. Larges. Larges.

V. THE MAYOR OF LONDON

The rights and privileges of the City of London were jealously guarded by the Mayor and citizens. The following extract shows the behaviour of the Mayor at a moment when the dignity of his office was challenged. It is taken from the work Dr. James Gairdner called Gregory's Chronicle, as it would seem to be in part compiled by a certain William Gregory, skinner, who was Mayor of London in 1451. The chronicle was edited by Dr. Gairdner for the Camden Society in 1876 under the title of Historical Collections of a London Citizen in the Fifteenth Century. *Its many graphic stories make it an invaluable source of information concerning London in the fifteenth century.*

(p. 222) THYS yere (1464), a-bute Mydsomyr, at the ryalle feste of the Sargantys of the Coyfe,[2] the Mayre of London was desyryde to be at that feste. And at denyr tyme he come to the feste with his offecers, a-greyng and a-cordyng unto hys degre. For with yn London he ys next unto the kyng in alle maner thynge. And in tyme of waschynge the Erle of Worcester was take be-fore the mayre and

---

[1] Hippocras : a spiced wine.
[2] Sergeants of the Coif, i.e. the most eminent lawyers.

9

sette downe in the myddys of the hy tabylle. And the mayre seynge that hys place was occupyd hylde hym con-tente, and went home a gayne with owt mete or drynke or any thonke, but rewarde hym he dyd as hys dygnyte requyryd of the cytte. And toke with hym the substance of hys bretheryn the aldyrmen to his place, and were sette and servyd also sone as any man couthe devyse, bothe of sygnet [1] and of othyr delycatys i-nowe, that alle the howse mervelyd howe welle alle tynge was done in soo schorte a tyme, and prayde alle men to be mery and gladde, hit shulde be a mendyd a nothyr tyme.

Thenn the offesers of the feste, fulle evylle a schamyd, informyd the maysters of the feste of thys mysse happe that ys be-falle. And they, consyderynge the grete dygnyte and costys and charge that longgyd unto the cytte, a-non sende unto the mayre a present of mete, brede, wyne, and many dyvers sotelteys.[2] But whenn they that come with the presentys say [3] alle the gyftys, and the sarvyse that was at the borde, he was fulle sore a schamyd that shulde doo the massage, for the present was not better thenn the servyse of metys was by fore the mayre, and thoroughe owte the hyghe tabylle. But hys demenynge was soo that he hadde love and thonke for hys massage, and a grette rewarde with alle. And thys the worschippe of the cytte was kepte, and not loste for hym. And I truste that nevyr hyt shalle, by the grace of God

VI. THE YOUNG PAGE

The service of Kings and nobles in Court and camp required a long apprenticeship. Chaucer's Squire shows us a young man in the concluding stages of his training. The following passage from The Life of Ipomydon (ed. Kölbing, Breslau, 1889) gives an excellent summary of the earlier training of the young page.

(l. 53) THOLOMEW a clerk he toke,
That taught the chyld uppon the boke,

[1] cygnet.   [2] a device, such as ' Gabriel greeting Mary ', or ' Man with a sickle, called Harvest ', elaborately worked in sugar paper, etc., which terminated each course.   [3] saw.

Both to synge and to rede,
And after he taught hym other dede.
Aftirward to serve in halle,
Both to grete and to smalle ;
Before the kyng mete to kerve,
Hye and low feyre to serve :
Bothe of howndis and haukis game.
Aftir he taught hym, all and same,   10
In se, in feld, and eke in ryvere,
In wodde to chase the wild dere,
And in the feld to ryde a stede,
That all men had joy of his dede.
All that lond of hym spake good,
For he was so myld of mood ;
Hende [1] he was, curteyse and fre,
A godelyer man myghte no man see.
Thy preysed hym bothe more and lesse,
Both man and woman, as I gesse ;   20
All lovyd hym that were hym by,
For he bare hym so curtessely.

VII. TOURNAMENTS

*Although chivalry was a dyirg institution, the glories of the Court of
Edward III had done something to arrest its decay. Jousts and
tourneys were still part of medieval life, and the citizen still could see
such sights as that told us by the chronicler in* The Brut, *where he
describes the jousts at Smithfield in* 1388.

(*p.* 343) IN this forsaide parlement, and in the twelfth
yere of King Richardes regne (1388), he let crye and ordeyne
generalle justise, that is called a turnement, of lordes,
knyghtis and skquires. And these justes and turnement
were holden at London in Smithfelde, for alle maner of
strayngers, of what londe and cunctre thei were, and thedir
thei were right welcome ; and to hem and to alle other
was holden opon housholde and grete ffestis ; and also
grete yftis were yeve to alle maner of straungers. And

---

[1] gracious.

thay of the kinges syde were alle of on sute : her cotis, her armyour, scheldes, and her hors and trapure, alle was white hertis, with crownes about her nekkis, and cheynes of golde hangyng there up-on, and the croune hangyng lowe before the hertis body ; the which hert was the kinges liveray that he yaf to lordes and ladies, knyghtis and skquiers, for to know his housholde from other peple. And at this first comyng to her justes, xxiiij ladies ladde these xxiiij lordes of the Garther with cheynys of goolde, and alle yn the same sute of hertis as is afore sayde, from the Tour on hors bak through the cite of London yn-to Smythfelde, there the justes schulde be do. And this fest and justes was holde general, and to alle tho that wolde come, of what land or nacion that evyr he were ; and this was holde duryng xxiiij dayes, of the kinges owne cost ; and these xxiiij lordes to answere to alle maner of pepil that wolde come thidir. And thedir come the Erle of seint Poule of Fraunce, and mony other worthi knyghtes with hym of divers parteys, fful welle arayed. And out of Holand and Henaude [1] come the Lorde Ostrenaunde, that was the Dukes sone of Holande, and mony other worthi knyghtes with hym, bothe of Holand and Henaude fulle welle arayede. And whenne these feste and justes was do and endid, the King thanked these st(r)ayngers and yaf ham mony grete yeftis ; and thanne thei token hir leve of the King and of other lordes and ladyes, and went hom ayen yn-to her owne cuntre, with grete love and moche thanke.

VIII. THE BURNING OF A HERETIC

Medieval justice indulged in a great deal of ostentatious display : the fraudulent baker might be seen, drawn through the streets, with his bread round his neck ; the vintner who sold bad wine was forced to drink some of it, while the remainder was poured over his head ; the felon was whipped through the streets and put in the pillory. More heinous crimes were more severely punished, and Gregory's Chronicle *gives the following account of what was a not uncommon sight to the medieval citizen.*

---

[1] Hainault.

(*p.* 233) ALLE soo thys same yere there was an herryke i-brende at the Towre Hylle, for he dyspysyd the sacrament of the auter ; hys name was Wylliam Balowe, and he dwellyd at Walden. And he and hys wyffe were abjuryd longe tyme be-fore. And my Lorde of London kepte hym in preson longe tyme, and he wolde not make noo confessyon unto noo pryste, but oonly unto God, and sayde that no pryste had noo more pouer to hyre confessyon thenn Jacke Hare. And he had no consyence to ete flesche aftyr Estyr, as welle as thoo that were bothe schryffe and houselyd.[1]

At the tyme of hys brennynge a Docter, Mayster Hewe Damelet, person of Syn Petrys in the Cornehylle, laboryd hym to be-leve in the hooly sacrament of the auter. And thys was the herytyke ys sayyng : ' Bawe ! bawe ! bawe ! What menythe thys pryste ? Thys I wotte welle, that on Goode Fryday ye make many goddys to be putte in the sepukyr, but at Ester day they can not a ryse them selfe, but that ye moste lyfte them uppe and bere them forthe, or ellys they wylle ly stylle yn hyr gravys.' Thys was that tyme of hys departyng from that worschipfulle docter.

IX. A NIGROMANCER

The treatment meted out to those who were rebels against Holy Church and in league with the devil may be illustrated by this vivid account of Dame Eleanor Cobham, Duchess of Gloucester, and her assistant. Eleanor was made to do penance by walking from Westminster to the City on three market days, bearing a taper in her hand, and afterwards was imprisoned in the Isle of Man. Her assistant's fate is briefly described below, from the account given in The Brut.

(*p.* 477) AND in this same yere (1441), the xv[th] day of Juyll, Kyng Henry the vj[th] come oute of Essexe to London, in at the port called Algate, and went over London Brigge and thurgh Suthwerk to his Maner of Kenyngton. And at his comyng in at Algate, the Maire, Aldermen and Comons, in theire best aray, welcomed the Kyng into the Cite ; and made grete Joye of his comyng. And godely

---

[1] as if by so doing he were shriven and had communicated.

the Kyng thanked the Maire and his brethern and all the Comons. And the Kyng was not so sone passed the Cite, bot that it hayled, rayned and eke lightned, that well was hym that was within house ; and so ayenst even it fared in the same Maner, wherof the peple were sore agast, and aferd of the grete tempest. And so it was spoken emonges the peple, that ther were som wikked fendes and spirites arered out of helle by conjuracion, forto noy the peple in the Reame, and to put theym to trouble, discencion and unrest. An then was it knowen that certeyn clerkes, and women that ar called ' wicches ', had made theire operacion and theire craft to destroy men and women, or whom they list, unto deth by theire fals craft and worching. Wherof Dame Alianore Cobham, which was the Duchesse of Gloucestre, was named principally of these actes and fals dedes forto destroy the Kyng, whom God save and kepe ! Bot as God wold save his hande-werk and servaunt, made it be knowen openly, all theire fals werkys and tresoun that they ymagyned and wroght, which was openly shewed afore all peple that wold com to Seint Paules Crosse on the Sonday, the twenty-third day of Juyll, by Roger that was hir Clerk, a Nigromancier, by the devels crafte and ymaginacion in his worching, which was shewed openly in the sermon-tyme, the day aboveseyd, to all peple that wold come to se it, of here scriptures, ymages of silver, of wexe, and of other metalles, and swerdys, with many other dyvers instrumentes of this fals craft of Nigromancy and the devels powere. And there Roger, this Clerk, stode upon an high stage, with all his Instrumentes about hym, spoyling of his garment ; and did upon hym a surplyce, with a crowne of papir upon his hede, forto forsake all his fals craft of the devell, and for to relapse all that he had doon and wrought by the devyll and his powere, in presence of the Archebisshop of Canterbury, the Cardy-nall, the Bisshop of Wynchestre, the Bisshop of London, the Bisshop of Salesbury, and many other grete clerkys beyng there present ; and of other lordes temporalles, therle of Huntingdon, therle of Northhumberland, and therle of Stafford, and moo other lordes of the Kynges Consayl, and the Maire and Aldermen, with the Comons of the Cite of London, and many moo people of dyvers partyes, and straungers of the Reame, and aliens of other straunge landes beyond the see, beyng in the Cite of London that tyme.

(*p.* 481) And the Seturday next, the seventeenth day of Novembre, Roger Bultyngbrok, Dame Alianore Cobhams Clerk of Nigromancy and sorcery, was brought to the Guyldhall of London, and there dampned [1] for his fals treson, and for his fals tresoun, and sorcery and Nigromancy ayenst all holy Chirch ; wherthurgh he was dampned to deth by landes lawe. And he was ledde to the Toure of London, and leyd vpon a hirdell, and drawen thurgh the Cite to Tybourne galowes, and there hanged, and let downe ageyne all quyk, and his bowelles cutte out of his body, and brent afore hym. And then was his hede smyten of, and his body quartered ; and oon sent to Oxenford, the secund sent to Cambrigge, the thridde to Bristowe, and the fourth to (   ) [2] ; and his hede was set upon London Brigge : and thus he ended his life in this world.

X. LAWYERS

' All things are possible for money ' ruefully writes a fifteenth-century man, and those engaged in litigation had constantly to bear this in mind. Litigation seems almost to have been a pastime of that century—everywhere we turn we read of it, and of the evils resulting. Among them the malpractices of lawyers and the falsity of jurors are recurrent themes. The following short passages from a pamphlet must illustrate in brief a vast subject. The pamphlet is printed among Wyclif's English Works, *edited by F. D. Matthew and published by the E.E.T.S. in* 1880.

(*p.* 182) ALSO false men of lawe disceyven moche this world, for thei tellen not sadly [3] and trewely how the lawe stondith, but norischen pledynge [4] and debate among men for to have a veyn name and wynnen hem a litil worldly stynkynge muk with Goddis curs, and wittyngly meyntenen the fals partie bi cavelacions,[5] and forbarien [6]

---

[1] judged. [2] blank in MS. [3] soberly.
[4] encourage law pleadings. [5] cavils, [6] obstruct.

pore men of right, that though a pore man hav nevere so muche right yet thei wole make many doseyns to forsweren hem on the book to gete hem self thank or wynnynge. . . . If ther be a trewe man in a contre he schal nat come to his queste [1] if he may devoyde [2] him, and if he seie the sothe [3] he schal have his hate, sclaundrynge, loss of his catel, or of his lif in this world ; and this laweieris thanken and flateryn and mayntenen false men and helpen them what they may . . . Lord, how schal God here them in their most nede, sith thei wolen not here a pore man, have he nevere so grete right.

XI. JURORS

(p. 183) JURROURIS in questis wolen forsweren them wittyngly for their dyner and a noble, [4] and that so customablice [5] that though a man have nevere so opyn right to a lordischipe anemptis [6] mannys lawe and also Goddis, that many questis wolen wittyngly swere that it is not his for a littel money. . . . Thus lordis and othere men ben nedid for this falsnesse to holden them at fees and othere grete costis, for ellis with their wiles and falsnesse thei wolen drive lordis and gentilmen out of their housis, heritage and alle their goodis ; and bi this falsnesse a fewe pore wrecchis myghten conqueren [7] into their owene hondis in schort tyme almost al the lordischipe that may be sold on any resonable manore.

XII. LONDON LICKPENNY

This poem has for centuries been ascribed to Lydgate, but modern authorities refuse to allow him the credit for this spirited piece of work. The version printed below comes from the Harleian MS. 542 f. 102, and is reprinted from Anglia xx, 410 ff., where Miss E. P. Hammond prints it side by side with the more frequently quoted version in 7 line stanzas, which is taken from Harleian MS. 367 f. 127.

In London there I was bent
I saw myself where truthe shuld be ateynte, [8]

---

[1] legal inquiry. [2] remove. [3] truth. [4] 6s. 8d.
[5] habitually. [6] in respect of. [7] acquire. [8] attained.

Fast to Westminstar ward I went,
To a man of law to make my complaynte.
I said, ' For Mary's love, that holy Seynt,
Have pity on the powre, that would procede,
I would gyve sylvar, but my purs is faynt,'
For lacke of money, I may not spede.

As I thrast thrughe out the thronge
Amonge them all, my hode [1] was gone,   10
Netheles I let not longe,[2]
To Kyngs Benche tyl I come.
By fore a juge I kneled anon,
I pray'd hym for God's sake he would take hede,
Full rewfully to hym I gan make my mone :
For lacke of money, I may not spede.

Benethe hym sat clerks, a great rowt,
Fast they writen by one assent.
There stode up one, and cryed round about
' Richard, Robert, and [John] of Kent.'   20
I wist not wele what he ment,
He cried so thike there in dede
There were stronge theves shamed and shent.
But they that lacked money mought not spede.

Unto the Common Place I yowde [3] thoo,
Where sat one with a sylken hode,
I dyd hym reverence as me ought to do,
And seyd all my goods by nowrd and by sowde,
I am defraudyd with great falshed :
He would not geve me a momme [4] of his mouthe ;   30
But for lacke of money I may not spede.

Then I went me unto the Rollis,
Before the clerks of the Chauncerie.
There were many qui tollis,
But I herd no man speke of me.

---

[1] hood.   [2] I did not long delay.   [3] went.
[4] the least sound that can be made by the lips.

Before them I knelyd upon my kne,
Shewed them myne evidence, and they began to reade.
They seyde trewer things might there nevar be ;
But for lacke of money I may not spede.

In Westminster Hall I found [out] one,   40
[Which] went in a longe gowne of Ray.[1]
I crowched, I kneeled before him anon,
For Mary's love of help I gan him pray.
As he had be wrothe he voyded [2] away,
Backward, his hand he gan me byd
' I wot not what thou menest,' gan he say
Ley downe sylvar, or here thow may not spede.

In all Westminstar Hall I could find nevar a one,
That for me would do, thowghe I shuld dye,
Without the dores, were Flemings grete woon,[3]   50
Upon me fast they gan to cry,
And sayd, ' Mastar, what will ye copen [4] or by ?
Fine felt hats, spectacles for to rede ? '
Of this gay gere, a great cause why.
For lake of money, I might not spede.

Then to Westminster Gate I went,
When the sone was at highe prime.
Cokes to me, they toke good intent,
Called me nere, for to dyne,
And proferyd me good brede, ale and wyne ;   60
A fayre clothe they began to sprede,
Rybbes of befe, both fat and fine.
But for lacke of money I might not spede.

Into London [5] I gan me hy
Of all the lond it bearethe the prise.
' Hot pescods ! ' one gan cry,
' Strabery rype ! ' and ' Chery in the ryse ! ' [6]

---

[1] a striped cloth.   [2] turned.   [3] in great number.
[4] barter.   [5] i.e. from Westminster into the City.
[6] cherries on the branch.

One bad me come near and by some spice.
Pepar and saffron they gan me bede,
Clove, grayns, and flowre of rise.   70
For lacke of money I might not spede.

Then into Chepe I gan me drawn,
Where I sawe stonde moche people :
One bad me come nere and by fine cloth of lawne,
Paris thred, Coton and umple.
I seyde there upon I could no skyle,
I am not wont there to in dede.
One bad me by an hewre, my bed to hele.
For lake of money I might not spede.

Then went I forth by London Stone,   80
Thrwghe out all Canwike [1] Strete ;
Drapers to me they called anon,
Grete chepe of clothe, they gan me hete.
Then came there one and cried, ' Hot shepes fete ! '
' Rushes faire and grene ! ' another began to grete.
Both melwell and makarell I gan mete :
But for lacke of money I myght not spede.

Then I hied me into Estchepe.
One cried ribes of befe, and many a pie.
Pewtar potts they clatteryd on a heape.   90
Ther was harpe, pipe, and sawtry.
' Ye ! by cokke ! Nay ! by cokke ! ' some began to cry ;
Some sange of Jenkyn and Julian to get them selvs mede,
Full fayne I wold hadd of that mynstralsie :
But for lacke of money I cowld not spede.

Into Cornhill anon I yode,
Where is moche stolne gere amonge.
I saw wher henge myne owne hode,
That I had lost in Westminstar amonge the throng.
Then I beheld it with lokes full longe,   100
I kenned it as well as I dyd my crede ;
To by myne owne hode agayne, me thought it wrong :
But for lacke of money I might not spede.

                    [1] Candlewick Street.

Then came the taverner and toke my by the sleve,
And seyd, ' Ser, a pint of wyn would yow assay ? '
' Syr ', quod I, ' it may not greve
For a peny may do no more than it may ! '
I dranke a pint, and therefore gan pay,
Sore a hungred away I yede,
For well London Lykke-peny for ones and eye :   110
For lake of money I may not spede.

Then I hyed me to Byllingesgate,
And cried, ' Wagge ! wagge ! yow hens ! '
I praye a barge man for God's sake,
That he would spare me myn expens.
He sayde, ' Ryse up man, and get the hens,
What ! wenist thow I will do on thee my almes dede ?
Here skapeth no man by-nethe two pens ' :
For lacke of money I myght not spede.

Then I conveyed me into Kent,   120
For of the law would I medle no more.
By caus no man to me would take entent,
I dight me to the plowe, even as I ded before.
Jesus save London, that in Bethelim was bore ;
And every trew man of law God graunt hym souls mede
And they that be othar, God theyr state restore :
For he that lackethe money, with them he shall not spede.

XIII. TRIAL BY COMBAT

The following extraordinary story taken from Gregory's Chronicle, p.
*199, shows the state of medieval law and of medieval civilization. Trial
by combat was a very old institution which the King's justices had for
centuries been engaged in curtailing, yet here in the fifteenth century, a
clever scoundrel could still invoke it, and by its aid save his own life
and imperil that of others.*

ALso that yere a thyffe, one Thomas Whytehorne, was
take in Neweforeste be-syde Beuley and put yn preson at
Wynchester. And when the day of delyverans com he

appelyd [1] many trewe men, and by that mene he kepte
hys lyffe in preson. And thoo [2] men that he appelyd were
take and put yn stronge preson and sufferde many grete
paynys, and was that they sholde confesse and a-corde
unto hys fals pelyng ; and sum were hongyd that hadde
noo frende shyppe and goode, and thoo that hadde goode
gate hyr charters of pardon. And that fals and untrewe
peler hadde of the kynge every day j d. ob.[3] And thys
he contynuyd al moste three yere, and dystryde many men
that were sum tym in hys company. And at the laste
he appelyd on [4] that outerly [5] sayde that he was fals in
hys appelynge, and sayde that he wolde preve hyt with
hys hondys, and spende hys lyfe and blode a-pone hys
fals body. And thys mater was fulle dyscretely take and
hyrde of bothe pelerrys parte, and of the defendente ys
parte also. And a notabylle man, and the moste pete-
fullyste [6] juge of al thys londe in syttyng a-pon lyffe and
dethe, toke thys sympylle [7] man that offeryd to fyght
with the peler, ande fulle curtesly informyd hym of alle
the condyscyons of the fyghtyng and duelle of repreffe
that shulde be by-twyne a peler of the kyngys, fals or
trewe, in that one party, and by-twyne the defendent,
trewe or false, in that othyr party. For in cas that the
peler prevaylyd in that fyght he shulde be put in preson
ayen,[8] but he shulde fare more better than he dyd be fore
tyme of fyghtynge, and be i-lowe of the kyng ij d. every
(day) as longe as hit plesyd the kyng that he shulde lyf.
For in prosses the kynge may by the lawe put hym to
dethe, as for a man sleer, bycause that hys pelyng, fals
or trewe, hathe causyd many mannys dethys, for a very
trewe man schulde with yn xxiiij howrys make opyn to
be knowe [9] alle suche fals hyd thyngys of felony or treson,
yf he be nott consentynge unto the same felowschyppe,
undyr payne of dethe ; and thys peler ys in the same cas,
wherefore he moste nedys dy by very reson. Thys ys for
the pelers party.

---

[1] accused.   [2] those.   [3] $1\frac{1}{2}d.$ [4] one.   [5] utterly, i.e. unequivocally.
[6] pitiful.   [7] ignorant.   [8] again.   [9] openly make known.

The defendaunte ys party ys, as that nobylle man, Mayster Myhelle Skyllyng, sayde ande informyde the defender, that he and the peler moste be clothyd alle in whyte schepys leter,[1] both body, hedde, leggys, fete, face, handys, and alle. Ande that they schulde have in hyr hondys ij stavys and grene hasche,[2] the barke beynge a-pon, of iij fote in lengthe, and at the ende a bat of the same govyn owte as longe as the more gevythe any gretenys. And in that othyr ende a horne of yryn, i-made lyke unto a rammys horne, as scharpe at the smalle ende as hit myght be made. And there whythe they schulde make hyr foule batayle a-pone the moste sory and wrecchyd grene that myght be founde a-bowte the towne, havyng nothyr mete ne drynke whythe, bot both moste be fastynge. And yf hyr frowarde wepyn[3] ben i-broke they moste fyght with hyr hondys, fystys, naylys, tethe, fete, and leggys ; hyt ys to schamfulle to reherse alle the condyscyons of thys foule conflycte ; . . . And yf the defendent sle that pelers, fals or trewe, the defendent shalle be hangyde by-cause of man sleynge, by soo moche that he hathe i-slayne the kyngys prover, for by hys meny[4] the kynge hadde mony[5] of suche as were appelyd, and that mony that rosse[6] of hyr stuffe or goodys that they hadde was put to the kynge almys, and hys amener[7] dystrybutyd hit unto the pore pepylle. But the kyng may by hys grace pardon the defendent yf he wylle, yf the defendent be welle namyd and of competent governaunce in the toune or citte there at hys abydyng ys ; but thys fulle seldon (is) sene by cause of the vyle and unmanerly fyghtynge. And by reson they shulde not ben beryd in noo holy sepulture of Crystyn mannys beryng, but caste owte as a man that wylfully sleythe hym selfe. Nowe remembyr thys foule batayle, whethey ye wylle doo hyt or noo. And bothe partys consentyde to fyght, with alle the condyscyons that long there too. And the fendent desyryd that the juge wolde sende unto Mylbroke there that he dwellyde,

---

[1] sheep's leather.   [2] ash.   [3] weapon.   [4] aid.
[5] money.   [6] came.   [7] almoner.

to inquere of hys gydynge and of conversacyon. And alle the men in that toune sayde that he was the trewyste laborer in alle that contre, and the moste gentellyste there with, for he was a Fyscher and tayler of crafte. And the peler desyryd the same, but he was not a-bydynge in no place passynge a monythe. And in every place there as inquesyscyon was made men sayde, ' Hange uppe Thome Whythorne, for he ys to stronge to fyght with Jamys Fyscher the trewe man whythe an yryn ¹ rammys horne.' And thys causyd the juge to have pytte ² a-pon the defendent.

The maner of fyughtynge of these two poore
wrecchys by-syde Wynchester.

The peler in hys a-rayment ande parelle whythe hys wepyn come owte of the Este syde, and the defendent owte of the Sowthe-Weste syde in hys aparayle, with hys wepyn, fulle sore wepynge, and a payre of bedys ³ in hys hond ; and he knelyd downe a-pone the erthe towarde the Este and cryde God marcy and alle the worlde, and prayde every man of forgevenys, and every man there beyng present prayde for hym. And the fals peler callyde and sayd ' Thou fals trayter ! why arte thou soo longe in fals bytter be-leve ? ' And thenne the defendent rosse upe and hym and sayde, ' My quarelle ys as faythefulle and alle soo trewe as my by-lyve, and in that quarelle I wylle fyght ', and with the same worde smote at the peler that hys wepyn breke ; and thenne the peler smote a stroke to the defendent, but the offycers were redy that he shulde smyte no more, and they toke a-way hys wepyn fro hym. And thenn they fought to gederys with hyr fystys long tyme and restyd hem, ande fought agayne, and thenn restyd agayne ; and thenn they wente togedyr by the neckys. And then they bothe with hyr tethe, that the lethyr of clothyng and flesche was alle to rente in many placys of hyr bodys. And thenn the fals peler caste that meke innocent downe to the grownde . . .

¹ iron.   ² pity.   ³ a set of beads : Every eleventh bead stood for a Paternoster, the others for Ave Marias.

that the sely innocent cryde owt. And by happe [1] more
thenne strengythe that innocent recoveryd up on hys
kneys and toke that fals peler by the nose with hys tethe
and put hys thombe in hys yee, that the peler cryde owte
and prayde hym of marcy, for he was fals unto God and
unto hym. And thenn the juge commaundyd hem to
cesse and hyr bothe hyr talys [2] ; and the peler sayde that
he hadde accusyd hym wronge-fully and xviij men, and
be-sought God òf marcy and of for-gevenys. And thenn
he was confessyd ande hanggyd, of whos soule God have
marcy. Amen.

As for the defendent was pardonyd of hys lyfe, leme,
and goodys, and went home ; and he become an hermyte
and with schorte tyme dyde.

XIV. THE TAVERNER

*' A tavern ', writes a sixteenth-century author, ' is the common con-
sumption of the afternoon, and the murderer or maker-away of a rainy
day. . . . It is the busy man's recreation, the idle man's business,
the stranger's welcome and the citizen's courtesy. It is the study of
sparkling wits, and a cup of canary their book.' This was not less
true in the fifteenth century. We have already seen Langland's picture
of the tavern (p. 74) : the next four extracts illustrate still further this
side of medieval life.*

*Langland, in the field full of folk, hears the taverners crying their
wares : 'A taste for nothing ! White wine and wine of Gascony . . . the
roast to defy ! ' This attractive addition to the noises of the medieval
town is heard again in the play of Mary Magdalene in the* Digby
Plays *edited by F. J. Furnivall, E.E.T.S. (E.S.), LXX, 1896, p.* 72.

I AM a taverner wytty and wyse,
That wynys have to sell gret plente.
Of all the taverners I bere the pryse
That be dwellyng with-inne the cete ;
Of wynys I have grete plente,
Both whyte wynne and red that ys so cleyr :
Here ys wynne of mawt [3] and Malmeseyn,

---

[1] fortune. [2] heard both their tales. [3] wine of Malta ?

Clary wynne [1] and claret, and other moo,
Wyn of Gyldyr [2] and of Galles, that made at the
    grome, (?)
Wyn of Wyan [3] and Vernage, I seye also;   10
Ther be no better, as ferre as ye can goo.

.   .   .   .

Here, lady, is wyn, a repast
To man, and woman a good restoratyff;
Ye shall not thynk your mony spent in wast
From stodyys and hevynes it woll you relyff.

XV. THE DEVILS CHAPEL

The moralists did not fail to castigate .the evils which they found attendant to the Ale-houses, and this extract from Jacob's Well *(E.E.T.S.* 1900, *edited by A. Brandeis), indicates their wholesale condemnation of ' the devil's school-house '.*

(*p.* 147) THE other day, I told you of the wose [4] of glotony in fyve fote of brede, now schal I telle you where this wose of glotonye begynneth and waxit. At the taverne often the glotonye begynneth. For the taverne is welle of glotonye, for it may be clepyd the develys scolehous and the develys chapel, for there his dyscyples stodyen and syngyn, bothe day and nyght, and there the devyl doth meraclys to his servauntys. God, in his chapel of holy cherche, makyth blynde men to se, crokyd to go, dombe to speke, deefe to here, and to have alle here ryghte wyttes; but the feend, in his chapel of the taverne, schewyth his myraclys. He takyth awey mannys feet, that he may noght go, and his tunge, that he may noght speke, alle his wyttes and his bodyly strengthe, thise myracles doth. the feend in the taverne.
Now here ye what lessoun he techyth his clerkys in the scole of the taverne. He techyth hem glotonye, leccherye, for-sweryng, slaundryng, bakbyting, to scorne, to chyde, to dyspyse, to reneye [5] God, to stele, to robbe, to fyghte,

---

[1] a kind of sweet wine.   [2] Guelder.   [3] Guienne.
          [4] ooze.   [5] deny.

to sle,[1] and manye othere swiche synnes. And thus he heldyth hem be the throte of glotonye in the scolehous of his taverne. He techyth his dyscyples to mysgoverne here tungys.

XVI. A FRIENDLY CAROUSE

This poem is taken, with one or two omissions, from a fifteenth-century MS. printed in T. Wright's Songs and Carols (*Percy Society*), *p. 91.*

'GOOD gossip myn, wher have ye be ?
Hit is so long sith I you see ;
Wher is the best wyne, tell you me !
  Can ye owght tell ? '
  'Ye, full well,
    Good gossippis myn, a ! '

I know a drawght of mery-go-down, [2]
The beste it is in all this town,
But yet I wolde not, for my gown,
  My husbond wyste.'   10
  'Ye may me triste,
    Good gossippis myn, a ! '

'Call forth owr gossippis by and by,
Elynore, Johan, and Margery,
Margret, Alis, and Cecely,
  For thei will cum,
  Both all and som,
    Good gossippis myn, a !

And eche of them will sumwhat bryng,
Gose, or pigge, or capons wynge,   20
Pastes of pygynnes,[3] or sum other thyng ;
  For we muste ete
  Sum maner mett,
    Good gossippis myn, a !

[1] slay.   [2] strong ale.   [3] pasties of pigeons.

Go beffore by tweyn and tweyn,
Wisely, that ye be not seen,
For I muste home and cum agayn,
  To witt, ywis,
  Wher my husbond is,
Good gossippis myn, a!   30

A strype or two God myght send me,
If my husbond myght here see me.'
' She that is aferde, lett her flee ',
  Quod Alis than ;
  ' I dred no man,
    Good gossippis myn, a ! '

' Now be we in the tavern sett,
A drawght of the best lett hym fett,
To bryng owr husbondis owt of dett,
  For we will spend   40
  Till God more send,
    Good gossippis myn, a ! '

Eche of them browght forth ther disshe ;
Sum browght flesshe, and sum (browght) fisshe.
Quod Margret meke : ' Now, with a wisshe :
  I wold Anne were here,
  She wold mak us chere,
    Good gossippis myn, a ! '

' How say ye, gossippis ? Is this wyn good ? '
' That is it ', quod Elynore, ' by the rode !   50
It chereth the hart and comforteth the blod.
  Such jonkers amonge
  Shall make us leve long.
    Good gossippis (myn, a) ! '

Anne bade me fill a pot of Muscadell,
' For of all wynes I love it well ;
Swet wynes kepe my body in hele ;
  Yf I had it nowght,
  I shuld tak thowght,
    Good gossippis myn, a ! '   60

' How loke ye, gossip, at the bordis end ?
Not mery, gossip ?   God it amend !
All shall be well, els God defend ;
   Be mery and glad,
   And sit not so sade,
     Good gossip myn, a ! '

' Wold God I had don after your counsell,
For my husbond is so fell [1]
He betith me lyke the devill of hell ;
   And the more I crye,   70
   The lesse mercy,
     Good gossippis myn, a ! '

Alis with a lowde voys spak than :
' Ywis,' [2] she said ' litill good he can,
That betith or striketh any woman,
   And specially his wyff ;
   God gebe hym short lyff,
     Good gossippis myn, a ! '

Margret meke said : ' So mot I thryve,
I know no man that is alyve   80
That gevith me two strokis, but he (shall) have fyve ;
   I am not afferd,
   Thowgh he have a berde,
     Good gossippis myn, a ! '

On cast down her shot,[3] and went away.
' Gossip,' quod Elynore, ' what dide she pay ?
' Not but a peny ' ; ' Loo, therfor I say,
   She shall no more
   Be of owr lore,
     Good gossippis myn, a !   90

---

[1] cruel.   [2] Certainly.   [3] One threw down her share.

Suche gestis we may have ynow,
That will not for ther shot alowe.[1]
With whom com she, gossip ? '   ' With you ? '
 ' Nay,' quod Johan,
 ' I com aloon,
   Good gossippis myn, a ! '

' Now rekyn owr shot, and go we hens ;
What cummeth to eche of us ? '   ' But thre pens,'
' Parde, this is but a small expens
   For suche a sorte,   100
   And all but sporte,
   Good gossippis myn, a ! '

' Torn down the stret, whan ye cum owt,
And we will cumpas rownd abowt.'
' Gossip,' quod Anne, ' what nedith that dowt ? [2]
   Your husbond is pleased,
   Whan ye be eased,
   Good gossippis myn, a !

Whatsoever any man thynk,
We com for nowght but for good drynk ;   110
Now let us go home and wynke,
   For it may be seen
   Wher we have ben,
   Good gossippis myn, a ! '

This is the thowght that gossippis take :
Ons in the wek, mery will they make,
And all small drynkis thei will forsake ;
   But wyne of the best
   Shall have no rest,
   Good gossippis myn, a !   120

---

[1] provide.   [2] fear.

Sum be at the tavern thrise in the weke,
And so be sum every day eke,
Or ellis thei will gron and mak them sek,
 For thyngis used
 Will not be refused;
  Good gossippis myn, a !

XVII. THE MAN ABOUT TOWN

The following account by Thomas Hoccleve of his life while still a young man employed in the office of the Privy Seal is taken from his autobiographical poem La Male Regle. *It gives us an inimitable picture of the dashing young man about town, and the constant struggle between work and play. The second passage is from his* De Regimine Principum. *This poem depicts the lot of the medieval scribe in considerable detail, and is one of the most important documents of its kind in existence. Both poems are printed from the excellent edition of Hoccleve's works, edited for the E.E.T.S. (E.S.) by F. J. Furnivall in 1892 and 1897.*

I

La Male Regle, Vol. I. p. 28.

My freendes seiden un-to me ful ofte,
My mis-reule me cause wolde a fit;
And redden ¹ me, in esy wyse and softe,
A lyte and lyte to withdrawen it;
But that nat mighte synke in-to my wit,
So was the lust y-rootid in myn herte.
And now I am so rype un-to my pit,²
That scarsely I may it nat asterte.³ . . .

Reson me bad and redde as for the beste,
To ete and drynke in tyme attemprely;   10
But wilful youthe nat obeie leste ⁴
Un-to that reed, ne sette nat ther-by.

---

¹ advised.   ² grave.   ³ escape.   ⁴ cared not to obey.

I taken have of bothe outrageously,
And out of tyme nat two yeer or three,
But xx^tl wyntir past, continuelly,
Excesse at borde hath leyd his knyf ¹ with me. . . .

The outward signe of Bachus and his lure,
That at his dore hangith day by day,
Excitith (us) to taaste of his moisture
So often, that man can nat wel seyn ' nay '.   20
For me, I seye I was enclyned ay
With-outen daunger thithir for to hye me,
But if swich charge up on my backe lay
That I moot it forbere, as for a tyme

Or but I were nakidly bystad ²
By force of the penyless maladie,
For thanne in herte kowde I nat be glad,
Ne lust had noon to Bachus hows to hie.
Fy ! Lak of coyne departith compaignie,
And hevy purs, with herte liberal,   30
Qwenchith the thirsty hete of hertes drie,
Wher chynchy ³ herte hath ther-of but smal.

I dar nat telle how that the fresshe repeir
Of Venus femel lusty children deere,
That so goodly, so shaply were, and feir,
And so plesant of port and of maneere,
And feede cowden al a world with cheere,
And of atyr passyngly wel byseye,⁴
At Poules Heed me maden ofte appeere
To talke of mirthe & to disport & pleye.   40

Ther was sweet wyn ynow thurgh-out the hous,
And wafres thikke ; for this conpaignie
That I spake of been sumwhat likerous,
Where as they mowe a draght of wyn espie—

---

¹ taken his place as a fellow-guest.
² For unless I were bare of coin.   ³ niggardly.   ⁴ arrayed.

Sweete, and in wirkynge hoot for the maistrie [1]
To warne a stomak with—thereof they dranke.
To suffre them paie had been no courtesie:
That charge I tooke, to wynne love and thanke. . . .

Of him that hauntith taverne of custume,
At shorte wordes, the profyt is this: 50
In double wyse his bagge it shal consume,
And make his tonge speke of folk amis;
For in the cuppe seelden founden is,
That any wight his neigheburgh commendith.
Beholde & see what avantage is his,
That god, his freend, and eek himself, offendith

But oon avauntage in this case I have:
I was so ferd with any man to fighte.
Cloos kepte I me; no man durste I deprave [2]
But rownyngly [3] I spak, nothyng on highte.   60
And yit my wil was good, if that I mighte
For lettynge of my manly cowardyse,
That ay of strookes impressid the wighte, [4]
So that I durste medlen in no wyse.

Wher was a gretter maister eek than y,
Or bet aqweyntid at Westmynstre yate,
Among the taverneres namely,
And cookes, whan I cam eerly or late?
I pynchid nat at [5] them in myn acate, [6]
But paied them all that they axe wolde;   70
Wherfore I was the welcomere algate,
And for a ' verray gentil man ' y-holde.

And if it happid on the Someres day
That I thus at the taverne hadde be,
Whan I departe sholde & go my way
Hoom to the privee seel, so wowed [7] me

---

[1] strength.   [2] abuse.   [3] in a whisper.   [4] weight.
[5] did not dispute.   [6] purchase.   [7] wooed.

Heete & unlust and superfluitee
To walke un-to the brigge & take a boot
That nat durste I contrarie them all three,
But did as that they stirred me, god woot.   80

And in the wyntir, for the way was deep,
Un-to the brigge I dressid me also,
And ther the bootmen took up-on me keep,
For they my riot knewen fern ago :
With them was I y-tugged to and fro,
So wel was him that I with wolde fare ;
For riot paieth largely everemo ;
He styntith nevere til his purs be bare.

Othir than ' maistir ' callid was I nevere,
Among this meynee, in myn audience.   90
Me thoghte I was y-maad a man for evere :
So tikelid me that nyce reverence,
That it me made larger of despense
Than that I thoght han been.   O flaterie !
The guyse of thy traiterous diligence
Is, folk to mescheef hasten & to hie. . . .

No force of al this ! go we now to watche
By nightirtale ¹ out of al mesure ;
For, as in that, fynde kowde I no matche
In al the Privee Seel with me to endure ;   100
And to the cuppe ay took I heede & cure,
For that the drynke appalle ² sholde noght.
But whan the pot emptid was of moisture,
To wake aftirward came nat in my thoght.

But whan the cuppe had thus my neede sped,
(And sumdel ³ more than necessitee,)
With repleet spirit wente I to my bed,
And bathid there in superfluitee.
But on the morn was wight of no degree
So looth as I to twynne fro my cowche.   110

¹ night-time.   ² slacken.   ³ something.

II

De Regimine Principum, Vol. III. p. 36.

MANY men, fadir, wenen that writynge
No travaile is; thei hold it but a game :—
Art hath no foe, but swich folk unkonynge :—
    But who-so list disport hym in that same,
    Let hym continue, and he shal fynd it grame : [1]
        It is wel gretter labour than it seemeth ;
        The blynde man of coloures al wrong deemeth.

A writer mot thre thynges to hym knytte,
And in those may be no disseverance ;
Mynde, ee and hand, non may fro othir flitte,   10
    But in them mot be joint contynuance.
    The mynd, al hoole with-outen variance,
        On the ee and hand awaytë mot alway,
        And thei two eek on hym ; it is no nay.

Who-so schal wrytë, may nat holde a tale
With hym and hym, ne synge this ne that ;
But alle his wittes grete and smale
    Ther must appere, and halden them ther-at,
    And syn he spekë may, ne syngë nat,
        But bothë two he needës moot forbere :   20
        His labour to hym is the alengere. [2]

Thise artificers, se I day be day,
In the hotteste of al her bysnysse,
Talken and synge, and makë game and play,
    And forth thir labour passith with gladnesse ;
    But we laboure in traveillous stilnesse
        We stowpe and stare upon the shepës skyn,
        And keepë muste our song and wordës in.

[1] painful.   [2] more grievous.

Wrytyng also doth grete annoyës thre.
Of which ful fewë folkës taken heede   30
Sauf we oure self ; and thisë, lo, thei be :
  Stomak is one, whom stowpyng out of dreede
  Annoyeth soore ; and to our bakkes neede
    Mot it be grevous ; and the thrid, our eyen,
    Up-on the-whytë mochel for to pryen.

What man that thre and twenti yere and more
In wryting hath continued, as have I,
I dar wel sayn it smerteth hym ful sore
In every veyne and place of his body ;
And eyen most it greeveth trewely   40
  Of any crafte that man can ymagyne :
  Fadir, in feith, it spilt hath wel-ny myne.

XVIII. A FRESH YOUNG GALLANT

*The Digby play of Mary Magdalene gives us this entertaining
picture of such a youth as we may imagine Chaucer often saw in the
streets near by his home in Aldgate Tower. Digby Plays, edited by
F. J. Furnivall, E.E.T.S. (E.S.) LXX, 1896 (p. 73).*

Hof, hof, hof, a frysch new galaunt
Ware of thryst, let that a-doune !
What ! wene ye, syrrys, that I were a marchant,
Be-cause that I am new com to town ?
With sam praty tasppysster wold I fayne rown ; [1]
I have a shert of reynnes [2] with slevys peneawnt,[3]
A lase of sylke [4] for my lady constant.
A ! how she is bewtefull and resplendant !
When I am from hyr presens, lord, how I syhe !
I wol a-wye sovereyns ; and soiettes I dys-deyne.   10
In wynter a stomachyr, In somer non att al ;
My dobelet and my hossys ever to-gether a-byde ;
I woll, or even, be shavyn, for to seme zyng [5]
With her a-zen the her,[6] I love mych pleyyng ;
That makyt me Ilegant and lusty in lykyng ;
Thus I lefe in this word ; [7] I do it for no pryde.

[1] chat.   [2] Rennes.   [3] hanging down loosely.   [4] a silken ornament.
[5] young.   [6] with hair against the hair.   [7] world.

XIX. A MEDIEVAL STREET

Trade and commerce, although so important an aspect of Town Life, do not readily lend themselves to our purpose. Chaucer, son of a vintner though he was, tells us very little ; and other writers only glance at the busy trading world. We must make an exception of The Libel of English Policy : *this has no value as verse, but is an excellent tractate on the outlook of a fifteenth-century trader, and should be read in its entirety by those interested. It has been authoritatively edited by Sir G. Warner, 1926. The few extracts which follow may serve to illustrate one or two sides of this fascinating subject.*

Langland's picture of the medieval street, with its crowds and noise, forms a fitting prologue (Prologue, B text, ll. 216 ff.).

BARONES an burgeis and bonde-men als
I seigh [1] in this assemble as ye shul here after.
Baxsteres [2] and brewesteres and bocheres manye,
Wollewebsteres [3] and weveres of lynnen,
Taillours and tynkeres and tolleres in marketes,
Masons and mynours and many other craftes.
Of alkin libbyng laboreres [4] lopen forth somme,
As dykers and delveres that doth here dedes ille,
And dryven forth the longe day with ' *Dieu vous save,*
    Dame Emme ' !
Cokes and here knaves [5] crieden ' Hote pies, hote !   10
Gode gris [6] and gees, gowe dyne, gowe ! '
Taverners until hem [7] tolde the same,
' White wyn of Oseye [8] and red wyn of Gascoigne,
Of the Ryne and of the Rochel [9] the roste to defye.'

XX. TRADERS' SIGNS

The medieval street with its medley of traders was a picturesque sight in itself, but this was enhanced by the large signs the citizens hung out to declare their calling. This extract is from Lydgate's Pilgrimage of the Life of Man, *edited by F. J. Furnivall, E.E.T.S., 1899, etc., p. 544.*

(*l.* 20,396) AND as in cytes and in townys,
Maystres off dyvers crafftys
Hang out, on polys and on rafftys,

---

[1] saw.   [2] bakers.   [3] wool-weavers.   [4] all kinds of labourers living.
[5] their boys.   [6] pigs.   [7] unto them.   [8] Alsace.   [9] Rochelle.

Dyvers sygnys hih and lowe,
Wher-by that men ther crafft may knowe ;—
As somme off hem hang out lyouns,
Somme Eglys and gryffouns,
Peynted on bordys and on stagys,
Dyvers Armys and ymages
(In cytes mo than nine or ten,)   10
Wherby men knowe thys craffty men ; [1]

. . . .

And at tavernys (with-outë wene)
Thys tooknys nor thys bowys grene, [2]
Thogh they shewë ffressh and ffayre,
The wyn they mende nat.

XXI. TRICKS OF THE TRADE

This is also from Lydgate's Pilgrimage, etc., *p.* 483. *It will serve
us a sample of the common complaint voiced by Langland, Gower,
and others of contemporary trade morality.*

I

(*l.* 18,080) WITH sobar cher and countenance,
My chaffer I can well sell,
And to symple folke I tell
That it is better than it is.
And wittingly I do a-mys
Touchynge the pris, how that it gothe,
And falsly swere many an othe,
Sober all-way, and sad of chere.
   And whan that I am a drapere, [3]
I hange out courteyns in the lyght,   10
For to blyndë folkës syght
That men may not sen at ye full
Nothar the colour nor the wull ;
Set it at hyghe pris therto,
And swere I myght ha sold it so

[1] crafts' men.
[2] ' Neither these tokens nor these green boughs ', referring to the
bush hung outside ale-houses, etc.   [3] Cf. *Piers Plowman*, below.

The lastë day, to a chapman.
Thus I begyll many a man
With this hand of whiche I tell
Bothë when I by and sell.

    This hand myght nat well be worse :   20
Some tyme ther-with I can sell horse,
And lyke a falce coursar, I can
With othis deceyve many a man.

II

A further example, perhaps the most vivid we have, from the pages of Langland must complete our picture. It is taken from the B. text, ll. 188 ff.

AND thanne cam Coveytise can I hym noughte descryve
So hungriliche and holwe sire Hervy [1] hym loked.
He was bitelbrowed [2] and baberlipped [3] also,
With two blered eyghen as a blynde hagge ;
And as a letheren purs lolled his chekes,
Wel sydder than his chyn thei chiveled for elde ; [4]
And as a bondman of his bacoun his berde was didraveled.[5]
With an hode on his hede, a lousi hatte above,
And in a tauny tabarde [6] of twelve wynter age,
Al totorne and baudy [7] and ful of lys [8] crepynge ;   10
But if that a lous couthe have lopen [9] the bettre,
She sholde noughte have walked on that welche,[10] so was
    it thredebare.
' I have ben coveytouse,' quod this caityve, ' I bi-knowe
    it here ;
For some tyme I served Symme atte Stile,
And was his prentis yplighte his profit to wayte.[11]
First I lerned to lye a leef other tweyne,[12]
Wikkedlich to weye was my furst lessoun.

---

[1] Harvey.   [2] beetle-browed.   [3] thick-lipped.
[4] And like a leathern purse his cheeks flapped about ; (they were) even longer than his chin and trembled with age.
[5] beslobbered.   [6] smock.   [7] dirty.   [8] lice.   [9] run away
[10] Welshcloth.   [11] look after.   [12] a leaf or two.

To Wy [1] and to Wynchestre I went to the faire,
With many manere marchandise as my Maistre me
    highte ;
Ne had the grace of gyle ygo amonge my ware,   20
It had be unsolde this sevene yere so me God helpe !
Thanne drowe I me amonges draperes my donet [2] to lerne,
To drawe the lyser [3] alonge the lenger it semed ;
Amonge the riche rayes [4] I rendred a lessoun,
To broche [5] hem with a pak-nedle and plaited hem to-
    gyderes,
And put hem in a presse and pynned hem therinne,
Tyl ten yerdes or twelve hadde tolled out threttene.
  My wyf was a webbe [6] and wollen cloth made ;
She spak to spynnesteres to spynnen it oute.
Ac the pounde that she payed by poised a quarteroun [7]
    more,   30
Than myne owne auncere [8] who-so weyghed treuthe.
I boughte hir barly malte, she brewe it to selle,
Peny ale and podyng ale [9] she poured togideres
For laboreres and for low folke that lay by hymselve.
  The best ale lay in my boure or in my bedchambre,
And who-so bummed [10] ther-of boughte it ther-after,
A galoun for a grote God wote, no lesse ;
And yit it cam in cupmel [11] this crafte my wyf used.
Rose the regratere [12] was hir righte name ;
She hath holden hokkerye [13] al hire lyf tyme.   40
  Ac I swere now, so the ik [14] that synne wil I lete,
And nevere wikkedliche weye ne wikke chaffare use,
But wenden to Walsyngham and my wyf als,
And bidde [15] the Rode of Bromeholme bryn geme oute of
    dette.'
  ' Repentedestow the evere,' quod Repentance, ' ne res-
titucioun madest ? '

---

[1] Weyhill, Hants.   [2] primer i.e. the elements of my craft.
[3] edge of the cloth.   [4] striped cloths.   [5] pierce.
[6] weaver.   [7] a quarter.   [8] steel-yard.   [9] thin ale and thick ale.
[10] tasted.   [11] a cup at a time.   [12] retailer.   [13] retail-trade.
[14] so may I thrive.   [15] pray.

'Yus, ones I was herberwed,'[1] quod he, 'with an hep
of chapmen,
I ross whan thei were arest and yrifled here males.'[2]
'That was no restitucioun,' quod Repentance, 'but a
robberes thefte.
Thow haddest be better worthy be hanged therfore
Than for al that thow hast here shewed.' 50
'I wende ryflynge were restitucioun,' quod he, 'for I
lerned nevere rede on boke,
And I can no Frenche in feith, but of the ferthest ende
of Norfolke.'
'Usedestow evere usurie,' quod Repentaunce, 'in alle
thi lyf tyme?'
'Nay, sothly,' he seyde, 'save in my youthe.
I lerned amonge Lumbardes and Jewes a lessoun,
To wey pens with a peys[3] and pare the hevyest,
And lene it for love of the crosse to legge a wedde and
lese it;[4]
Suche dedes I did wryte gif he his day breke.
I have no maneres thorw rerages than thorw *miseretur &
comodat.*[5]
I have lent lordes and ladyes my chaffare,[6] 60
And ben her brocour after and boughte it my-self.
Eschaunges and chevesances[7] with suche chaffare I dele,
And lene folke that lese wol a lyppe[8] at every noble.
And with Lumbardes lettres I ladde golde to Rome,
And toke it by taille here and tolde hem there lasse.'
'Lentestow evere lordes for love of her mayntenaunce?'
'Ye, I have lent lordes loved me nevere after,
And have ymade many a knyghte bothe mercere & drapere,
That payed nevere for his prentishode noughte a peire
gloves.'

---

[1] staying. [2] bags. [3] weight.
[4] and lent it for love of the cross, (for the borrower) to give me
a pledge and to lose it (i.e. the pledge).
[5] I have more manors by arrears than by practising liberality.
[6] merchandise. [7] Exchange and clevisance, as here used, denote
usury. [8] part.

' Hastow pite on pore men that mote nedes borwe ? '   70
' I have as moche pite of pore men as pedlere hath of
    cattes,
That wolde kille hem, yf he cacche hem myghte, for
    coueitise of here skynnes.'
    ' Artow manlyche [1] amonge thi neighbores of thi mete
    and drynke ? '
    ' I am holden,' quod he, ' as hende [2] as hounde is in
    kychyne,
Amonges my neighbores, namelich such a name ich have.'

XXII. THE APPRENTICE

*The following passage is interesting, both for the light it throws on
the social status and consequent exclusiveness of the ordinary town-gilds,
and also on the power of the bondman's Lord, and on the ' standing
together ' of the fraternity against outside interference once an apprentice
had been made one of their craft. The extract comes from a long poem
of the early fifteenth century dealing with the mason's gild.*

THE fowrthe artycul thys moste be,
That the mayster hym wel be-se [3]
That he no bondemon prentys make,
Ny [4] for no covetyse do hym take ;
For the lord that he ys bond to,
May fache [5] the prentes whersever he go.
Gef yn the logge [6] he were y-take,
Muche desese [7] hyt myghth there make,
And suche case hyt myghth befalle
That hyt myghth greve summe or alle ;   10
For alle the masonus that ben there
Wol stonde togedur hol y-fere. [8]
Gef suche won yn that craft schulde dwelle,
Of dyvers desesys ye myghth telle.
For more ese thenne, and of honeste,
Take a prentes of herre degre.

---

[1] hospitable.   [2] courteous.   [3] take care.
[4] nor.   [5] fetch.   [6] mason's lodge.   [7] trouble.
                        [8] wholly combined.

11

By olde tyme, wryten y fynde
That the prentes schulde be of gentyl kynde,
And so sumtyme grete lordys blod
Toke thys gemetry that ys ful good.　　20

XXIII. THE FIFTEENTH CENTURY

The following passage from Jacob's Well, *p.* 133, *gives an instructive picture of town-life as seen by a fifteenth-century moralist.*

THE other day, I tolde you of five fote brede wose [1] in coveytise, An other day a-forn also of other five fote of wose, And now I schal telle yow of the thre laste fote brede wose in coveytise.

On fote brede wose in fals marchaundyse, and that is five inche thicke. The firste inche is lyther bergaynyng; that is, whan thou seest a man muste sellyn his thyng for nede and for myscheef, and the sellere is noght wyse, and so thou hast it half for nought, and the same thou wylt sellyn it hym that hath nede therto to byin it for double more than it is worth, and thus thou pylest [2] thi neyghbours of here good lytherly.[3] The secunde inche is leesyng [4] and forsweryng in thi sellyng, sparyng none othys,[5] saying that thi thyng is myche bettere than it is, and that it coste the myche more than it dyde; and in thi bygyng onythyng thou lackyst it, in sweryng grete othys that it is fawty, be it nevere so good, to have it for lytel price. The thridde inche is, whanne thou hauntyst false mesurys and weyghtys, in bying be the more, and sellyng be the lesse; and, thowgh thi mesure or weyghte be trewe, git thou takyst it large inward, and gevyst it scarse owtward agens trewthe. The fourth inche is fals schewyng of chaffare.[6] Whanne thou dyghtyst it so, and makyst it to seme bettere than it is, in a therk [7] place, as drapers don and othere. The fifth inche is hydyng of the treuthe; that is, whan thi thyng is fawty, thou hydest the defawte fro hym that byeth it, and makyst it to seme good. And corsoures

---

[1] oose.　　[2] robbest.　　[3] treacherously.　　[4] lying.　　[5] oaths.
[6] merchandise.　　　　　[7] dark, see above page 145.

that have false hors, thei wyll, wyth false othys, swere that
it hath no defawte, and thus is falshed usyd on yche syde,
and trewe men dysseyvid.

The secunde fote brede of wose in coveytise is crafte
of foly, that is nine inche thycke. . . . The secunde inche
is jugoulours, for thei getyn here good wyth false japys and
lesynges, and getyn here lyvyng wyth wrong. The thridde
inche is faytours [1] that getyn mete and monye of pyteous
folk, wyth wyles, as to makyn hem seme crokyd, blynde,
syke, or mysellys, and are noght so. The fourth inche is
lacche-drawerys that undon mennys dorys. Gif thei fynde
the good-man at hom, thei say here good is brent,[2] or takyn
awey wyth thevys. Thei seyn thei were ryche men, and
now thei have ryght nought. Summe seyn thei have lost
hors and harneys begonde the se : summe seyn thei are
gentyll-men, and here londys are sett to wedde,[3] and so
thei wyll noght go, tyl thei have sumwhat. And gif the
wyif be alone, thei folwyn here in-to the spense,[4] that
for dreed sche is fayn to gyven hem what sche may. The
fifth inche is harlotrie,[5] makyng japys a-forn folk, in pleying
at the spore, at the bene, at the cat, in ledyng berys and
apys, or in swich other unthryft. The sixth inche is
herowdys [6] of armys that in justyng or in turnementys
wayten who doth best, and his name thei crye, and therfore thei have gyftes, to mayntene pompe and pryde.
The seventh inche is champyouns dwellynge wyth lordys,
feyghtynge in here querels, and getynge here lordys the
maystrye in wrong agens the ryght. The eighth inche is
tollerys [7] that dystressyn men to payin agen resoun, and
takyn more toll than trewth wolde. The ninth inche is
hangemen, havynge no pyte to hange men, no to smyten
of here hevedys, for joye of here wynnyng.

The thredde fote brede wose in coveytise is foly [8] pley ;
that is, at the tabelys and at the dyse. This fote wose
wexith nine inche thycke. The firste inche is coveytise,
for he that pleyith coveytyth to wynne. The secunde

[1] idle beggars.   [2] burnt.   [3] pledge.   [4] larder.   [5] buffoonery.
[6] heralds.   [7] toll-takers.   [8] foolish.

inche is raveyne,[1] for he that kepyth stylle fro his felawe
that he wynneth of hym, it is but raveyn. The thridde
inche is manye othys. The ferthe inche is getyng of veyn
godys wyth lesynges,[2] and gret synne, and ydel speche.
The fifth inche is slaundre of God and of His seyntys, or gif
the dese com noght at pay, he seyth God ne His sayntys
helpyn hym noght, but deryn[3] hym. The sixth inche is
evyl exaumple that thei geve to othere, to don as thei do.
The seventh inche is spendyng here tyme in wast and
in foly, and apeyrin[4] here soulys, whil thei myght do
werkys of profyght. The eighth inche is corrupcyoun to
hem that usyn to beholden myche here pley, for thei
myspendyn here tyme also in veyn. The ninth inche is
unbuxumnes[5] to holy cherch. It forbyddeth suche pleyis,
and namely[6] to preestys. He that wynneth ony mony
at the tablys or at the dyse, he muste restore it agen, or
dele it for here soule.

XXIV. A POET'S TRIALS

*The noisy streets are well described in this poem, first printed in
T. Wright's Reliquiae Antiquiae I, p. 140. It comes from a fourteenth-
century MS. (Arundel 292, f. 72 v.), and is of particular interest
if we remember that Chaucer, from his lodging in Aldgate Tower,
may easily have experienced sensations such as those so vividly described by the agonized poetaster.*

SWARTE smekyd[7] smethes smateryd with smoke
Dryve me to deth wyth den of here dyntes;
Swech noys on nyghtes ne herd men nevere,
What knavene cry and clateryng of knockes,
The cammede kongons[8] cryen after col! col!
And blowen here bellewys that al here brayn brestes.[9]
Huf! puf! seith that on, haf! paf! that other,
Thei spyttyn and spraulyn and spellyn many spelles.[10]
Thei gnauen and gnacchen, they gronys to-gydere,
And holdyn hem hote with here hard hamers.   10

---

[1] rapine.   [2] lies.   [3] deride.   [4] injuring.   [5] disobedience.
[6] especially.   [7] smutted.   [8] crooked caitiffs.   [9] brain brusteth.
[10] tell many tales.

Of a bole hyde [1] ben here barm-fellys,
Here schankes ben schakeled for the fere flunderys, [2]
Hevy hamerys thei han that hard ben handled,
Stark strokes thei stryken on a stelyd stokke, [3]
Lus ! bus ! las ! das ! rowtyn be rowe, [4]
Swech dolful a dreme the devyl it to-dryve !
The mayster longith a lityl, and lascheth a lesse,
Twineth hem tweyn and towchith a treble, [5]
Tik, tak ! hic, hac ! tiket, taket ! tyk, tak !
Lus, bus ! lus, das ! swych lyf thei ledyn,   20
Alle clothemerys, Cryst hem gyve sorwe !
May no man for brenwateres [6] on nyght han hys rest.

XXV. POET TO PATRON

*The poet's woes may serve to remind us of the presence of the scholar
and writer in the medieval town. A previous extract (p. 142) has
shown us the life of a professional writer in the King's service. The*
Paston Letters *give much easily available information of the dual rôle of
chaplain and secretary played by priests employed by wealthy laymen.*

*Authors, even when like Lydgate they had monastic support to fall
back upon, found the favour of some rich patron almost a necessity.
Froissart declared it was the support of Philippa of Hainhault which
' made and created me ' ; Lydgate wrote for many patrons, including
Henry V, etc. A great deal of information about these matters will
be found in two articles by Samuel Moore in the* Publications of the
Modern Language Association of America, *Vols. 27 and 28. The
widespread dependence of author on patron is there well brought out
by a detailed study of the conditions obtaining in E. Anglia at the
middle of the fifteenth century. Finally, while dealing with culture
and learning, one or two extracts from University life are necessary.*

*The following amusing poem of Lydgate occurs at the beginning
of Book III of his* Falls of Princes. *Another text has been printed
by Miss E. P. Hammond in* Anglia, *Vol. 38, 1914, to which I am
indebted for explanations of several references which Lydgate indulges
in to ' wind about with circumstance ' his plea for money. His patron
was the famous Humphrey, Duke of Gloucester, perhaps the most
generous patron of letters in the fifteenth century.*

---

[1] bull-hide. [2] fiery flinders. [3] steely stock. [4] snore they by the row.
[5] The master pauses a while, catches up a smaller hammer and
mingles with the twin hammers the treble of his own.
[6] burning-waters, i.e. the hissing of the iron when plunged into
water.

RIGHT myghty prince, and it be youre wille,
  Condescende leyser for to take
To se th' entent of this litel bille,
  Whiche whan I wrote my hand felt I quake.
Tokyn of mournyng I wered clothis blake,
  Cause my purs was falle in grete rerage,[1]
Lyneng outward, his guttis were out shake,
  Only for lak of plate and of coyngnage.

I sought lechis for a restauratif,
  In whom I fonde no counsolacioune   10
To a poticary for a confortatyf,
  Dragge nor dya was none in Bury towne,
Bottum of his stomak was tourned up so downe,
  A laxatif dide hym so grete outrage,
Made hym slendir by a consumptioune,
  Only for lak of plate and coyngnage.

Shippe was ther none,[2] nor saile rod[3] of hewe,
  The wynd froward to make hym therto lond,
The floode was passed and sodainly of newe
  A lowe ground ebbe was fast by the strond,   20
That no maryner durst take on hond
  To cast an anker, for straytnes of passage;
The custom skars, as folke may undrestond,
  Only for lak of plate and of coyngnage.

There was no token sent downe from the Towre,[4]
  As any gossomer the countrepase was light,
A fretyng etyk[5] caused his langure
  By a cotidan,[6] whiche hield hym day and nyght.
Sol et luna[7] was clipsed of hir light,
  Ther was no crosse, ne prynte of no visage,[8]   30
His lyneng derk, there were no platis bright,
  Only for lak of plate and of coyngnage.

---

[1] arears.   [2] Coin had I none (the gold coins at this date bore on
their obverse a picture of the king in a ship).   [3] red.
[4] i.e. the Mint.   [5] devouring fever.   [6] daily fever.   [7] Gold and silver.
[8] There were no silver coins in his purse (silver coins at this time
bore a cross on their reverse, and a crowned head on the obverse).

Harde to lyke hony out of a marble stone,
  For there is nother lycour nor moysture,
An ernest grote [1] whan it is drunk and gone,
  Bargayne of merchauntis stant in adventure.
My purse and I be callid to the lure,[2]
  Of indigence oure stuff leyde in morgage,
But my lord may al my sorowe recure,
  With a receyte of plate and of coyngnage.   40

Nat sugred (plate) made by the apotecarye,
  Plate of light metal yevith a mery sowne;
In Bokelesbury [3] is no suche letuary,
  Gold is a cordialle gladdest confeccioun.
Ageyne etikes of olde consumpcioun,
  Aurum potabile, folk ferre ronne in age,
In quyntencense, best restauracioun,
  With silver plate, enprinted with coyngnage.

The Auctoure Makith a l'envoie excusyng Hymsilff of
His Writynge.

O sely bille, why artow nat ashamed,
  So maleapert to shew out thy constraynt,   50
But povert hath so nygh thy tonne atained,[4]
  That *nichil habet* is cause of thy compleynt.
A drye tysik makith old men ful feynt,
  Rediest way to renewe theyr corage
Is a fressh dragge, of no spices meynt,
  But of bright plate enprynted with coyngnage.

Thow mayst afferme, as for thyn excuse,
  Thy bareyn saile is sike and solitarye,
Of crosse nor pile there is no recluse,
  Prynte nor impressioun in all thy seyntwarye.   60

---

[1] a bargain penny.   [2] reclaimed by my master.   [3] the Grocer's street
    [4] But poverty has so nearly exhausted my resources.

To conclude briefly and nat to tarye,
There is no noyse herd in thyne hermitage,
God send sone a gladder letuary,
With a clere sowne of plate and of coyngnage.

XXVI.   THE MEDIEVAL SECRETARY

The lot of the medieval secretary was not always a happy one. He was an educated man, yet did not rank with the gentry and would not rest easily with the servants. William of Worcester or William Botoner was such a man. He had entered the service of the unlearned and quarrelsome Sir John Fastolf and the following letters show how unhappy he was both while his master lived and after. The second extract (which comes from George Ashby's Poems, edited by Mary Bateson for the E.E.T.S. (E.S.) 1899. p. 3), may be compared with that on page 142 which gives us Hoccleve's account of the secretary's life.

I

'UT SERVUS AD ARATRUM'

I

[*W. Botoner (William of Worcester) to John Paston.* '*P.L.*' *No.* 214]

2 *September* 1454

AFTYR dewe recomendacion wyth my simple service precedying, please your maistershyp to wete, that as to such remembraunce that ye desyre me to contynew forth to the uttermost, I shall wyth gode wille, so as my maister wille licence me, as oft as I can, th' officer to hafe leysure to be wyth me, for ye know well I can not do it alone, etc.

And where as ye of your pleasure wryte me or calle me Maister Worcester, I pray and requyre yow foryete that name of maistershyp, for I am not amended by my maister [1] of a ferthyng yn certeynte, but of wages of housold in

---

[1] I am no better for being master.

comune *entaunt come nows plaira.*[1] By Worcestr or
Botoner I hafe (vs.) yerly, all costs born, to help pay for
bonetts that I lose. I told so my maister thys weke, and
he seyd me yerstenday he wyshed me to hafe be a preest,
so I had be disposed, to hafe gofe me a lyvyng by reson of a
benefice, that anothyr most gefe it, as the Byshop, but
he wold ; and so I endure *inter egenos ut servus ad
aratrum.*[2]

Forgefe me, I wryte to make yow laugh ; and our
Lord bryng my maister yn a better mode for othyrs as
for me.

At Caister, ijd. day of September.

I pray yow displeser not your servaunt be so long, for
my maister lettet hym.

Your,

W. Wyrcestyr.

II

[*W. Botoner to John Paston. 'P.L.' No. 267*]

1456

. . . My maister demaundyth me sondry tymes when ye
shall be here. I coude not sey till thys day be passed.
William Geney shall be here to morn, so wold Jesus ye
were her then. I asked licence to ryde ynto my contree,
and my maistr dyd not graunt it ; he seyd hys wille
was for to make, etc. Y ansuerd, it fyt not me to
know it. God gefe hym grace of holsom councell, and
of a gode disposicion ; *non est opus unius diei, nece unius
septimanæ. . . .*[3]

Wryt hastly, vj. day Januar.

W. Botoner.

---

[1] 'As much as we please.' Botoner fed with the servants.
where there was a plentiful, if rough, supply of food.

[2] 'Among the destitute, as a serf at the plough.'

[3] 'It will take more than one day—or one week for the matter
of that—(to amend Fastolf's temper).'

III

[*W. Botoner to John Paston.* ' *P.L.*' *No.* 296]

12 *Oct.* 1456

Please you to wete that I hafe remembred of the langage
that I hafe late lerned W. Barker had to yow and othyrs of
his accomptes apposyng,[1] and of that they be not hole
bethyn [2] us, but yn division, etc.   Sir, as I may sey yow,
hyt was nevere othyrwyse, ne nevere ys lyke to be ; for
now they hafe so with Lowys, he that ys next shall be yn
the same as was yn gelosye ; for when my maister com-
aundyth such as of force (by reson of her [3] occupacion)
most be nere hym, to do a message to hys felow, or question
of hym, hyt shall be ymagyned amonges our felyshyp that
he doth make maters to my maister.   And so it ys
ymagyned of me when I wryte lettres to London, to Bok-
kyng or Barker, that yn such maters as please hem not,
than it ys my doing ; yff it take well to theyr entent, then
it ys her doyng.   And yn gode feyth, so it was ymagyned
of me and othyrs that wrote, by my maister comaundment,
to Castre, to the parson of Blofeld, Geffrey Spyrlyng, and
othyrs, that of such maters as was lykyng to hem and
coude be sped by help of my maister frendes as by theyr
solicytyng, than it was seyd that it was theyr avice, labour,
and doyng And yff the maters went not to my maister
entent, ne that they coude not bryng aboute the mater,
then it was imagyned and jangled that it was my wrytyng
and doyng.   I bare nevere my maister purs, ne condyt
nevere chargeable mater alone of hys yn lawe, for my
discrecion ne connyng know not whate such maters menyth.
. . .   I am eased of my spyrytes now that I hafe expressed
my leude [4] menyng, because of my felow Barker, as of such

---

[1] The apposing of accounts was the calling of the responsible
person to reckoning.

[2] between.   [3] their.   [4] uneducated.

othyr berkers ayenst the mone,[1] to make wysemen laugh at her folye. Our Lord kepe yow.

Wryt at Castre the xij day of October.

Your

W BOTONER. . . .

Foryefe me of my leude lettre wrytyng, and I pray yow laugh at it.

IV

[W. Botoner to a friend. ' P.L.' No. 347]

About 1460

My maister [2] also (God yelded is [3] sowle) graunted to me a liffelode accordyng to my degre, that I, my wiffe, and my childre, schulde have cause to prey for hym. My wiffes uncle was present in his chapell at Castre as wele as my wiffe, and comaunded her oncle to chese [4] the londe. This is trowthe be the blissed Sacrament that I receyved at Pasch. And because I demaunded my right and duute of my Maister Paston, he is not plesed. I have lost more thanne x. mark worthe londe in my maister servyce, by God, and not I be [5] releved, alle the worlde schal knowe it elles that I have to gret wrong. Wolde God I kowde plese bothe Maister Paston and my oncle in reson, who preeerve you.

Wrete hastely the vij. day of Feveryere.

Your,

W. BOTONER, dit WURCESTER.

II

I GAN remembre and revolve in mynde
My bryngyng up from chyldhod hedyrto,
In the hyghest court that I coude fynd,
With the kyng,[6] quene,[7] and theyr uncle also,

---

[1] against the moon. [2] Sir J. Fastolf. [3] repay it to his.
[4] choose. [5] unless I be.
[6] Henry vi. [7] Margaret of Anjou.

The duc of Gloucetre, God hem rest do,
   With whome I have be cherysshyd ryght well,
   In all that was to me nedefull every dell.

Wrytyng to theyr sygnet full fourty yere,
As well beyond the see as on thys syde,
Doyng my servyce aswell there as here,   10
Nat sparyng for to go, ne for to ryde,
Havyng pen and inke evyr at my syde,
   Redy to acomplysshe theyre commandment,
   As truly as I coulde to theyr entent.

And in theyr service I spendyd all my youth,
And now in pryson throwen in myn age,
Havyng of me no pyte ne routh,[1]
Revylyng me with unfyttyng language,
As thaugh I were neyther wytty ne sage,
   Whiche grevyd me sore and was gretly sad,   20
   To be in povert and of goodes bad,

That before was well in goodes and rest,
And no man was ayenst me dysplesyd,
And all my dayes was among the best.

XXVII. BOOKS AND THEIR OWNERS

The following verses are copied from various fifteenth-century MSS.
and are here reprinted from Reliquiae Antiquae II, 163, *except the*
fourth, which is by John Awdlay. The second was written by the
Countess of Worcester (1440).

I

YEE that desyre in herte and have plesaunce
Olde stories in bokis for to rede,
Gode matiers putt hem in remembraunce,
And of the other take yee none hede ;
Byseching yowe of your godely hede,
Whane yee this boke have over-redde and seyne,
To Johan Shirley restore yee it ageine.

---

[1] pity nor ruth.

II

And I yt los, and yow yt fynd,
I pray yow hartely to be so kynd,
That yow wel take a letel payne,   10
To se my boke brothe home agayne.

Thys boke is one,
   And God's kors [1] ys anoder;
They that take the ton,
   God gefe them the toder.

III

He that stelys this booke
Shul be hanged on a hooke.
He that this booke stelle wolde,
Sone be his herte colde.
That it mow so be,   20
Seith *Amen* for cherité.

IV

No mon this book he take away,
Ni kult owte noo leef; I say for why,
For hit is sacrelege, sirrus, I yow say
Beth acursed in the dede, truly.
   Yef ye wil have any copy,
Askus leeve and ye shul have.

V

This is the boke of William Tucke,
Christ graunte to hym yn erth good lucke;
And or he dye to send hym grace,   30
In Hevyn so hye to purchase a place.

VI

Where from ever thys boke be com,
Yt ys Wyllyam Barbors off Newe Bokenham.

[1] curse.

Who-so-ever thys booke fynde,
I pray hym have thys in hys mynde ;
For Hys love that dyed on tre,
Save thys booke and bryng yt to me !—
Wylliam Barbor off newe Bokenham.

XXVIII. THE MODEL UNDERGRADUATE

The following letters give us a little welcome light on the life of an Oxford undergraduate of the fifteenth century. Unfortunately, between the first letter and the rest of the series, we have nothing extant, so we only know the beginning and end of Walter's University career. But even so, the details of his going up to Oxford, the costs of part of his stay there, and the arrangements for his ' determining ' feast on being made a Bachelor of Arts are full of interest.

[*Margaret Paston to the family chaplain, James Gloys.*
' *P.L.*' *No.* 716.]

18 *January,* 1473.

I PRAY you hertely, yeve [1] it be no dysese [2] to you, that ye will take the labour to bring Walter thyr he schuld be, and to purvaye for hym that he may be sette in good and sad [3] rewle. For I were loth to lese hym, for I trust to have more joye of hym than I have of them that bene owlder ; though it be more coste to me to send you forth with hym, I hold me plesed, for I wote [4] wele ye schall best purvaye for hym, and for suche thynges as is necessar to hym, than another schuld doo, after myne intent. And as for ane hors to lede hys gere, we thynke it were best porvaye one atte Camberage, lesse than ye canne gythe onye carreours from thens to Oxynforth more hastyly. . . . And also I pray you wryte a letter in my name to Watere, after that ye have knowne myne entent by fore this to hym ward ; so that he doo welle, lerne well, and be of good rewle and disposycion, ther shall nothyng faylle hym that I may helpe with, so that it be nessessare to hym,

¹ if.   ² trouble.   ³ sober.   ⁴ know.

and bydde hym that he be not to hasty of takyng of orderes [1]
that schuld bynd hym, till that he be of xxiii. yeere of agee
or more, thoff he be consaled the contrare, for oftyn rape [2]
rewith. I will love hym better to be a good secular man
than to be a lewit [3] prest.

II

[Walter Paston to his Mother. 'P.L.' No. 816.]

19*th May*, 1478.

RYHGT reverent and worchypfull moder, I recomaund me
on to yowr good modershypp, besechyng yow to geve me
yowr dayly benediccyon, desyeryng hartyly to heer of
yowr prosperyte, whych God preserve to Hys plesure, and
to yowr hartys desyyr, &c. I marvel soor that yow sent
me noo word of the letter wych I sent to yow by Master
Wylliam Brown at Ester. I sent yow word that tym
that I xold send yow myn exspenses partyculerly ; but as
at thys tym the berar her of had a letter sodenly that he
xold come home, and there fore I kowd have no leysur
to send them yow on that wys ; and there fore I xall
wryt to yow in thys letter the hool som [4] of my exspenses
sythyns.[5] I was with yow tyll Ester last paste, and also
the reseytys, rekenyng the xx.s. that I had of yow to Oxon
wardys with the Buschopys fyndyng.

The hool some of reseytys ys £5 17s. 6d., and the holl
some of exspenses ys £6 5s. 5¾d., and that comth over the
reseytys in my exspenses I have borowd of Master Edmund,[6]
and yt drawyth to viii.s. And yet I recone none exspenses
sythyns Ester. But as for them, they be non grete ;
and therfor I besech yow to send me mony by Syr Richard
Cotman,[7] brynger of thys letter, or ellys by the next
masenger that yow kan have to me.

---

[1] Major orders, which would pledge him to a life of celibacy.
[2] haste.   [3] worthless.   [4] whole sum.
[5] since.   [6] his tutor or master (see next letter).
[7] a priest.

III

[Edmund Alyard to Margaret Paston. 'P.L.' No. 829.]

4 *March*, 1479.

RIGHT worshepful mastres, I recommande me unto yow as lowly as I kan, thankyng yow for your goodnes at all tymis; God graunt me to deserve it, and do that may plese yow.

As for your son Water, his labor and lernyng hathe be, and is, yn the Faculte of Art, and is well sped there yn, and may be Bacheler at soche tyme as shall lyke yow, and then go to lawe. I kan thynk it to his preferryng, but it is not good he know it on to the tyme he shal chaunge; and as I conceyve ther shal non have that exibeschyon to the Faculte of Lawe. Therfore meve ze the executores that as soche tyme as he shal leve it, ye may put anodyr yn his place, soche as shal lyke you to prefer. If he shal go to law, and be made Bacheler of Art be fore, and ye wolle have hym hom this yere, ther may he be Bacheler at Mydsomor, and be with yow yn the vacacion, and go to lawe at Mihelmas. Qwhat it shal lyk yow to commande yn this or eny odir, ye shal have myn service redy.

I pray yow be the next masenger to send me your entent, that swech as shal be necessary may be purveyed yn seson. And Jesu preserve yow.

At Oxinforth, the iiii. day of March.

Your scoler,

EDMUND ALYARD.

IV

[Walter to his brother Sir John Paston. 'P.L.' No. 830.]

22 *May*, 1479.

AFTER all dw reverens and recomendacions likyth yt yow to understond that I reseyvyd a letter fro my broder John, where by I understod that my moder and yow wold

know what the costes of my procedyng [1] schold be. I sent
a letter to my broder John, certyfyyng my costes, and the
causys why that I wold procede ; but as I have sent word
to my moder, I purpose to tary now tyll yt be Mychylmas,
for yf I tary tyll than, sum of my costys schall be payyd ;
for I supposed, whan that I sent the letter to my broder
John, that the Qwenys broder schold have procedyd at
Mydsomer, but he woll tary now tyll Michylmas ; but
as I send word to my moder, I wold be Inceptor [2] before
Mydsomer, and there fore I besechyd her to send me sum
mony, for yt woll be sum cost to me, but not mych. . . .
And if ye know not what thys term menyth, ' Inceptor ',
Master Edmund, that was my rewler at Oxforth, berar
here of, kan tell yow, or ellys any oder gradwat.

V

[Walter to his brother John Paston. 'P.L.' No. 831.]

30 *June*, 1479.

AND yf ye wyl know what day I was maad Baschyler, I
was maad on Fryday was sevynyth, and I mad my fest on
the Munday after. I was promysyd venyson ageyn my
fest of my Lady Harcort, and of a noder man to, but I
was deseyvyd of both ; but my gestes hewld them plesyd
with such mete as they had, blyssyd be God, Hoo have
yow in Hys kepyng. Amen.

[1] to his B.A. degree.
[2] To incept meant to complete the taking of a degree.

SECTION FOUR

CHURCH LIFE

The vital part played by religion in the life of the people of medieval England cannot be exaggerated. The Church embraced all classes, and nearly every single inhabitant of town and village was at least in nominal communion with her. Both spiritually and materially the power and ubiquitous nature of the Church was ever before men's eyes. The monasteries, with their great churches and their clustered buildings, soared up above the peasant's hovel or the towns-man's wooden house : the vast manors of the religious orders employed innumerable serfs and retainers ; the progress of bishop or abbot through the country-side on his way to West-minster, or overseas to Rome, gave the gaping villager a glimpse of the abundant opulence of those great princes of the Church.

In matters spiritual, as has been suggested (see p. 55), the Church came into contact with even the humblest at the supreme moments of life. The clergy administered the sacraments and lived amongst their flocks—some for good, some scandalously. But always, as the layman looked at the Church, there came to his mind the dread power which these ministers could and did exercise : their priestly functions overawed him, and in the main he was obedient.

I. A MEDIEVAL SAINT

The ranks of the medieval clergy included strange contrasts. The account here given of the life of Edmund Rich, afterwards Archbishop of Canterbury, may be contrasted with the darker pictures which are a commonplace of medieval literature. It is taken from Higden's Polychronicon, *edited by J. R. Lumby, Rolls Series, pp. 215 ff.*

167

THAT yere deide seynt Edmond of Pountenay and Bonefas was archebisshop after hym. This Edmond was i-bore [1] at Abyngdoun bysides Oxenforde, and had holy fadir and moder ; his fader heet [2] Edward, Riche by his surname ; by assent of his wif he hadde relygious lyf at Evesham. His moder heet Mabily, sche usede the heire [3] and an haubergeoun, and faught in flesche and agensy her flesche. Edmond was i-bore clene of al wem [4] of childhode, a seynt Edmondes day the kyng and martir, and lay al that day fro the morwe tide to eve as they he were a swowe,[5] so that they that were there wolde have i-buried hym ne hadde his moder with seide hem. He was i-cleped Edmond, that is, gracious and clene, for he was i-bore in a seynt Edmondis day, and also for while his moder gede with childe with hym sche wente a pilgrimage and bad here bedes [6] at seynt Edmond his tombe, and there sche was firste war that the child was on lyve. From his firste childhod this used his wittes to the studie of goodnes by occupacioun of gostliche [7] lyvynge, for [8] good usage and custom schulde afterward have the maistrie and voyde alle wikked dedes ; they [9] he were schynynge withalle the floures of vertues, git he chees the clennes that maketh a man be next to God. In token therof he made his avow to Oure Lady ; by his moder counsaille he used the heyre, and faste every Friday to brede and to water, and used every Sonday and holy day to seie al the Sawter or [10] he wolde dyne. In his childhood he lernede his gramere and was so disesed with the heed ache that he hadde non hope to spede afterward in lore. His moder spak to hym and seide, ' Sone, I trowe that the lewednesse and unsemeliche tonsure that thou usest is cause of thy woo ' : (thanne afterward he usede tonsure as a clerk, and was hool of al that woo). In a tyme he walked by hym self in a mede bysides Oxenforde, and a faire child appered to hym and seide, ' Heyl, my leef, I wondre that thou knowest me

---

[1] born.   [2] was called.   [3] hair-shirt.   [4] blemish.
[5] in a swoon.   [6] told her beads.   [7] holy.   [8] so that.
[9] though.   [10] ere.

nough, and nameliche while I am alwey by thy side in
scole and in other places; therfore what thou sixt [1] in
my forheede i-wrete, prynte it everiche [2] nyght in thyn
owne forheed.' The writynge was ' Jesus Nazarenus rex
Judeorum ', that is, ' Jesus of Nazareth kyng of Jewes ':
therafter he lerned to have oure Lordes passioun alwey in
his mynde. Ones for besynesse of a lessoun that he moste
rede he forgat it, than whan the day gan to spring the
olde enemy bonde faste his hondes for he schulde nought
blesse hym self, and he prayde in his herte, and the enemy
fil doun from hym bytwene the bed and the wal, and he
conjured hym by the schedynge of Goddis blood that he
schulde telle wherwith he myghte be moste i-chastede :
' With that thou hast now i-nempned ',[3] quod the fend.
Another tyme he hadde forgete to say his orisoun, ' O
beata et intemerata ', and seynt John the Evangelist
appered to hym in his slepe, and manassede hym to smyte
with a pamere.[4] And for holy writ seith that he that
reccheth [5] nought of the smale falleth awey litel and litel,
he wolde everiche day schryve hym and clense hym of
venial synnes. They he were nought *infra sacros* [6] he
was a maister of aart, and usede to here a masse and seie
his houres everiche day or he wolde rede, and was profitable
to his scolers, for he taughte hem to here masse also.
When he feng [7] money of his scolers he leyde it in a wyn-
dowe, and seide, ' Pouder to pouder and askes to askes ';
but the money was ofte i-take awey with his felawes in
game other [8] elles priveliche with theofes. Whanne he
redde arsmetrik [9] his moder that was deed appered to
hym in his sleep, and axede of hym and seide, ' What
figures beeth thees that thou studiest ynne ? ' and he
answerde, ' Suche and suche '; and than sche peynted
thre cercles in her right hond, as they sche wolde mene
the Fadir and Sone and Holy Goost, and seide, ' Sone,
studie thou in these figures after this time.' Seelde [10]

[1] seest. [2] every. [3] named. [4] a rod. [5] cared not.
[6] Though he was not *infra sacros*, i.e. of holy orders.
[7] took. [8] or. [9] arithmetic. [10] Seldom.

he sat in chirche, but he badde his bedis stondynge other knelynge ; ffor he was a nobil prechour, a scharp arguer, and a mylde lyster.[1] For he was avised and took heede of fallas,[2] and was war and wys in asoyllynge of questiouns, and dede greet profit in redynge. For greet abstinens his heer fil awey of his berd and heed, so that his lippes semed i-clove ; he used alwey grete mete, and lefte flesche on Monday and Wednesday, and also in Septuagesme, that is in al the Lente from tyme that Alleluia is i-cloped, he wolde taste no flesche the day to before the day that he wolde synge his masse ; and so ofte it happed that he eet no flesche in a monthe al hool : he eet but seelde twyes a day ; he thoughte not of lettuaries[3] and of medicynes. For greet knelynge his kneen were harde as the sooles of his feet. Everiche day he seide thre payre of matyns and of houres of the day ;—of oure Lady, of the Holy Gost, with Placebo and Dirige. A night after his firste sleep he wolde aryse and seie certeyn psalmes and prayers. Gif eny envious word come in place, he wolde chaunge the theme, and passe to the betir matire ; he wolde have no benefice with cure but oon. He made large spences for he wolde nought be helde covetous and a wrecche. He woulde nought be in pledynge of causes. He wolde have men of seculer court with hym to the mete, for he wolde wynne hem to the blisse of hevene. He wolde nought visite his hous of office, nother here acountes of his ministres ; he spende alwey more than he hadde. He chalangede of his servauntes clennes of body by covenaunt y-wryte, so that gif eny of hem fyl into leccherye, he schulde fonge[4] his huyre and take his leve and be agoo. Tethynges and offrynges and redempciouns of synnes he spende onliche[5] in mylde[6] uses. He hadde tofore hym y-peynt the ymage of oure Lady, and al aboute hym the passioun of oure Lord. And so the lessoun come of the book, and tofore the ymage he had his bedes, and of either come greet devocioun. The tyme of etynge and

---

[1] reader.   [2] deceitfulness, fallacies.   [3] lectuaries.
[4] receive.   [5] only.   [6] charitable.

slepynge and rydynge, whanne he myghte nought studie, he tolde hit al y-lost. As ofte as he openede his bibel he wolde worschippe hit with a cros. Whanne the legacye of the cros was commytted to hym he took no procuracies [1] that hym were y-graunted, but agenst the usages of othere suche legates he travaylde on his owne cost. He prechede at Oxenforde, at Gloucetre, and at Wircetre, and reyn that fyl on the peple he made hit torne agen with his prayeres. Hit happede as he sleep in his studie that a candel fyl doun on his bible and brende, but whanne he wook and syghte no brennynge was y-sene. Also with his penne he made thris croys on a kybe [2] that he hadde, and hit vansched awey. His heyres that he werede were y-throwe into the fuyre whan they were olde, but they myghte nought brenne. And in the heyres that he werede unnethe [3] myghte ony worme be y-founde. Sometyme messangers were i-sent from Caunterbury to Salisbury for Edmond tresorer of that place schulde come and be arche-bisshop of Caunterbury. The deen of Salisbury he spak with hem and seide, ' Ye beeth welcome and ye dooth worschippe to oure cherche ; but ye beeth evel come, for ye take oure tresoure.' Hym schamed nought to drawe of his owne hosen and schoon. Everiche man that he mettre in the way that wolde be schryve to hym,[4] he wolde light doun of his hors and hire his schrifte, and spare for no lette of comynge to his in, neyther for wynde ne for rayn ne for other wedir. He ferde as the olyve tree that holdeth to itself the bitternesse in the rynde, and heldeth out the other the swetnes of the oyle, so he was hard to hymself and esiliche and goodliche to other men. He beet his brest ofte with his hond, and his knees agenst the grounde, so that clerkes that leye in selers [5] under hym myghte unnethe sleepe. For worschippe of oure Lady he worschipped alle wommen, but therby was he nevere i-wemmed.[6] But in a tyme oon blamed hym that was hoomly with hym for a faire wyf that he wolde

[1] procurations (fees).   [2] chillblain.   [3] scarcely.
[4] shriven by him.   [5] cellars, i.e. lower chambers.   [6] stained.

ofte speke with, and he answerde and seide, 'Seie thou
nought how faire sche was; I knowleche sche hath ofte
i-sete by me, but by her was I nevere more tempted than
I was by the wal. . . .' He hated fongers [1] of giftes, and
seide on Frensche, 'Entre prendre et pendre is but oon
lettre alone. . . .' His laste sikenesse gan for to wexe
grevous and strong, and he wente out of Pountenye to
Soysy, and byhight hem that he wolde come agen at seynt
Edmondes day. Whan the sacrament of the aughter was
in-brought to hym he seyde, 'Thou art my Lord, the I
have i-loved, in the I have i-trowed, the I have y-prechid,
the I have i-sought, and non other. Men tellith that it
gooth into the wombe, bot y telle that hit goth into the
soule and thought.' Than he wesche the woundes of the
ymage of the crucifixe, and kussed hem ful swete, and seide,
'Ye schal kecche up water in joye of oure Savyour his
welles.'

II. SLOTH THE PARSON

*'The poure personn of a toun' is admirably drawn by Chaucer.
Langland presents us with the other side of the medal: the drinking,
hunting 'squarson' who lingered on in the English country-side long
after the Reformation.* (Piers Plowman, B. text, V. 392 ff.)

THANNE come Sleuthe al bislabered,[2] with two slymy
　　eighen,[3]
'I most sitte', seyde the segge,[4] 'or elles shulde I nappe;
I may noughte stonde ne stoupe, ne withoute a stole knele.
Were I broughte abedde, . . .
Sholde no ryngynge do me ryse ar I were rype to dyne.'[5]
He bygan 'Benedicite' with a bolke,[6] and his brest knocked,
And roxed,[7] and rored, and rutte [8] atte laste.
'What! awake, renke!' [9] quod Repentance, 'and rathe [10]
　　thee to shrifte',
'If I shulde deye bi this day, me liste noughte to loke;

---

[1] takers.　　　[2] beslobbered.　　　[3] slimy eyes.　　　[4] fellow.
[5] If I am once in bed, no ringing will arouse me till I am ready
for dinner.
[6] sighed.　[7] stretched himself.　[8] snored.　[9] man.　[10] hasten.

I can [1] noughte perfitly my Pater Noster, as the prest it
    syngeth, 10
But I can rymes of Robyn Hood, and Randolf Erle of
    Chestre,
Ac neither of owre Lorde ne of owre Lady, the leste that
    evere was made.
    I have made vowes fourty, and forgete hem on the
    morne ;
I parfourned nevere penaunce, as the prest me highte,
Ne ryghte sori for my synnes yet was I nevere ;
And if I bidde any bedes, but if it be in wrath,
That I telle with my tonge is two myle fro myne herte.
I am occupied eche day, haliday and other,
With ydel tales atte ale, and otherwhile in cherches ;
Goddes peyne and his passioun—ful selde thynke I
    thereon. 20
    I visited nevere fieble men, ne fettered folke in puttes ; [2]
I have levere [3] here an harlotrie, or a somer-game of
    souteres, [4]
Or lesynges [5] to laughe at, and belye my neighbore,
Than al that evere Marke made, Mathew, John, and Lucas ;
And vigilies and fastyng-dayes, alle thise late [6] I passe,
And ligge abedde in Lenten, and my lemman in myn armes,
Tyl matynes and masse be do, and thanne go to the freres ;
Come I to "*Ite, missa est*", [7] I holde me yserved.
I nam noughte shryven some tyme, but-if sekenesse it make,
Nought tweies in two yere, and thanne up gesse [8] I schryve
    me. 30
    I have be prest and persoun passynge thretti [9] wynter,
Yete can I neither solfe [10] ne synge, ne seyntes lyves rede ;
But I can fynde in a felde or in a fourlonge an hare,
Better than in *Beatus vir* or in *Beati omnes*
Construe oon clause wel, and kenne it to my parochienes.[11]

---

[1] know.   [2] prisons.   [3] rather.   [4] cobbers.   [5] lyings.
[6] let.   [7] The closing words of the Mass.   [8] upon guess.   [9] thirty.
[10] solfa, i.e., sing the scale of notes.
[11] But I can find a hare in a field or furrow better than I can
construe plainly one clause of *Beatus vir* or *Beati omnes*, and explain it to my parishioners.

I can holde love-dayes,[1] and here a reves rekenynge,
Ac in canoun, ne in the decretales, I can noughte rede a
    lyne.'[2]

III. 'IF GOLD RUSTE WHAT SHAL IREN DOO?'

Wyclif constantly inveighs against the bad example set by many of the clergy. Here is a characteristic passage, illustrating his point of view and the excesses existing among some clerics of his time. Wyclif's English Works, *ed. F. D. Matthew, E.E.T.S., 1880.*

(*p.* 168)   PRESTIS also sclaundren [3] the peple bi ensaumple of ydelnesse and wanntonnesse; for comynly thei couchen in softe beddis whanne othere men risen to their labour and blabren [4] out matyngs and masse as hunteris, withouten devocion and contemplacion; and hien faste to mete richely and costly arrayed of the beste, and than to slepe. And soone a-noon to tablis,[5] and chees, and taverne, and betynge of pavement,[6] and than speken of lecherie, of depravynge of goode men, that wolen not sue their companye; and thanne cometh dronken-nesse, chidynge and fighttynge and many tymes mansleynge: and bi these prestis and their wantownesse moche peple is brought to lecherie, glotonye, ydelnesse and thefte.

IV. A WANDERING PRIEST

.This well-known passage from Piers Plowman (*text. vi. 1 ff.*) *gives an account of the life of one section of the medieval clergy, wandering about picking up a casual living, yet unfitted by training and by profession to do any manual task. The gradual infiltration of ' bondsmen's brats ' into the ranks of the clergy was more and more apparent during this and the next century.*

THUS ich a-waked, God wot whanne ich wonede [7] on
    Cornehulle,
Kytte and ich in a cote clothed as a lollere,[8]

---

[1] a day appointed to settle disputes amicably.
[2] But in the Canon (of the Mass) or in the Decretals (edicts and decrees forming part of Canon Law), I cannot read a line.
[3] scandalize. [4] carelessly say. [5] backgammon.
[6] lounging about, [7] dwelt. [8] a lounger: an idle fellow.

And lytel y-lete [1] by leyve me for sothe,
Among lollares of london and lewede heremytes;
For ich made of tho men as reson me tauhte.[2]
For as ich cam by Conscience with Reson ich mette
In an hote hervest whenne ich hadde myn hele,
And lymes to labore with and lovede wel fare,
And no dede to do bote drynke and to slepe.
In hele and in unite on me aposede; [3]   10
Romynge in remembraunce thus Reson me aratede.[4]
'Canstow serven', he seide, 'other [5] syngen in a churche,
Other coke for my cokers, other to the cart picche,
Mowe other mowen other make bond to sheves,
Repe other be a repereyve [6] and a-ryse erliche,
Other have an horne and be haywarde and liggen [7] oute
     a nyghtes,
And kepe my corn in my croft fro pykers and theeves?
Other shappe shon other clothes other shep other kyn
     kepe,
Heggen other harwen, other swyn other gees dryve,
Other eny other kyns craft that to the comune nedeth, 20
Hem that bedreden be by-lyve to fynde?'
'Certes', ich seyde 'and so me God helpe,
Ich am to waik [8] to worche with sykel other with sythe,
And to long, leyf me lowe for to stoupe,
To worchen as a workeman eny whyle to dure.'
'Thenne havest thow londes to lyve by' quath Reson,
     'other lynage riche
That fynden the thy fode? for an ydel man thow semest,
A spendour that spende mot other a spille-tyme,
Other beggest thy bylyve a-boute at menne hacches,
Other faitest up-on Frydays other feste-dayes in
     churches,   30
The whiche is lollarene lyf that lytel ys preysed,

---

[1] lightly esteemed.
[2] for I wrote about those men, as Reason taught me.
[3] Being in health (of body) and soundness of mind, one cross-
examined me.   [4] questioned.   [5] or
[6] reap-reve; overseer of reapers.   [7] lie.   [8] weak,

Ther ryghtfulnesse rewardeth ryght as men deserveth,
  Reddit unicuique iuxta opera sua.[1]
Other thow art broke, so may be, in body other in membre,
Other ymaymed [2] thorw som mys-hap wher-by thow myght
  be excused ? '
' Whanne ich yong was ', quath ich ' meny yer hennes,
My fader and my frendes founden me to scole,
Tyl ich wiste wyterliche [3] what holy wryt menede,
And what is best for the body as the bok telleth,
And sykerest [4] for the soule by so [5] ich wolle continue. 40
And yut fond ich nevere in faith sytthen my frendes
  deyden,
Lyf that me lyked bote in thes longe clothes.[6]
Yf ich by laboure sholde lyve and lyflode deserven,
That labour that ich lerned best ther-with lyve ich sholde ;
  In eadem vocatione in qua vocati estis, manete.[7]
And ich lyve in Londone and on Londone bothe,
The lomes [8] that ich laboure with and lyflode deserve
Ys *pater-noster*, and my prymer, *placebo* and *dirige*,[9]
And my sauter [10] som tyme, and my sevene psalmes.[11]
Thus ich synge for hure soules of suche as me helpen, 50
And tho that fynden me my fode vouchen saf, ich trowe,
To be welcome whanne ich come other-whyle in a monthe,
Now with hym, and now with hure, and thus-gate ich begge
With-oute bagge other botel bote my wombe one.[12]
And al-so more-over me thynketh, syre Reson,
Men sholde constreyne ne clerke to knavene werkes ;[13]
For by lawe of *Levitici* that oure Lord ordeynede,

---

[1] *Ps.* lxi. 13 (Vulgate).   [2] maimed.   [3] clearly.
[4] surest.   [5] provided that.   [6] *i.e.* his long clerical robe.
[7] 1 *Cor.*vii. 20.   [8] tools.
[9] *Placebo* and *dirige* : The services for the dead are signified by
these two words, which are the opening words of Vespers and Dirge
or Matins of the Dead (*Ps.* cxiv. 9 and v. 8). The Primer was
an elementary book of religious instruction.
[10] Psalter.   [11] The seven penitential psalms.
[12] Without bag or bottle (the beggar's usual accompaniments)
but only my belly.
[13] No clerk should be made to do labourer's work.

Clerkes that aren crouned [1] of kynde understondyng,
Sholde nother swynke, ne swete, ne swere at enquestes,
Ne fyghte in no vauntwarde, ne hus foe greve ; 60
 Non reddas malum pro malo.
For it ben aires of hevene alle that ben crouned,
And in queer, and in kirkes, Cristes owene mynestres,
 Dominus pars hereditatis mee ; & alibi : Clementia non
 constringit.
Hit by-cometh for clerkus Crist tor to serven,
And knaves uncrouned to cart and to worche.
For shold no clerk be crouned bote yf he ycome weit
Of franklens and free men and of folke ywedded.
Bondmen and bastardes and beggers children,
Thuse by-longeth to labour and lordes kyn to serven 70
Bothe God and good men as here degree asketh ;
Some to synge masses, other sitten and wryte,
Rede and receyve that reson ouhte spende ;
Ac sith bondemenne barnes han be mad Bisshopes,
And barnes bastardes han ben archidekenes,
And sopers [2] and here sones for selver han be knyghtes,
And lordene sones here laborers and leid here rentes to
 wedde, [3]
For the ryght of this reame ryden a-gens oure enemys,
In confort of the comune and the kynges worshep,
And monkes and moniales [4] that mendinauns [5] sholden
 fynde, 80
Han mad here kyn knyghtes and knyghtfees purchased,
Popes and patrones poure gentil blod refuseth,
And taken Symondes sone seyntewarie [6] to kepe.
Lyf-holynesse and love han ben longe hennes,
And wole, til hit be wered [7] out or otherwise ychaunged.
For-thy rebuke me ryght nouht Reson, ich yow praye ;
For in my conscience ich knowe what Crist wolde that ich
 wrouhte.
Preyers of a parfyt man and penaunce discret
Ys the leveste [8] labour that oure Lord pleseth.

---

[1] tonsured. [2] soap-sellers. [3] pledge. [4] nuns.
[5] poor persons. [6] sanctuary [7] worn. [8] dearest.

V. THE CONGREGATION OF THE FAITHFUL

Piers Plowman (C. text X. 203 ff.) gives us the following account of the state of religion, and of the Church in Langland's day.

Ac these eremytes that edefyon thus by the hye weyes,
Whilom were workmen, webbes and taillours,
And carters, knaves, and clerkus with-oute grace,
Helden ful hungry hous and hadde muche defaute,
Long labour and lyte wynnynge and atte laste aspiden,
That faitours [1] in frere clothynge [2] hadde fatte chekus.
For-thi [3] lefte thei here laboure these lewede [4] knaves,
And clothed hem in copes clerkus as hit were,
Other on of som ordre othere elles a prophete ; [5]
A-gens the lawe he lyveth yf latyn be trewe ;   10
   Non licet vobis legem voluntati, sed voluntatem conjungere legi.
Now kyndeliche, [6] by Crist beth suche callyd ' lolleres ',
As by Englisch of oure eldres of olde menne techynge.
He that lolleth is lame, other his leg out of joynte,
Other meymed [7] in som membre, for to meschief hit souneth. [8]
And ryght so sothlyche suche manere eremytes
Lollen agen the byleyve and lawe of holy churche.
For holy churche hoteth [9] alle manere puple
Under obedience to bee and buxum to the lawe.
Furst, religious, of religion here ruele to holde,   20
And under obedience to be by dayes and by nyghtes ;
Lewede men to laborie ; and lordes to honte
In frythes [10] and in forestes for fox and other bestes
That in wilde wodes ben and in wast places,
As wolves that wyryeth men, wommen, and children ;
And up-on Sonedays to cesse, godes servyce to huyre,
Bothe matyns and messe and, after mete, in churches
To huyre here evesong every man ouhte.

---

[1] cheaters, lying vagabonds.   [2] friar's clothing.   [3] Therefore.
[4] worthless. [5] Or as one of some order (of friars), or else a prophet.
[6] Naturally.   [7] maimed.   [8] for it sounds like some mischance.
[9] orders.   [10] woods.

Thus it by-longeth for lorde, for lered, and lewede,[1]
Eche halyday to huyre hollyche the service, 30
Vigiles and fastyngdayes : forthere-more to knowe,
And fulfille tho fastynges bote infirmite hit made,[2]
Poverte, other othere penaunces, as pilgrymages and
 travayles.
Under this obedience arn we echone ;
Who-so brekyth this, be wel war bot yf he repente,
Amende hym, and mercy aske, and meekliche hym shryve,
Ich drede me, and he deye hit worth [3] for dedlich synne
A-counted by-fore Crist, bote conscience excuse hym.
Loke now where [4] these lolleres and lewede eremytes,
Yf thei breke thys obedience that ben so fer fro churche ? 40
Wher see we hem on Sonedays the servyse to huyre,
As, matyns by the morwe ? Tyl masse by-gynne,
Other Sonedays at evesonge seo we wel fewe !
Othere labory for here liflode as the lawe wolde ?
Ac at mydday meel-tyme ich mete with hem ofte,
Comynge in a cope as he a clerke were ;
A bacheler [5] other a beaupere [6] best hym by-semeth ;
And for the cloth that kevereth hym cald is he a frere,
Wassheth and wypeth and with the furste sitteth.
Ac while he wrought in thys worlde and wan hus mete
 with treuthe, 50
He sat atte sydbenche and secounde table ;
Cam no wyn in hus wombe thorw the weke longe,
Nother blankett in hus bed, ne white bred by-fore hym.

VI. THE PARDONER AND HIS AUDIENCE

Chaucer's racy Prologue to the Pardoner's Tale (*Group C, ll.*
329 ff.) is well-known, but it gives such an inimitable picture of one
of these rascals that it is reprinted here.

' LORDINGS ', quod he, ' in chirches whan I preche,
I peyne me to han an hauteyn speche,[7]

---

[1] for learned and unlearned.
[2] To fulfil those fasts, unless infirmity has caused it to be impossible.
[3] when he dies it will be.   [4] whether.   [5] a young graduate.
[6] reverend father.   [7] I take pains to preach in a lofty vein.

And ringe it out as round as gooth a belle,
For I can al by rote [1] that I telle.
My theme is alwey oon, and ever was—
" *Radix malorum est Cupiditas.*"
First I pronounce whennes that I come,
And than my bulles shewe I, alle and somme.
Our lige lordes seel on my patente,
That shewe I first, my body to warente,   10
That no man be so bold, ne preest ne clerk,
Me to destourbe of Cristes holy werk ;
And after that than telle I forth my tales,
Bulles of popes and of cardinales,
Of patriarkes, and bishoppes I shewe ;
And in Latyn I speke a wordes fewe,
To saffron with my predicacioun, [2]
And for to stire men to devocioun.
Than shewe I forth my longe cristal stones,
Y-crammed ful of cloutes and of bones ;   20
Reliks been they, as wenen they echoon. [3]
Than have I in latoun [4] a sholder-boon
Which that was of an holy Jewes shepe.
" Good men ", seye I, " tak of my wordes kepe ; [5]
If that this boon be wasshe in any welle,
If cow, or calf, or sheep, or oxe swelle
That any worm hath ete, or worm y-stonge, [6]
Tak water of that welle, and wash his tonge,
And it is hool anon ; and forthermore,
Of pokkes and of scabbe, and every sore   30
Shal every sheep be hool, that of this welle
Drinketh a draughte ; tak kepe eek what I telle.
If that the good-man, that the bestes oweth, [7]
Wol every wike, er that the cok him croweth,
Fastinge, drinken of this welle a draughte,
As thilke holy Jewe our eldres taughte,

---

[1] know all by heart.   [2] To spice my preaching.
[3] each one.   [4] a mixture of metals much like brass.   [5] heed.
[6] If it has eaten a snake, or been stung by one.   [7] owns.

His bestes and his stoor shal multiplye.
And, sirs, also it heleth jalousye ;
For, though a man be falle in jalous rage
Let maken with this water his potage,   40
And never shal he more his wyf mistriste,
Though he the sooth of hir defaute wiste ;
Al had she taken preestes two or three.

Heer is a miteyn eek, that ye may see.
He that his hond wol putte in this miteyn,
He shal have multiplying of his greyn,
Whan he hath sowen, be it whete or otes,
So that he offre pens, or elles grotes.

Good men and wommen, o thing warne I yow,
If any wight be in this chirche now,   50
That hath doon sinne horrible, that he
Dar nat, for shame, of it y-shriven be,
Or any womman, be she yong or old,
That hath y-maad hir housbond cokewold,
Swich folk shul have no power ne no grace
To offren to my reliks in this place.
And who-so findeth him out of swich blame,
He wol com up and offre in Goddes name,
And I assoille ¹ him by the auctoritee
Which that by bulle y-graunted was to me."   60
By this gaude ² have I wonne, yeer by yeer,
An hundred mark sith I was Pardoner.
I stonde lyk a clerk in my pulpet,
And whan the lewed peple is doun y-set,
I preche, so as ye han herd bifore,
And telle an hundred false japes more.
Than peyne I me to strecche forth the nekke,
And est and west upon the peple I bekke,³
As doth a dowve sitting on a berne.
Myn hondes and my tonge goon so yerne,⁴   70
That it is a joye to see my bisinesse.
Of avaryce and of swich cursednesse

---

¹ absolve.   ² trifle.   ³ nod.   ⁴ actively.
13

Is al my preching, for to make hem free
To yeve her pens, and namely [1] un-to me.
For my entente is nat but for to winne,
And no-thing for correccioun of sinne.
I rekke never, whan that they ben beried,
Though that her soules goon a-blake-beried !
For certes, many a predicacioun
Comth ofte tyme of yvel entencioun ;   80
Som for plesaunce of folk and flaterye,
To been avaunced by ypocrisye,
And som for veyne glorie, and som for hate.
For, whan I dar non other wyes debate,
Than wol I stinge him with my tonge smerte
In preching, so that he shal nat asterte [2]
To been defamed falsly, if that he
Hath trespased to my brethren or to me.
For, though I telle noght his propre name,
Men shal wel knowe that it is the same   90
By signes and by othere circumstances.
Thus quyte I folk that doon us displesances ;
Thus spitte I out my venim under hewe
Of holynesse, to seme holy and trewe.
    But shortly myn entente I wol devyse ;
I preche of no-thing but for coveityse.
Therfor my theme is yet, and ever was,
    " *Radix malorum est cupiditas.*"
Thus can I preche agayn that same vyce
Which that I use, and that is avaryce.   100
But, though my-self be gilty in that sinne,
Yet can I maken other folk to twinne [3]
From avaryce, and sore to repente.
But that is nat my principal entente.
I preche no-thing but for coveityse ;
Of this matere it oughte y-nogh suffyse.
    Than telle I hem ensamples many oon
Of olde stories, longe tyme agoon :

---

[1] especially.   [2] escape.   [3] separate.

For lewed peple loven tales olde ;
Swich thinges can they wel reporte and holde.   110
What ! trowe ye, the whyles I may preche,
And winne gold and silver for I teche,
That I wol live in povert wilfully ?
Nay, nay, I thoghte it never, trewely !
For I wol preche and begge in sondry londes ;
I wol not do no labour with myn hondes,
Ne make baskettes, and live therby,
Because I wol nat beggen ydelly.
I wol non of the Apostles counterfete ;
I wol have money, wolle, chese, and whete,   120
Al were it yeven of the poverest page,
Or of the poverest widwe in a village,
Al [1] sholde hir children sterve for famyne.
Nay ! I wol drinke licour of the vyne,
And have a joly wenche in every toun.
But, herkneth, lordings, in conclusioun ;
Your lyking is that I shal telle a tale.
Now, have I dronke a draughte of corny ale,
By God, I hope I shal yow telle a thing
That shal, by resoun, been at your lyking.   130
For, though myself be a ful vicious man,
A moral tale yet I yow telle can,
Which I am wont to preche, for to winne.
Now holde your pees, my tale I wol beginne.'

VII. THE MASS

This poem, one of many similar poems written in the fifteenth century, illustrates the way in which literature was pressed into the service of the Church. These rhymed stanzas perhaps enforced on many minds what the droning homily of the priest often failed to communicate. It forms part of a long poem on the virtues of the Mass, written by Lydgate. (Minor Poems of J. L., *p.* 87, *ed. H. N. Mac-Cracken, E.E.T.S.* (*E.S.*) 1910.)

Ye folkys all, whyche have devocioun
   To here masse, furst do your besy cure

---

[1] Although.

With all your inward contemplacion,
   As in a myrrour presentyng in fygure
The morall menyng of that gostly armure,
When that a preest, with mynystres more and lasse,
   Arayeth hymsylf, by record of scripture,
The same howre when he shall go to masse ;

Furst, with your eyen verray contemplatyfe,
   Calleth to mynde, of hoole affeccioun,   10
Howe the masse here in thys present lyfe
   Of gostly gladnesse ys chyef direccioun,
   To have memory of Crystes passioun,
As doctors remembre in theyr doctryne,
   Geyne gostly sekenesses oure restauracioun,
Our bawme, our tryacle, our helthe, our medycyne.

Of hygh dyscrecion, yef ye lyst consydre,
   As ye arn bound of verray trowthe and ryght,
Best preservasioun that ye do nat slydre
   In all that day for lak of goostly lyght,   20
   Furst every morow, or Phebus shyne bryght,
Lat pale Aurora condute yow and dresse
   To holy churche, of Cryste to have a syght,
For chyef preservatyf gayne all goostly sykenesse.

Entryng the churche with all humylyte
   To here masse a morow at your rysyng,
Dysposyth your self, knelyng on your kne,
   For to be there at your begynnyng,
   From the tyme of hys revestyng,
Departeth nat, tyll tyne that he have do.   30
   To all your werkes hit shalbe gret furtheryng
To abyde the ende of In Principio.

Kepe yow from noyse and janglyng importune,
   The howse of God ys ordeynyd for prayere,
With syght and sylence sadly doth contynew,
   In your defaute that no man noyse here,

Gase nat abowte, demure of looke and chyere,
As I sayd erst, tyll tyme the preest have do,
  Your good, your catall shall encrese yfeere,
So ye abyde tyll In Principio.   40

In sacryfyces of the old lawe
  With the heede [1] men offred up the tayle,
From a good gynnyng men shuld nat withdrawe
  Tyll hit were endyd, Moyses gafe counsayle.
A werke begon ys of more avayle
Yef a good ende accorde well therto,
  For encrese of your goostly travayle
Abyde at masse tyll In Principio.

VIII. THE VIRTUE OF THE MASS

*The virtues of the Mass have given rise to a whole body of literature
in prose and verse. The following, printed from* Reliquiae Antiquae,
*is a sample of the teaching of the medieval Church on this most im-
portant subject.*

SUMTYME ther was a poure man,
I shal thou telle, as I can,
That labouryd and travaylyd for hus lyf;
He had a good woman to hus wyf.
The poure man, I thou say,
Was temptyd with a fend nyth and day;
He was in poynt to for-doun hymselve
Aboutyn a ten tyme or twelve.
Hys wyf was evermore at hus hand,
And so sche gan hym withstand.   10
She was wys of here werk,
And preyid hym for to gon to kerk,
Of here persone to ben shreve;
Therafter they shuldyn the better leve.
This man tok hys wyvys reed,
And to the persone gan hym sped,
And told hym al hys evyl dede,
And preyid hym to redyn hym sum rede.

[1] head.

The persone thout of that cas,
He sau ful perlyous it was ;   20
Gyf he for-dede hymself so,
He were for-lore for ever mo.
He bad that man al that yer
Comyn every day a messe to her ;
' And gyf thu wylt do so,
Thi destene thu shalt over-go.'
The poure man seyd, nay,
Hym most travaylyn every day ;
He hadde non other levyng,
But of hys dayis travaylyng.   30
' Gyf I shuld a messe cum to,
That dayis werk me most for-go.'
The persone seyd, ' Be my fay !
I shal gef the a peny every day,
And cum and here thin messe snelle,[1]
Quan I rynge the messe belle.'
The poure man, withoutyn nay,
Com to messe every day
Quan he herde the belle rynge,
And had a peny to hys spendynge.   40
Thus he contynuyd al that yere,
Come every day a messe to here ;
And quan the messe was do,
Wente agen hus laboure to ;
Til it was ny the yerys ende,
A feyre there was holdyn hende.
This poure man had suyn [2] to selle,
And theder he wold, as I you telle,
On morwe he ros and gan hym dresse ;
Hys wyf bad hym bydyn and here messe.   50
He answerd and seyd, nay,
He shuld here messe by the way ;
Ther stod a chyrch as he shuld gon,
Ther wolde here hys messe done.

---

[1] quickly.   [2] swine.

' For yf I byde the personus masse,
The feyre shal be mekyl [1] passe.'
He tok hys suyn and forth gan gone,
For by the chyrch hys thout was one.
Quan he com at the chyrche gate,
He fond a clerk stondynge ther-ate.   60
The poure man seyde the clerk to :
' Is here ony messe to do ? '
The clerk seyde, ' Nay, i-wys,
Of a messe thu myth well mys.'
The poure man seyde agen there,
' A messe wolde I fayn here.'
The clerk seyde, ' So mote I the !
I have herd this day thre.
Quat wylt thu geve, so Cryst the save !
And tak the qwych thu wylt have.'   70
The man seyde, ' So mote I the !
A peny shal I gevyn the.'
He seyde, ' Nay, withoutyn lak,
No lece [2] than the tabard on thi bak.'
The man seyde, ' That were me lot for-bere ;
Be neyin I have but sympul gere !
But rather than I shulde fayl,
Have it here for thi travayl ? '
He kest of his tabbard anon ;
The clerk gan it on done.   80
The clerk seyde, ' So mote (I) the !
I have herd messes thre ;
On of the Trinyte that is most,
Anothere of the Holy Gost,
The third of oure lady fre ;
Tak qwych thu wylt to the.'
The man seyde, ' So mot I the !
I holde me to the Trinyte.'
The clerk seyde, ' Cryst the save !
And graunte the al the mede that I shuld have ! '   90

[1] well-night.,   [2] less.

The man went fort with hys suyn,
And dede hys feyre wel an fyn ;
And as he came homward agyn,
He herde mekyl cry an dyn.
Summe crydyn and seydyn, alas !
Ther was fallyn a ferly [1] cas ;
A man that never was evyl of play
Hadde for-done hymself that day.
Than was it the clerk that I of tolde,
That had the medes of the messe solde ;   100
Here he hadde the destenee [2]
That the poure man shulde abe.
Than the man thoute in hus prevyte,
That was hys owyn destene,
And thro the vertu of the masse
It was away fro hym passe.
He went hom and dede hym shryve,
And was a good man al hus lyve.
Be this example men moun se
Quat vertuwys in the messe be ;   110
Therefore I rede, be my fay !
We heren messe qwyl we may,
And so summe messys for to seyne
To bryngyn our frendes out of peyne.
Now God that suffrod for us ded,
And leftyt here thi body in bred,
Thu gyf us grace to servyn the,
Here in erthe qwyl we be.
Amen ! Amen ! for charyte !

IX. THE PERILS OF CHURCH MUSIC

Wyclif shows no mercy to anything he considers detrimental to true religion, and among other abuses he fastens on the elaborate ceremonial and music of the cathedra's and greater monastic institutions. The following is a good example of his argument, and is taken from Wyclif's English Works, *edited by F. D. Matthew, E.E.T.S. (O.S.)* 1880.

---

[1] wonderful.   [2] destiny.

(*p.* 191) ALSO bi song the fiend lettith [1] men to studie and preche the gospel; for since mannys wittis ben of certeyn mesure and myght, the more that thei ben occupied aboute siche mannus song the lesse moten thei be sette aboute goddis lawe; for this stirith men to pride and jolite and othere synnys, and so unableth them many gatis [2] to understonde and kepe holy writt that techeth mekenesse, mornynge for oure synnys and other mennus, and stable lif and charite. And yet God in al the lawe of grace chargith not siché song, but devocion in herte, trewe techynge and holy spekynge in tonge . . . but mannus foly and pride stieth [3] up ever more and more in this veyn novelrie. First men ordeyned songe of mornynge [4] whanne thei weren in prison, for techynge of the gospel, . . . to putte awey idelnesse and to be not unoccupied in goode manere for the tyme; and that songe and oure [5] acordith not, for oure [5] stirith to jolite and pride, and here [6] stirith to mornynge and to dwelle lenger in wordis of Goddis lawe. Than were matynes of oure Lady ordeyned of synful men, to be songen with heighe criynge to lette men fro the sentence [7] and understanding of that that was thus songen, and to maken men wery and undisposid to studie Goddis lawe for akyng of hedis; and of schort tyme thanne weren more veyn japis [8] founden— deschaunt, countre note and orgon and smale brekynge, [9] that stirith veyn men to daunsynge mor than to mornynge; and, therefore, ben many proude and lecherous lorelis [10] founden and dowed [11] with temperal and worldly lordi- schipis and gret cost. But thes foolis schulden drede the sharpe wordis of (St.) Austyn that seith: as oft as the song liketh me more than doth the sentence that is songen, so oft I confesse that I synne grevously. . . . When ther ben fourty or fyfty in a queer,[12] thre or foure proude and lecherous lorellis schullen knacke [13] the most devout servyce that no man schal here the sentence, and

[1] hinders. [2] ways. [3] rises. [4] mourning. [5] ours. [6] theirs. meaning. [8] tricks. [9] descant, harmony, organ and florid music. [10] rascals. [11] endowed. [12] choir. [13] shall perform with flourishes.

alle othere schullen be doumbe and loken on them as
foolis. And then (they) preisen [1] Sir Jacke,[2] or Hobbe,
and William the proude clerk ; ' How smale thei knacken
there notis ', and seyn that they serven well God and
Holy Cherche.

X. THE NOVICE

*Besides the part played by the Church in its efforts to bring the Faith
to all by devoted labour in town and country, we have to remember
that up and down the land were numerous monasteries and nunneries.
Here, more or less immured from the world, lived the Regulars as they
were called : men and women vowed to a life of poverty, chastity
and obedience. The fifteenth century undoubtedly saw them long past
their hey-day : laxity of their rule and disorders of various kinds
had brought them a long distance from the original conceptions of their
founders such as S. Benedict. Langland, Chaucer, and other writers
are full of matter which reveal to us the ordinary man's reflections on
this decay, while such works as that of Thomas Gascoigne (Loci
e Libro Veritatem) show what more learned minds were thinking.
The six following extracts will indicate some aspects of the life of the
cloister.*

*John Lydgate, who was a monk of the famous abbey of Bury St.
Edmunds, has given us an excellent account of the life of a novice,
particularly interesting because it shows us the influence of the monastic
routine on the ordinary boy (for his earlier life, see p. 43), who has
little real vocation for the contemplative life.* Minor Poems of Lydgate,
E.E.T.S. (E.S.) 1910, p. 354 ff.

ENTRYNG this tyme into relygioun,
  Onto the plowe I put forth myne hond,
A yere complete made my professioun,
  Consideryng litel charge of thilke bond ;
  Of perfeccioun ful gode exaumple I fond,
Ther techyng good, in me was (all) the lacke,
With Lothes wyf I loked often abak.

Taught of my maystres by vertuous disciplyne
  My lookes restreyne, and kepe clos my syght,

---

[1] praise.
[2] the priest. *Sir* was a courtesy title given to all priests at this time.

Of blyssed Benet to folowe the doctryne,   10
   And bere me lowly to every maner wyght,
   By the advertence of myn inward syght,
Cast to godward of hole affeccioun,
To folowe thempryses of my professioun.

His holy rewle was onto me rad,
   And expouned in ful notable wyse,
By vertuous men, religious and sad,
   Ful weel experte, discrete, prudent, and wys
   Of observaunces of many a gostly empryse;
I herd all weel; but, touchyng to the dede,   20
Of theis when taught I toke litel hede!

Of religioun I wered a blak habite,
   Only outward as by apparence,
To folowe that charge I savoured but ful lyte,
   Save by a maner connterfete pretence;
   But in effecte ther was none existence,[1]
Like the image of Pygmalyon,
Shewed I lyfly, and was made but of ston.

Upon the ladder, with staves thryes thre
   The ix. degrees of vertuous mekenesse   30
Called in the Reule ' grees [2] of humylite ',
   Wheron t' ascende my feet me lyst not dresse,
   But by a maner feyned fals humblenesse,
So covertly, when folkes were present,
One to shewe outward, another in myn entent.

First, where as I forsook myne owne wylle—
   Shette with a lock of obedience,
T' obeye my sovereynes, as it was ryght and skylle,
   To folowe the skole of perfygt pacience,
   To myn eymes doon worshep and reverence—   40
Folowyng the revers, I toke all another weye,
What I was boden, I koude weel disobeye.

[1] reality.   [2] steps.

With tonge at large and brotel [1] conscyence,
  Ful of wordes, dis-ordinat of language,
Rekeles to kepe my lyppes in silence,
  Mouth, eyen, and eres token ther avauntage,
  To have ther cours onbrydeled by outrage,
Out of the reynes of attemperaunce,
To sensualyte gaf I the governaunce.

Watche out of tyme, ryot and dronkenesse.   50
  Unfructuous talkyng, intemperat diete,
To veyn fables I dyd myn eres dresse,
  Fals detraccioun (also) was to me swete,
  To talke of vertu me thought it was not mete
To my corage nor my compleccioun,
Nor naught that sowned toward perfeccioun.

One with the firste to take my disporte,
  Last that arose to come to the quere,
On contemplacioun I fond but small comforte,
  Holy histories did to me no chier,   60
  I savoured more in good wyne that was clere,
And every houre my passage for to dresse,
As I seyd erst, to ryot or excesse.

I kowde grucche, and fond no cause why,
  Causeless ofte compleynyng on my fare,
Geynst my correcciouns answered frowardly,
  Without reverence, list no man to spare,
  Of all vertu and pacience I was bare,
Of rekles youthe I list non hede to take,
What Cryst Jesu suffred for my sake.   70

Which now remembrying in my later age,
  Tyme of my childhode, as I reherse shall,
Wythinne xv (yeres), holdyng my passage
  Myd of a cloyster, depicte upon a wall,
  I saugh a crucifyx, whos woundes were not smalle,
With this (word) ' vide ', wreten there besyde,
' Behold my mekenesse, O child, and leve thy pryde.

[1] evil.

The which word, whan I dyd undirstond,
  In my last age takyng the sentence,
Theron remembryng, my penne I toke in honde, 80
  And gan to wryte with humble reverence,
  On this word, ' vide ' with humble diligence,
In remembraunce of Crystes passioun,
This litel dite, this compilacioun. . . .

XI. THE NUN'S DAY

The following extracts are from a versified fifteenth-century version of the rule of S. Benedict, edited by E. A. Kock, for the E.E.T.S. (O.S.) in 1920. *The whole day of the religious was carefully planned— the fitting observance of the various daily services being of primary importance. This passage from p.* 99 *explains to the nuns for whom it was written how they are to spend their waking hours.*

ALL that wons [1] in religioun
Aw [2] to have sum ocupacioun
Outher in kirk of hali bedes [3]
Or stodying [4] in oder stedes.[5]
For ydilnes, os sais Sant Paul,
Es grete enmy unto the saul.
And therfor es ordand that thai
Sum gude warkes sal wirk alway,
And sum certane times of the yer
To wirk with hand, os men may her.   10
Fro pase,[6] thurgh al cristyndome,
Til the kalandes of october cum,
Unto prime [7] sone sal thai rise,
And sine [8] ilkon wirk on ther wise
What so es most nedeful labore
Until the tyme of the third oure.
And lessons sal thai rede than next
Fro the third our unto the sext.
And efterward thurgh wirchep
Fro oures and mes [9] wend unto mete.   20

[1] dwell. [2] aught. [3] prayers. [4] studying. [5] places. [6] Easter.
[7] divine office said about 5 or 6 a.m. [8] afterwards. [9] hours and mass.

And efter mete, then sal thai slepe,
And silence al samen [1] sal thai kepe,
So that none do other disese, [2]
Bot ilkon paid other to plese,
Sone efterward, when this es done
And thai haf said the our of none, [3]
Until [4] their werk then sal thai gang
Unto the tyme of evynsang,
To scher or bind, if it be nede,
Or dike or els do other dede.   30
For unto travel wor we born,
And al our elders us be-forn.
Bot travel aw mesurd to be [5]
Til ilkon efter ther degre,
To men or women, old or ying,
Ilkon to do divers thing.
Fro october, os I are sayd,
Unto lentyn es thus purvayed:
In orisons and in ther oures
And lessons salbe ther laboures.   40

In lentyn tyme then sal thai rise
Arly, and say ther servyse
And orisons til godes honoure,
Until it be past the third oure.
Than to the tent our [6] sal thai wirk,
And sine til non serve in the kirk.
And in lentyn aw tham to luke
That ilkon have ordand a buke,
Whilk salbe red right to the end,
Als the cours of the rewl hase kend. [7]   50
And who so groches [8] oght here-o-gayn [9]
Salbe punest with grevus payne.

<hr/>

[1] together.   [2] discomfort.
[3] divine office of none, about 3 p.m.   [4] unto.
[5] but work ought to be regulated.   [6] tenth hour.
[7] taught.   [8] grumbles.   [9] against this.

Who tenter to trofils [1] and wil not rede
And thai overtayn [2] with that dede,
With payn thai sal amendes make,
So that other ensaumpil [3] take.

XII. IN THE REFECTORY

Unnecessary talking was never encouraged among monks and nuns :
only the officials of the house, whose duties necessitated it, were able
to converse freely. Even at meals and at intervals afterwards, as the
following lines show, talking was strictly limited, and an elaborate
sign language was in use in some monastic establishments.

(*p.* 95)   The covent, when thai set at mete,
For to rede sal thai not for-gete.
On the Sunnday sal on begin,
And al that wouke scho sal not blin. [4]
Unto hir felos sal scho say,
Besekand that thai for hir pray.
And sone when that scho enters in,
This vers to say scho sal be-gin :
' Domine, labia mea aperies—
Lord, opin my lippes als gastly lech, [5]   10
And my moth sal thi lovyng tech.'
Hir soverain sal blis hir gud spede,
And so scho sal be-gin to rede.
Than of al nose [6] thai salbe stil
And grathly [7] tak entent hir til.
If any of tham nede oght to have,
Softly with signes thai sal it crave. [8]
And scho that redes sal sithen [9] ete
With tham that serves at the mete.
And in order thai sal not rede,   20
Bot who so best can do that dede,
And most likandly tels and leres
Unto tham that the lesson heres.

---

[1] attends to trifles.   [2] caught.   [3] warning.
[4] cease.   [5] as a holy physician.   [6] noise.   [7] straightway.
[8] For a full list of such signs, see Aungier's *Syon Monastery,*
pp. 405-9.   [9] afterwards.

Of time of mete now es to lere,
In times and sesons of the yere.
Fro pas [1] right unto Witsunnday
At the sext our ete sal thai,
The whilk es midday for to mene,
And sine [2] sal thai soupe bedene.
In somer, fro Witsunday be past,   30
Wedinsday and Friday sal thai fast,
Bot if [3] thai other swink or swete
In hay or corn with travel grete.
And if thai non slike travel done,
On thos days sal thai fast to none.
And on other days, als I air saide,
At mydday sal ther mete be graide.[4]
Bot al this salbe purued playn
At the ordinance of ther soverayn.
What seson so scho putes tham to,   40
With-outin groching sal thai do.
Fro time that December be-gin
Until clene lentyn cum in,
At hi none sal thai ete ;
Ther lesons sal thai not for-gete.
In lentyn sal non to mete gang,
Or efter the our of evyn-sang ;
And al servys than sal thai sai
Efter mete bi light of day,
So that al be rewlid right   50
At wend to bede bi dais lyght.

In times when thai sal soup infere,[5]
Then sal thai set efter soppere
Al in a stede,[6] whor thai wil sit,
And rede lessons of hali writ
Or els of lives of hali men,
That gastly [7] comfort may tham ken.
Tales of trofils [8] thai sal non tel,
Ne other maters than of mel,[9]

[1] Easter.   [2] afterwards.   [3] unless.   [4] ready.
[5] together.   [6] place.   [7] ghostly.   [8] trifles.   [9] speak.

That may let haly orisoun 60
Or drive tham fro devocioun.
On fastyngdais, in ilka place,
Efter evynsang a litil space
In a stede thai sal set down
And mak a schort colaciown.
And als son os thai haf done,
Al samen sal thai wend ful son
Unto complin, mor and myn.
And efter the our of complin
In ther hertes al sal thai hurd,[1] 70
And non have lef to spek a word,
Bot gestes [2] or other thinges it gar [3]—
Bot thai spek it myght be-war—
Or if ther soverayn say tham to
Nedeful thinges thai er to do.
Unto hir sal thai answer than
Als curtesly als ever thai kan.
And prevely so sal thai say,
That non tham here bot scho and thay.
And other speking salbe none 80
Fro tyme that thai have complyn done.

XIII. THE CONVENT'S DAILY FOOD

(*p.* 91) Who to the kechin sal tak tent [4]
Sal ordan wele for the covent
Ever-ilk-a day two maners of mete,
Bi-caus that who so may not ete
Of the ton for nokins [5] nede,
Of the tother thai may tham fede.
So til [6] a covent suffes [7] may
Two maner of potege [8] ilka day.
If thai hafe appils or other thing
Ordand of their awn growyng, 10
Then sal thai make servys of slike [9]

---

[1] treasure up. [2] unless guests. [3] necessitate. [4] pay attention.
[5] no manner of. [6] to. [7] suffice. [8] soup. [9] such.

14

Unto ever-ilkon in-like.
To ilka lady suffise may
A pond of bred a-pon a day,
Wheder thai wil ete ons or twise.
If it be ordand on this wise,
That ever-ilkon wil of hir lave [1]
The third part til hir sopper save,
And to the celerer wil it seme
Swilk servys for to saf and yeme. [2]   20
And who so wendes gret travel til
Salbe servyd at ther soverans [3] wil,
With mor or les that es to mene, [4]
Bot ever that non outrage be sene ;
For no thyng es als gret enmy
Unto Godes folk als glotony.
And tharfor thus sais Jesus Crist,
Als witnes wele the evaungelest :
' Videte ne grauentur corda vestra
crapula et ebrietate—   30
Greves not your hartes for no nede
With glotony and dronkenhede.'
And les mesur in ilka thing
Salbe usid to childer gyng. [5]

The mesure salbe of ther drink
Set efter ther soverayn think, [6]
Efter thai travel arely and late,
And after the plais es cald or hate ;
Bot at [7] thai never assent until
Thair flesch yernyng fully to fil.   40
Softly sal thai tast, and fair,
Drynk that may ther hedes inpair,
Als myghty wyne or nobil aile.
For the wisman tels slik a taile :
' Wyne that es myghty and strang
Mase witty [8] men forto wirk wrang.'

[1] loaf.   [2] guard.   [3] prioress's.   [4] that is to say.   [5] young.
[6] their prioress's will.   [7] only that.   [8] wise.

Tharfor es wit, to lest and mast,
Wine or aile softly to tast.
And if thai in slik places be,
That thai of nother half plente,   50
Swilk os thai find then sal thai fande,[1]
And love God hertly of his sande.[2]

XIV. THE WELCOME GUEST

This extract is taken from the charming fourteenth-century version of the Breton Lai le Freine *(Tale of the Ash). It gives us a most human and sympathetic account of a medieval country-side and of medieval manners. The whole poem has been admirably translated by Miss Edith Rickert in her* Romances of Love. *This passage is taken from the edition of H. Weber in his* Metrical Romances, of the XIII, XIV and XV Centuries, 1810. *Vol. I, p.* 361.

(*l.* 115) THE levedi hadde a maiden fre,
Who ther y-nurtured hade y-be,
And fostered fair ful mony a yere;
Sche saw her kepe this sory chere,
And wepe, and syke,[3] and crye, ' Alas ! '
And thoghte to helpen her in this cas.
And thus sche spake, this maiden ying,
' So n'old I wepen for no kind thing [4]:
But this o child wol I of-bare
And in a convent leve it yare.   10
Ne schalt thou be aschamed at al;
And whoso findeth this childe smal,
By Mary, blissful quene above,
May help it for Godes love.'

The ïevedi graunted anone therto,
And wold wele that it were y-do.
Sche toke a riche baudekine [5]
That hir lord brought fram Constentine,
And lapped the litel maiden therin;
And toke a ring of gold fin,   20

---

[1] try.   [2] gifts.   [3] sigh.
[4] Not for anything would I grieve thus !   [5] a rich mantle.

And on hir right arm it knitt
With a lace of silke therin pitt [1]:
And whoso hir founde schuld have in mende,
That it were comen of riche kende.

The maide toke the childe hir mide,
And stale away in an eventide,
And passed over a wild heth;
Thurch feld and thurch wode hye geth
Al the winter-long night.
The weder was clere, the mone was light,   30
So that hye com by a forest side:
Sche wax al weri and gan abide.
Sone after she gan herk
Cokkes crowe, and houndes berk.
Sche arose and thider wold;
Ner and nere she gan behold
Walles and hous fele hye seighe,[2]
A chirche, with stepel fair and heighe.
Then nas ther noither strete no toun,
Bot an hous of religioun: 40
An ordre of nonnes, wele y-dight,
To servy God both day and night.
The maiden abode no lengore;
Bot yede hir to the chirche-dore,
And on knes she sat adoun,
And seid wepeand hir orisoun:
' O Lord, she seyd, Jesu Crist,
That sinful man bedes herst,[3]
Underfong [4] this present,
And help this seli [5] innocent,   50
That it mot y-cristned be,
For Marie love, thi moder fre!'

Hye loked up, and bi her seighe
An asche, bi hir, fair and heighe,

---

[1] fastened.   [2] many she saw.
[3] who hearest the prayers of sinful man.   [4] accept.   [5] blessed.

Wel y-bowed, of michel priis ;
The bodi was hollow as mani on is.
Therin she leyed the child, for cold,
In the pel[1] as it was bifold ;
And blisted[2] it with al her might.
With that it gan to dawe light ;   60
The foules up, and song on bough,
And acre men yede to the plough.
The maiden turned oyain anon,
And loke the waye heo hadde er gon.

The porter of the abbay aros,
And dede his office in the clos ;
Rong the belles and taperes light,
Leyd forth bokes, and al redi dight.
The chirche dore he undede,
And seighe anon in the stede   70
The pel liggen in the tre,
And thoughte wele that it might be
That theves hadde y-robbed somwhare,
And gon therforth, and lete it thare.
Therto he yede and it unwond,
And the maiden child therin be fond.
He tok it up betwen his hond,
And thonked Jesu Cristes sond :
And hom to his hous he it brought,
And tok it his douhter, and hir bisought,   80
That hye schulde kepe it as sche can,
For sche was melche and couthe theran.[3]
Sche bad it sonke and it nold,[4]
For it was neighe ded for cold.

Anon fer sche alight,
And warmed it wele aflight.
Sche yaf it sonke opon hir barm[5]
And seththen[6] laid it to slepe warm

[1] fur.   [2] blessed.
[3] For she had her own child at the breast and understood these
things.   [4] would not.   [5] bosom.   [6] afterwards.

And when the masse was y-don,
The porter to the abbesse com ful son :　　　90
' Madame, what rede ye of this thing ?
To-day, right in the morning,
Sone after the first stounde,[1]
A litel maiden-childe I founde
In the holwe assche therout ;
And a pel him about,
A ring of gold also was ther,
How it com thider I not nere.' [2]
The abbesse was awonderd of this thing :
' Go, hye seyd, on heigheing,[3]　　　100
And fiche it hider, I pray the,
It is welcom to God and to me.
I chil it help as I can,
And segge it is mi kinswoman.'
The porter anon it gan forth bring,
With the pel, and with the ring.
The abbesse lete clepe [4] a prest anon,
And lete it cristen in fun-ston [5] :
And for it was in an asche y-founde,
Sche cleped it Frain in that stounde,　　　110
The Freyns of the asche is a *freyn*
After the language of Breteyn,
Forthi, *le Frein* men clepeth this day
More than asche, in iche cuntray.

XV. SONG AGAINST THE FRIARS

*The Friars were omnipresent in medieval England. They had
arrived here little over a century before Chaucer's birth, but even by
the mid-fourteenth-century had lost much of their original zeal and had
allowed themselves to become a byword. The following passages have
been chosen to represent, as far as is possible, various sides of their
activities as viewed by friends and foes.*

' Freres and feendes ben but lyte asonder ', *says Chaucer; and
almost every writer on religious conditions in this and the following*

---

[1] hour.　　　[2] I do not know.　　　[3] quickly.
[4] ordered to be called.　　　[5] font-stone.

century says the same thing, though often with far greater emphasis.
Wyclif and Langland both loathed the Friars, and were constantly
railing against them. The following song, printed from T. Wright's
Political Poems and Songs, *Rolls Series, Vol. I, p. 263, will serve*
as an example of the flood of satirical verse which overwhelmed the
four orders in their later decadent days.

PRESTE, ne monke, ne yit chanoun,
Ne no man of religioun,
Gyfen hem so to devocioun,
    As done thes holy frers.
For summe gyven ham to chyvalry,
Somme to riote and ribaudery;
Bot frers gyven ham to grete study,
    And to grete prayers,
  Who so kepes thair reule al,
    bothe in worde and dede;   10
  I am ful siker [1] that he shal
    have heven bles to mede. [2]

Men may se by thair contynaunce,
That thai are men of grete penaunce,
And also that thair sustynaunce
    Simple is and wayke.
I have lyved now fourty yers,
And fatter men about the neres [3]
Yet sawe I never than are these frers
    In contreys ther thai rayke.   20
  Meteles so megre are thai made,
    and penaunce so puttesham doun,
  That ichone is a hors-lade,
    when he shal trusse of toun.

Allas! that ever it shuld be so,
Suche clerkes as thai about shuld go.
Fro toun to toun by two and two,
    To seke thair sustynaunce.
By God that al this world wan,
He that that ordre first bygan,   30

[1] sure.   [2] as a reward.   [3] loins?

Me thynk certes it was a man
　　Of symple ordynaunce.
　For thai have noght to lyve by,
　　thai wandren here and there,
　And dele with dyvers marcerye,
　　right as thai pedlars were.

Thai dele with purses, pynnes, and knyves,
With gyrdles, gloves, for wenches and wyves:
Bot ever bacward the husband thryves
　　Ther thai are haunted tille.　　　　　　　40
For when the gode man is fro hame,
And the frere comes to our dame,
He spares nauther for synne ne shame,
　　That he ne does his wifle.
　Gif thai no helpe of houswyves had,
　　when husbandes are not inne,
　The freres welfare were ful bad,
　　for thai shuld brewe ful thynne

　　．　　．　　．　　．　　．　　．　　．　　．　　．

Trantes thai can, and many a jape ;
For somme can with a pound of sape　　　　50
Gete him a kyrtelle and a cape,
　　And som what els therto.
Wherto shuld I othes swere ?
Ther is no pedlar that pak can bere,
That half so dere can selle his gere,
　　Than a frer can do.
　For if he gife a wyfe a knyfe
　　that cost bot pennys two,
　Worthe ten knyves, so mot I thryfe,
　　he wyl have er he go.　　　　　　　　　60

　　．　　．　　．　　．　　．　　．　　．　　．　　．

Thai say that thai distroye synne,
And thai mayntene men moste therinne ;
For had a man slayn al his kynne,
　　Go shryve him at a frere.

And for lesse then a payre of shone
He wyl assoil him clene and sone,
And say the synne that he has done
    His saule shal never dere.
  It semes sothe that men say of hayme [1]
    in many dyvers londe,   70
  That that catyfe, cursed Cayme,
    first this order fonde.

Nou se the sothe whedre it be swa,
That frer Carmes come of a k.,
The frer Austynes come of a.,
    Frer Jacobynes of i.,
Of m. comen the frer Menours;
Thus grounded Caym thes four ordours,[2]
That fyllen the world ful of errours,
    And of ypocrisy.   80
  All wyckednes that men can telle
    regnes ham among;
  Ther shal no saule have rowme in helle,
    of frers ther is suche throng.

Thai travele yerne [3] and bysily,
To brynge doun the clergye;
Thai speken therof ay vilany,
    And therof thai done wrong.
Whoso lyves oght many yers,
Shal se that it shal falle of frers,   90
As it dyd of the Templers,
    That wonned here us among.
  For thai held no religioun,
    bot lyved after lykyng,
  Thai were distroyed and broght adoun,
    thugh ordynance of the Kyng.

   .   .   .   .

[1] them.   [2] Wyclif was fond of this device, and frequently used it when disparaging the Friars. The Carms are the Carmelites or White Friars; the Austynes, the Austin Friars; the Jacobins, the Dominicans or Black Friars; and the Menours, the Franciscans or Grey Friars.   [3] eagerly.

Tham felle to lyve al on purchace,
Of almes geten fro place to place,
And for alle that tham holpen has,
 Shuld thai pray and syng.   100
Bot now this londe so neght soght is,
That unnethe may prestes seculers
Gete any service for thes frers,[1]
 That is wondre thing,
 This is a quaynt custome
 ordeyned ham among,
 That frers shal annuel prestes [2] bycome,
 and so gates [3] selle ther song.

Ful wysely can thai preche and say;
Bot as thai preche no thing do thai.   110
I was a frere ful many a day,
 Therfor the sothe I wate.[4]
Bot when I sawe that thair lyvyng
Acordyd not to thair preching,
Of I cast my frer clothing,
 And wyghtly went my gate.
 Other leve ne toke I none,
 fro ham when I went,
 Bot toke ham to the devel ychone [5]
 the priour and the covent.   120

XVI. A DOMINICAN FRIARY

The rapid change which translated the poor friars into some of the wealthiest of bodies was much remarked on in medieval times. Langland and Wyclif are full of scorn for the activities of the friars of their day, and Chaucer gives many sly hints of the low esteem in which they were held by the ordinary man. Pierce the Plowman's Crede *furnishes us with this detailed account of the magnificence of their buildings. Our extract is taken from the Oxford edition of W. W. Skeat, 1906, p. 7.*

---

[1] The land is so closely scrutinized by the Friars that the secular priests can scarcely find employment.

[2] i.e. sayers of services for the dead for a year : Mass priests or chantry priests, as they are called.

[3] in that way. [4] the truth I know. [5] gave them all to the devil.

THANNE thought y to frayne the first of this foure ordirs,
And pressede to the Prechoures to proven here wille.
Ich highede to her house to herken of more ;
And whan y cam to that court y gaped aboute.
Swich a bild bold, y-buld opon erthe heighte,
Say I nought in certaine sithe a longe tyme.
Y gemede upon that house and gerne theron loked,
How the pileres weren y-peynt and pulched ful clene,
And queynteli i-corven with curiouse knottes,
With wyndowes well y-wrought wide up o-lofte.   10
And thanne y entrid in and even-forth went,
And all was walled that wone though it wid were,
With posternes in pryvytie to passen when hem liste ;
Orcheyardes and erberes euesed well clene,
And a curious cros craftily entayled,
With tabernacles y-tight to toten all abouten.
The pris of a plough-lond of penyes so rounde
To aparaile that pyler were pure lytel.
Thanne y munte me forth the mynstre to knowen,
And a-waytede a woon wonderlie well y-beld,   20
With arches on everiche half and belliche y-corven,
With crochetes on corners with knottes of golde ;

Then I thought to question the first of these four orders (i.e.
the Dominicans or Preachers), and pressed forward to them to
test their will. I hastened to their house to hear further, and
when I came to the court-yard I gaped about me, for a building
so built, perched high on the earth, I had not seen for a long time.
I gazed carefully upon that house, and looked eagerly how the
pillars were painted and thoroughly polished, and quaintly carved
with curious bosses, and the wide windows aloft were well-made.
And then I entered in and went straight on, and all that dwelling-
place, wide though it was, had a wall round it, pierced with private
posterns, which they could pass when they would. There were
orchards and gardens with fair borders, and a curious cross carved
with great skill, with canopied shrines arranged to spy all about.
The price of a ploughland, in round pennies, were little enough to
provide for that building.
Then I ventured forth to explore the minster, and beheld a
building wonderfully well built, with arches on every side, beautifully
carved, having crockets at the corners with gold bosses. There

Wyde wundowes y-wrought y-written full thikke
Schynen with schapen scheldes to schewen aboute,
With merkes of marchauntes y-medled bytwene,
Mo than twenty and two twyes y-noumbred.
Ther is none heraud that hap half swich a rolle,
Right as a ragman hath rekned hem newe.
Tombes opon tabernacles tyld opon lofte,
Housed in hirnes harde set a-bouten,   30
Of armede alabaustre clad for the nones,
Made upon marble in many maner wyse;
Knyghtes in her conisantes clad for the nones,
All it semed seyntes y-sacred opon erthe;
And lovely ladies y-wrought leyen by her sydes
In many gay garmentes that weren gold-beten.
Though the tax of ten yer were trewly y-gadered,
Nolde it nought maken that hous half, as y trowe.
Thanne kam I to that cloister and gaped abouten
How it was pilered and peynt and portreyd well clene,   40
All y-hyled with leed lowe to the stones,
And y-paved with peynt til iche poynt after other;
With kundites of clene tyn closed all aboute,
With lauoures of latun lovelyche y-greithed.

were spacious windows with many inscriptions, shining with coats
of arms to gleam about, and with the badges of merchants mingled
in between. There were more than two-and-twenty, twice reckoned
over. There is no herald that has such a roll, even as a catalogue
has newly reckoned them.

Tombs made of marble in many different ways were set up on
high in enclosed nooks and corners, and closely set about and
adorned with alabaster canopies for the occasion. Knights clad in
their surcoats all seemed like saints, hallowed on earth, and lying
by their sides were beautifully wrought ladies, in many gay gar-
ments, adorned with beaten gold. Though the taxes for ten
years were fully gathered, they would not even half purvey for
that house as I thought.

Then I came to the cloister and gaped about, seeing how it was
pillared and painted and beautifully adorned, and covered with
lead down to the stones, and paved with painted tiles, each piece
after the other. Conduits of bright tin all enclosed, and beautifully
fitted washing places of metal were there. I trow the produce
of the land in a great shire would not furnish that place from end

I trowe the gaynage of the ground in a gret schire
Nolde aparaile that place oo poynt til other ende.
Thanne was the chaptire-hous wrought as a greet chirche,
Corven and covered and queyntliche entayled,
With semlich selure y-set on lofte,
As a Parlement-hous y-peynted aboute.   50
   Thanne ferd y into fraytour and fond there an other,
An halle for an heygh kinge an housholde to holden,
With brode bordes abouten y-benched wel clene,
With windowes of glas wrought as a chirche.
Thanne walkede y ferrer and went all abouten,
And seigh halles full hygh and houses full noble,
Chambers with chimneyes and chapells gaie ;
And kychens for an hyghe kinge in castells to holden,
And her dortour y-dight with dores ful stronge ;
Fermery and fraitur with fele mo houses,   60
And all strong ston wall sterne opon heithe,
With gaie garites and grete and iche hole y-glased ;
And othere houses y-nowe to herberwe the queene.
And yet thise bilderes wiln beggen a bagg-ful of whete
Of a pure pore man that maie onethe paie
Half his rente in a yer and half ben behynde !

to end. Also the chapter house was constructed like a great church,
with carvings and coverings and quaintly sculptured, with a fitting
ceiling set above it, and painted everywhere as it were the Parliament House.
   Then I went to the refectory and found there another hall, fit
for a high king to hold his household in, with broad tables about
and full well furnished with benches, and with windows as if it
were a church. Then I walked farther, and went about everywhere,
and saw very high halls and most noble houses, chambers with
fireplaces and gay chapels and kitchens fit for a high king's castle ;
the dormitory was furnished with great strong doors; the
infirmary and refectory and many more buildings; and a strong
stone wall, stalwart on a height, and with watch-towers, and each
loop-hole glazed ; and other houses enough to harbour a queen.
And yet these builders will beg a bag of wheat of a very poor man
that may scarcely pay half his rent in the year and leave half owing.

XVII. A FRIAR'S SERMON

The Friars were well known as preachers, especially the Dominicans ; and Friar Brackley here gives us a sample of the kind of sermon the ordinary preacher delivered. The whole subject of the medieval sermon has recently been admirably dealt with in a monograph entitled Preaching in Medieval England, *by G. R. Owst, Cambridge,* 1926.

[*A Whitsunday Sermon of Friar Brackley* ' *P.L.*' *No.* 372.]

FRENDS, this holy tyme, as owr moder Holy Chirch maketh mension, the Holy Gost came from hevyn, and lighted in the disciples of Crist, inflamyng them with connyng, and strenghyng them with grace. And be cause the doctrine and prechyng of them shuld go thurghought all the werd, furst thei wer to be enfourmed and taught connyng, and to be strenth with awdacide and grace, and than to be endewed and yovyn all manner of langags that thei myght prechyn to all maner of naciones, so that tho naciones that thei preched to myght understond them, and every naciones his owyn tonge ; and so thees Appostilles, after that thei wern enspired with the Holy Gost, wher so ever thei preached, were ther never so many naciones present, ich nacion thought that thei spokyn in ther owyn langage —etenim illud loquebantur variis linguis Apostoli.

Frends, iij. thyngs be necessary in prechyng to hym that shall prechyn thurgh the werd as the Appostell dede · —that is to sey, connyng, boldnesse, and langags. If thei had had connyng and none audacite, but have fered to have preched, it shuld litill a profited, as we have examplles dayly at Cambridge, exempli (gratia) de Clerico quis studuit sermonem, &c. And if thei have bothyn connyng and audacite, and have none eloquensye ner copiousnesse of langage, so that he preche that his audiens is most exercised in, that thei may understand hym, elles it profiteth not.

Therfor thes holy Appostill(es), be for thei shuld prechyn,

furst thei wer to be confirmed and strenghed. Our Lord strenghed them be under nemyng, enformyng, and helpyng, culpando ut in Evangelium recumbentibus, &c. He strenghed them with his help and grace whan he brethed in them, seyng 'Accipite Spiritum Sanctum ; et quorum remiseritis peccata, remittuntur eis, et quorum retinueritis retenta sunt ', &c. He strenghed them also be his doctrine whan he seid ' Petite et accipietis ; si quid petieritis Patrem in nomine meo, dabit vobis.' How that ye shuld prayn to God and askyn, I taught you on Estern day. Therfor ye shall pray to God be good werkyng, right full lebyring, and in good deds perseveryng.

Frends, ye owe for to ask of God that your joy may ben a full joy and perfight ; we may never have a full joy in this werd, wher as ever among folwyth hevynesse. A man joyth sumtyme in gold and sylver, and in gret substaunce of erdly gods, in bewte of women, but this joy is not perfyght—but this joy is not stabill, but it is mutabill as a shadow ; for he that this joyth in the bewte of his wyffe, it may fortune to morwyn he shall folwyn her to chirch up on a bere. But if ye wull knowyn what is a full and a wery joy, truly forgevenesse of synne and ever-lestyng blisse, wher as is never sikenesse, hunger, ner thurst, ner no maner of disseas, but all welth, joy, and prosperite, &c. Ther be iij. maner of joys, the on void, a nother half full, the thred is a full joy. The furst is plente of werdly gods, the seconde is Gostly grace, the threde is everlestyng blisse. The furst joy, that is affluens of temporall gods, is called a veyn joy, for if a man wer set at a bord with delicate mets and drynks, and he sey a cawdron boyllyng a forn hym with pykke and bronston, in the which he shuld be throwyn naked as sone as he had dyned ; for he shuld joy mych in his deliciose mets, it shuld be but a veyn joy.

Right so doth the joy of a covetouse man, if he sey what peyn his sowle shuld suffre in helle for the myskepyn and getyn of his good, he shuld not joy in his tresore, ut in Libro Decalogorum, ' Quidam homo dives ', &c.

Semiplenum gaudium est quando quis in praesenti gaudet et tunc cogitans de futuris dolet, ut in quodam libro Graeco, 'Quidam Rex Graeciae', &c. Her ye may se but half a joy; how (who) shuld joy in this werd, if he remembred hym of the peynes of the toder werd? 'Non glorietur fortis in fortitudine sua, nec sapiens in sapientia sua, nec dives in divitiis suis.' De quibus dicitur, qui confidunt in multitudine divitiarum suarum, quasi oves in inferno positi sunt. 'Qui gloriatur, in Domino glorietur.' Therfor lete us joy in hope of everlestyng joy and blis. 'Gaudete quia nomina vestra scripta sunt in caelo,' ut gaudium vestrum sit plenum. A full joy is in hevyn. Et in hoc apparet quod magnum gaudium est in caelo, quoniam ibi est gaudium quod 'oculus non vidit, nec auris audivit, et in cor hominis non ascendit, quae Deus praeparavit diligentibus', et ideo, fratres, variis linguis loquens (precor) ut gaudium vestrum sit plenum, vel habeatis gaudium sempiternum.

II

Friar Brackley's own opinion of the value of his preaching may be gathered from the following excerpt from a letter of his to one of the Pastons about 1460 ('P.L.' No. 349).

RYTE reverent Sire, &c.; William Yelverton Judex and hise wyf were here with here meny and here hors in our ladyes place, &c. on Saterday at evyn, and yedyn hens on Monday after none, whan summe had dronkyn malvyseye and tyre, &c. And I preched on the Sonday before hem, not warnyd tyl after mete. And than for lak of M. Vergeant, or our wardeyn Barnard, I sodeynly seyd the sermon. And byfore I had ryte ovyr and soleyn chere of hem bothe, &c.; but after the sermon he seyd openly to the prior, heryng myche folk in the chirch, 'I haf herd hym oftyn here and ellys where, but this ys the best that ever I herd hym sey,' &c., and at evyn drank to me, and made me good chere, &c.

XVIII. A THEOLOGICAL WRANGLE

The following account, from Gregory's Chronicle, *p.* 228, *is an excellent example of one of the continuous quarrels that raged between the Regulars and the secular priests throughout the fourteenth and fifteenth centuries. The Regulars, and especially the Friars, enjoyed many advantages over the ordinary priest, and bitter animosity was frequently displayed. Here we have at length the story of one of these feuds.*

ALLE soo that yere be-ganne a gre cyssym by twyne fryers and prystys, but the Fryer Charmys, that ys to saye the Whyte Freers, be-ganne hyt fryste at Poules Crosse. He that be-ganne thys matyr was borne in Flete Strete, a skyner ys sone, and hys name ys Syr Harry Parker ; he blamyd men for there grete copy [1] of hyr goodys, and in specyalle he blamyd benefysyd men that had grete benyficys and prestys that had temporalle lyffelod. [2] For he sayd and affermyd that non of the twelve Apostolys nor Cryste hadde no thyng in propyr but alle in comyn, and sayd and affyrmyd by hys connyng, [3] as strong as he cowthe, that Cryste was a begger and had nought but by way of almys. And that made men to groge [4] and to muse passyng soore.

But the Sonday aftyr there was a docter of devynyte, Maystyr Wylliam Ive, the mayster of Whytyngdon ys College, sayde agayne the fryer, and prevyd that Cryste was poore and kepte noo grete tresoure, but as for beggyng he utterly denyde hyt, and by hooly scrypture prevyd hit soo that men undyrstode that the fryer erryd sore agayne Hooly Chyrche ; ande thenne the fryers gan malyngne a gayne thys docter. Thenne in Advente they prevyde [5] a docter of the Whyte Fryers, Mastyr Thomas Haldon, and that he schulde preche agayne the Mayster Wylliam Ive before sayd, and there he talkyd moke [6] of the beggyng of Cryste, and put the pepylle that the same mater schulde ben determenyd in there scholys by twyne hym and a Grey Fryer at the White Fryers in Flete Strete the Wanysdaye seven nyght aftyr. And the Sonday folowyng, a

---

[1] abundance.   [2] temporal sources of income.   [3] knowledge.
[4] grumble.   [5] provided   [6] much.

15

docter of devynyte, Mayster Edwarde Story, person of Alle Halowys the More in London, and aftyr confessor unto the Quene, and aftyr that Byschoppe of Carlylle, prechyd at Poulys Crosse, and as moche as he myght wolde have passefyde [1] the mater, and sayde that hyt was blasphemy soo to reherse and say by oure Lord Cryste. But that same Sonday the fryers set uppe byllys at every chyrche dore that the docter sayde nott trought,[2] but the trought shulde be schewyd ande sayd by Doctor Mayster John Mylverton, the pryor of the same place, and he was provyncyalle of the same ordyr. And that aftyr noone in hys sarmon he raylyd soore and grevysly to fortefy hys bretheryn ys sayyngys, that sum laye men were wrothe with the fryers and whythedrewe hyr almys from them ; and sum men were not plesyd with hyr curettes, and sayde that they hadde noo ryght to have any offerynge byt lyffe by almys as Cryste dyde ; ande thys men were devydyd,[3] sum welle and sum ylle.

But the Wanysday the docter, Mayster Halden, kepte the scholys with in the Fryers and dysputyd a gayne a Gray Fryer as he promysyd ; and at that scholys were many grete docters and clerkys to geve hym audyens. And they thought he yode [4] soo farre that Mayster Alcocke, a doctor of lawe and commyssary unto the Dene of Synt Martyns in the Graunte, assytyd [5] the fryer tnat he shulde appere by fore the Arche Byschoppe of Cauntylbury at Lambeffe. And the fryer sayde he wold not obbey his cytacyon, for alle fryers ben exempte for alle the byschoppe ys power, but [6] hit were for eresy ; and the docter of lawe sytyd hym for eresy.

Thenne at the begynnyng of the terme aftyr Estyr the fryer apperyd by fore Mayster Docter Wynterborne, my lordys offycer and juge in suche causys and othyr as for spyrytualte. And ther were many worthy docters a gayne the fryer, but he lenyd evyr unto [7] hys prevelege, but he schewyd non but a bylle [8] unselyd. Thenne the mater was

---

[1] pacified. [2] truth. [3] divided. [4] went.
[5] cited. [6] unless. [7] defended constantly. [8] letter.

put to my Lorde of London, by so moche that alle thys
trobylle was done in hys dyossy,[1] and the Chaunceler
of Inglond, that was my Lorde of Warwycke ys brother,
toke party a-gayne the fryers ; and the day folowynge the
Provyncyalle and Docter Haldon come to Poulys by fore
my Lorde of London and brought hyr prevelegys with
hem, but the prevelege wolde not serve that tyme for noo
cause of eresy. And my lorde lawfully a-sytyd them to
appere by fore hym that same aftyr non, but they come
not, for the provyncyalle toke hys· way a-non towarde
Rome. And Docter Haldon toke noo leve of the byschoppe.
And thenn my Lord Chaunceler hyrde that they were gone,
and send for the yong fryer Harry Parker and commaundyd
hym to preson. And he was take from preson and sende
unto my Lorde of London. And the Sonday aftyr the
same fryer, Harry Parker, objuryd [2] that he sayd, and
sayde as we saye, that Cryste ys lorde of ovyr alle thynge,
and he confessyd alle so that very nede causyd them to
saye that Cryste beggyd, by cause that [3] men shulde take
the ordyr of fryers moste parfytyste of alle orders.

But one fryer couthe not be ware [4] by a nother, for
with a whyle in the vacacyon tyme a Blake Fryer prechyd
alle moste the same. And he was exampnyd by fore my
Lorde of London, and was made to preche agayne and
revokyd. Thenne my Lord of London cursyd thes two
docters, Mayster John Mylverton and Docter Thomas
Halden, at Poulys Crosse for there contymacy,[5] and hyt
happyd that Docter Ive dyde the execucyon of the curse,
and that grevyd the fryers soore, and sayde that he was
sette alle in malys ; but thys Docter Ive myght not chese.[6]

Ande be fore thys tyme the fore sayde Docter Ive kepte
the scolys at Poulys that ys undyr the chapter house,
and there he radde many fulle nobylle lessonnys to preve
that Cryste was lorde of alle and noo begger, and he dyde
hyt aftyr the forme of scholys, for he hadde hys abyte and
hys pelyon,[7] and a vyrger with a sylvyr rodde waytynge

---

[1] diocese.   [2] abjured.   [3] so that.   [4] warned.
[5] contumacy.   [6] choose.   [7] his habit and his pillion (of a D.D.).

uppon hym. And the same fryer of Menors that answeryd the Whyte Fryer answeryd hym onys, and many tymys he dyspute and radde in that scholys; he kepte hyt more than two yere. Thenn the fryers straynyd curtesy whoo sholde answery hym. And ssum fryers desyryd to answerye hym, but at the day of hyr desyre they apperyd not. And thenn men layde grete wagers the Provyncyalle wolde come home and doo many thyngys, and causyd that a fryer of Rome made a tretysse of the beggyng of Cryste, that welle was hym that myght have a copy of hyt, and they were to sylle at many placys in Rome, and sum were sende home to the Whyte Freers, but yet hit happyd that they come to thys Docter Ive, that he undyr stode the consayte welle i-nowe and sayde fulle lytylle or nought.

Thenn the Pope havyng woundyr of the complaynt of thys fryer, and inqueryde of suche men as come late owte of Inglonde of the mater; and whenne he undyrstode the mater, he wrote downe to the Arche Byschoppe of Cauntyr-bury and to the Byschoppe of London, and thonkyd hem that they were so trewe to Cryste and Hooly Chyrche, and desyryd to have alle the hoole mater and proscesse i-sende unto hym by wrytynge. And so hyt was, every thyng as ny as they couthe ymageny, puttyng alle favyr and parcyallyte and malysce a syde.

But the very trewe processe thys nobylle Doctor Ive wrote unto the Pope the maner, sayyng, and prechyng in hyr sermonys, bothe hys doyng and sayyng, as welle as the fryers, and the actys of bothe scholys. And nine docters of devynyte and bachelers of devynyte subscrybyd hyr namys with hyr owne hondys, and testefyde that alle was trewe that thys sayde Docter Ive hadde wretyn, for hyt was exampnyd and radde by fore alle the byschoppys that tyme beyng at London, and by the same docters and clerkys that subscrybyd. And that large and grete letter was sende with the byschoppys letters. And yf that Doctor Ivys letter hadde ben i-selyd with sum lordys sele spyrytualle, or an notarys syne there on, the freer had ben brende [1] in shorte tyme ; hit hadde non othyr sele but hys owne sygnett.

And the kynge toke a grete party on thys mater, for thes fryers hadde causyd moche trobylle a monge hys pepylle, and therefore he desyryd that holy fadyr the Pope to chastysse suche trespasserrys and brekers of the pesse, and send forthe a letter with the othyr letters.

Thenne the Pope ressayvyd thes letters, and undyrstode alle the hoole processe, and made hys cardynallys to exampne the fryer, and by hys answerynge they found nine moo poyntys that he erryd on, and sone aftyr he was put into the castylle of Angylle in stronge preson, and laye there yn alle most three yere. And evyr hys frendys and the fryers lokyd aftyr hys comyng home, but he may not, for he hathe bund hym sylfe unto the Pope by an yryn oblyacyn faste i-selyd a-boute hys two helys. And then he lackyd mony and frende schyppe, [and] submyttyd hym to the Pope ; but whenn he shalle cum hom I wotte not, but for sothe hys artyculys ben dampnyd, whether he be or nought I wot ner ; I truste ye shalle knowe aftyr in tyme comyng by Goddys grace, hoo have us alle in hys blessyd kepyng. Amen for cheryte.

[1] burnt.

SECTION FIVE

FOREIGN LIFE

Some mention, perhaps, should be made of the scenes and events which were the accompaniment of medieval travel. It is true that the majority of medieval men and women did not travel very much : the nearest market town, or the local or country shrine often marked the limits of their journeyings. These may be illustrated by the adventures of the Canterbury pilgrims, and our extract from the *Tale of Beryn* will serve to conclude Chaucer's well-known descriptions, while Langland gives yet another of his graphic pictures.

Travel abroad was a more difficult matter ; but here again the King's service and that of Holy Church accounted for many Englishmen abroad. The *locus classicus* for the medieval traveller must always be the account of the celebrated Sir John Mandeville, and consequently his memoirs have been largely drawn on.

I. PILGRIMS AT CANTERBURY

We know a great deal about medieval travellers on pilgrimage from the pages of Chaucer, but unfortunately he never described the great moment when they arrived at the end of their journey and knelt at the shrine of Thomas à Becket. That, however, has been done by an inferior hand, but not without skill or interest in The Tale of Berin, *edited by F. J. Furnivall and W. G. Stone, E.E.T.S. (E.S.) 1887. Our extract is from lines 130 ff.*

THE knyght & al the feleshipp, & no thing for to ly,
When they wer all I-loggit, as skill wold, & reson,
Everich aftir his degre, to Cherch then was seson
To passen & to wend, to maken hir offringis,
Righte as hir devocioune was, of sylvir broch & ryngis.
Then atte Chirche dorr the curtesy gen to ryse,

Tyl the knyght, of gentilnes, that knewe righte wele the
  guyse,
Put forth the Prelatis, the Person, & his fere.[1]
A monk, that toke the spryngill [2] with a manly chere,
And did right as the maner is, moilled [3] al his patis,[4] 10
Everich aftir othir, righte as they wer of states.
The ffrere feyned fetously [5] the spryngil for to hold,
To spryng [6] oppon the remnaunt,—that for his cope he
  nold
Have lafft that occupacionne in that holy plase,—
So longid his holy conscience to se the Nonnys fase.
The knyghte went with his compers toward the holy shryne,
To do that they were com fore, & aftir for to dyne ;
The Pardoner & the Miller, & other lewde sotes,
Sought hem selffen in the Chirch, right as lewde gotes ;
Pyrid [7] fast, & pourid, highe oppon the glase,   20
Countirfeting gentilmen, the armys for to blase,
Diskyveryng fast the peyntour, & for the story mourned,
And a red it also right as nolde Rammys hornyd : [8]
' He berith a balstaff ',[9] quod the toon,[10] ' & els a rakis
  ende.'
' Thou faillist ', quod the Miller, ' thowe has nat wel thy
  mynde ;
It is a spere, yf thowe canst se, right with a prik to-fore,
To bussh adown his enmy, & thurh the Sholdir bore.'
' Pese ! ' quod the hoost of Southwork, ' let stond the
  wyndow glasid !
Goith up, & doith yeur offerynge ! yee semeth half amasid !
Sith yee be in company of honest men & good,   30
Worchith [11] somwhat aftir, & let the kynd of brode [12]
Pas for a tyme ! I hold it for the best ;
Ffor who doith after company, may lyve the bet in rest.'
  Then passid they forth boystly,[13] goglyng with hir hedis,

---

[1] companion.   [2] holy water brush.   [3] wetted.   [4] their heads.
[5] attempted skilfully.   [6] sprinkle.   [7] Peered.
[8] and explained it as right as are horned rams ; cf. the proverb,
' as right as a ram's horn '.   [9] quarter-staff.   [10] the one.
[11] worship.   [12] native breeding.   [13] boisterously.

Knelid a down to-fore the shryne, & hertilich [1] hir bedis
They preyd to Seynt Thomas, in such wyse as they couth ;
And sith, the holy relikis, ech man with his mowith
Kissid, as à goodly monke the names told & taught.
And sith to othir placis of holynes they raughte,
And were in hir devocioun tyl service wer al doon ; · 40
And sith they drowgh to dynerward, as it drew to noon.
  Then, as maner & custom is, signes [2] there they
    boughte,—
Ffor men of contre shulde know whom they hadde oughte,—
Ech man set his sylvir in such thing as they likid
      .   .   .   .
They set hir signes oppon hir hedis, and som oppon hir
    cappe.

II. ABJURING THE REALM

This extract is taken from The Brut, *p. 442, and describes an
unusual ending to what was a common sight on the roads in England
in the Middle Ages—a felon being taken to the coast in order that he
might abjure the realm.*

AND in the same yere, a fals Breton, between Ester and
Witsontyde, mordrede a good wedowe in hir bedde, the
which hadde found hym, for almesse, withoute Algate,
in the suburbes of London.   And he bar a-way all that
sche hadde, and after toke girth [3] of holy churche at
Saint Georges in Suthwerk ; but at the last he toke the
Crosse,[4] and for-suore the Kyng land.   And as he went
his way, it happid hym to come by the same place wher
he did that cursede dede.   And women of the same parish
come oute to hym with stones and with canell dong and
there made an ende of hym in the high streit, so that

---

[1] heartily.   [2] i.e. the pilgrim's token.   [3] sanctuary.
[4] i.e. abjured the Realm. On so doing a felon was ascribed a
port from whence he was to embark overseas. He had to proceed
thereto, keeping strictly to the highway, and so long as he did so
his life was protected by the King's authority. But, as M. Jus-
serand has told us, ' accident played an important part in the life
of the fourteenth century '. . . . !

he went no ferthere ; not-with-stondyng the Constablis and other men also, which had hym in governaunce, to convey hym forth in his way. For there was a grete companye of them ; and on hym thei had neither mercie nor pite ; and thus this fals thefe endede his life in this worlde, for his falsnesse.

III. BEGGARS BY THE WAY

From Piers Plowman, *C. text X.* 98 *ff.*

Ac beggers with bagges the whiche brewhouses ben here
    churches,
Bote thei be blynde other broke other elles be syke,
Thauh he falle for defaute that faiteth [1] for hus lyf-lode,
Reccheth [2] nevere, ye ryche thauh suche lorelles sterven.
For alle that han here hele and here eyen syghte,
And lymes to laborye with and lolleres lyf usen,
Lyven a-gens Godes lawe and lore of holy churche.
And yut arn ther other beggers in hele, as hit semeth,
Ac hem wanteth here witt, men and women bothe,
The whiche aren lunatik lollers and leperes a-boute, 10
And mad as the mone sitt more other lasse.[3]
Thei caren for no cold ne counteth of no hete,
And arn meuynge [4] after the mone, moneyles thei walke,
With a good wil, witlees meny wyde contreys,
Ryght as Peter dude and Paul, save that thei preche nat,
Ne myracles maken ; ac meny tymes hem happeth
To prophecien of the puple [5] pleyinge, as hit were,
And to oure sight, as hit semeth suththe,[6] God hath the
    myghte
To geven eche a wyght wit, welthe, and his hele,
And suffreth suche so gon, hit semeth, to myn Inwitt,[7] 20
Hit arn as hus aposteles,[8] suche puple other as his privye
    disciples.
For he sente hem forth selverles in a somer garnement,

[1] begs.   [2] Cares.   [3] And more or less mad, according as the moon sits.   [4] wandering.   [5] people.   [6] truth.   [7] imagination.   [8] They are like his apostles.

With-oute bred and bagge as the bok telleth,
  Quando misi vos sine pane et pera.
Barfot and bredles beggeth thei of no man
And thauh he mete with the meyre amyddes the strete,
He reverenceth hym ryght nouht no rather than another ;
  Neminem salutaver itis per viam.
Suche manere of men Matheu ous techeth,
We sholde have to house and help hem when thei come ; 30
  Et egenos vagosque induc in domum tuam.
For hit aren murye-mouthede men, mynstrales of hevene,
And Godes boyes,[1] bordiours [2] as the bok telleth,
  Si quis videtur sapiens, fiet stultus ut sit sapiens.
And alle manere mynstrales men wot wel the sothe,
To under-fonge hem faire by-falleth for the ryche,[3]
For the lordes love and ladies that thei with lengcn.
Men suffren al that suche seyn and in solas taken,[4]
And yut more to suche men doth er thei passe,
Gyven hem gyftes and gold for grete lordes sake. 40
Ryght so, ye riche rather ye sholde, for sothe,
Welcomen and worsshepen and with youre goode helpen
Godes mynstrales and hus messagers and hus murye bor-
  diours ;
The whiche arn lunatik lollares and leperes a-boute,
For under Godes secre seel here synnes ben ykeuered.
For thei bereth no bagges ne none botels under clokes,
The whiche is lollaren lyf and lewede eremytes,[5]
That loken ful louheliche [6] to lacchen [7] mennes almesse,
In hope to sitten at even by the hote coles,
Unlouke hus legges abrod other lygge at hus ese, 50
Reste hym, and roste hym and his ryg [8] turne,
Drynke drue and deepe [9] and drawe hym thanne to bedde ;
And when hym lyketh and lust,[10] hus leve ys to aryse ;
When he ys rysen, rometh out and ryght wel aspieth

---

[1] servants. [2] jesters. [3] To receive them liberally is the duty
of the rich. [4] Men allow all that such men say to pass, and take it
as amusing. [5] Which is the life of lollers and ignorant hermits.
[6] humbly.   [7] obtain.   [8] back.
[9] Drain the pot to the dregs.   [10] wishes to.

Whar he may rathest [1] have a repast, other a rounde of
    bacon,
Sulver, other sode mete, [2] and som tyme bothe ;
A loof, other half a loof, other a lompe of chese ;
And carieth it hom to hus Cote, and cast [3] hym to lyve,
In ydelnesse, and in ese, and by others travayle.

IV. THE PILGRIM'S VOYAGE

*The pilgrimage to the shrine of S. James of Compostella, in the
north of Spain, was undertaken every year by large numbers of Englishmen. They could go there by the long and dangerous journey through
France and over the Pyrenees, or by the almost equally dangerous sea
passage. Here is the account of one who made his pilgrimage by sea,
collected in a volume entitled* The Stacions of Rome, *etc., edited by
F. J. Furnivall, E.E.T.S. (O.S.)* 1867, *p.* 37.

MEN may leve alle gamys
That saylen to Seynt Jamys,
Ffor many a man hit gramys, [4]
    When they begyn to sayle ;
Ffor when they have take the see
At Sandwyche or at Wynchylsee,
At Brystow, or where that hit bee,
    Theyr hertes begyn to fayle.

Anone the mastyr commaundeth fast
To hys shypmen, in alle the hast,   10
To dresse hem [5] sone about the mast,
    Theyr takelyng [6] to make ;
With ' Howe ! hissa ! ' then they cry ;
' What, howe ! mate, thow stondyst to ny,
Thy felow may nat hale the by ' ; [7]
    Thus they begyn to crake. [8]

A boy or tweyn anone upstyen, [9]
And overthwart the sayle-yerde lyen.

[1] soonest.   [2] silver, or boiled meat.   [3] contrives.
[4] grieves.   [5] busy themselves.   [6] tackling.
[7] haul fast thee.   [8] cry.   [9] climb.

'Y how! taylia!' the remenaunt cryen,
   And pulle with alle theyr myght.   20
'Bestowe the boote,[1] boteswayne, anon,
That our pylgryms may pley theron;
For som ar lyke to cowgh and grone
   Or [2] hit be full mydnyght.'

'Hale the bowelyne! now, vere the shete!'
Cooke, make redy anoon our mete;
Our pylgryms have no lust to ete,
   I pray God yeve [3] hem rest.'
'Go to the helm! what, howe! no nere!' [4]
'Steward, felow, a pot of bere!'   30
'Ye shalle have, sir, with good chere,
   Anon alle of the best.'

'Y howe! trussa! hale in the brayles! [5]
Thow halyst nat, be God, thow fayles!' [6]
'O se howe welle owre good shyp sayles!'
   And thus they say among.
'Hale in the wartake!' [7] 'Hit shal be done.'
'Steward, cover the boorde anone,
And set bred and salt therone,
   And tary nat to long!'   40

Then cometh oone and seyth: 'Be mery,
Ye shall have a storme or a pery.' [8]
'Holde thow thy pese! thow canst no whery,[9]
   Thow medlyst wondyr sore.'
Thys menewhyle the pylgryms ly,
And have theyr bowlys fast theym by,
And cry aftyr hote malvesy:[10]
   Thow helpe [11] for to restore.

And som wold have a saltyd tost,
Ffor they myght ete neyther sode [12] ne rost;   50

---

[1] stow the boat.   [2] ere.   [3] give.   [4] no nearer to the wind!
[5] furling ropes.   [6] slacken off.   [7] a kind of rope.   [8] squall.
[9] curse?   [10] malmsey.   [11] their health.   [12] boiled.

A man myght sone pay for theyr cost,
  As for oo day or twayne.
Som layde theyr bookys on theyr kne,
And rad so long they myght nat se.
' Allas, myne hede wolle cleve on thre ! '
  Thus seyth another certayne.

Then commeth owre owner, lyke a lorde,
And speketh many a royall worde,
And dresseth hym to the hygh borde,
  To see alle thyng be welle.   60
Anone he calleth a carpentere,
And byddyth hym bryng with hym hys gere,
To make the cabans here and there,
  With many a febylle [1] celle.

A sak of strawe were there ryght good,
Ffor som must lyg theym [2] in theyr hood :
I had as lefe be in the wood,
  Without mete or drynk.
For when that we shall go to bedde,
The pumpe is nygh oure beddes hede ;   70
A man were as good to be dede
  As smell therof the stynk !

V. A GREAT MEDIEVAL TRAVELLER

The travels of Sir John Mandeville were among the most popular of medieval English writings.   Until recent years the account printed here below of the authorship of the volume was accepted, but recent researches make it clear that the real author was not an Englishman but a certain Jean de Bourgogne.   The question is further complicated by the fact that both these names may only be coverings for the real author Jean d'Outremeuse.   The most recent edition by P. Hamelius for the E.E.T.S., 1919, contains a convenient summary of the available evidence.   The extracts given here are taken from the edition of J. O. Halliwell, 1883.   They will give the reader an admirable summary of medieval credulity and superstition regarding foreign countries and peoples.

---

    [1] flimsy.   [2] lie them down.

(*p.* 4) AND for als moche as it is longe tyme passed, that ther was no generalle passage ne vyage over the see ; and many men desiren for to here speke of the holy lond, and han thereof gret solace and comfort ; I John Maundevylle, knyght, alle be it I be not worthi, that was born in Englond, in the Town of Seynt Albones,[1] passed the see in the yeer of our Lord Jesu Crist MCCCXXII, in the day of Seynt Michelle : and hidre to have ben longe tyme over the see, and have seyn and gon thorghe manye dyverse londes, and many provynces and kingdomes and iles, and have passed thorghe Tartarye, Percye, Ermonye[2] the litylle and the grete ; thorghe Lybye, Caldee and a gret partie of Ethiope ; thorghe Amazoyne, Inde the lasse and the more, a gret partie ; and thorghe out many others iles, that ben abouten Inde ; where dwellen many dyverse folkes, and of dyverse maneres and lawes, and of dyverse schappes of men. Of whiche londes and iles, I schalle speke more pleynly hereaftre. And I schalle devise you sum partie of thinges that there ben, whan time schalle ben, aftre it may best come to my mynde ; and specyally for hem, that wylle and are in purpos for to visite the Holy Citee of Jerusalem, and the holy places that are thereaboute. And I schalle telle the weye that thei schulle holden thidre. For I have often tymes passed and ryden the way, with gode companye of many lordes : God be thonked.

And yee schulle undirstonde, that I have put this boke out of Latyn into Frensche, and translated it agen out of Frenche into Englyssche, that every man of my nacioun may undirstonde it. But lordes and knyghtes and othere noble and worthi men, that conne[3] Latyn but litylle, and han ben beyonde the see, knowen and undirstonden, gif I erre in devisynge, for forgetynge, or elles ; that thei mowe redresse it and amende it. For thinges passed out of longe tyme from a mannes mynde or from his syght, turnen sone into forgetynge : Because that mynde of man ne may not ben comprehended ne witheholden,[4] for the freeltee of mankynde.

[1] St. Albans.   [2] Armenia.   [3] know   [4] retain.

VI. CIRCUMNAVIGATING THE EARTH

(*p.* 182) I SEYE you certeynly, that men may envirowne
alle the Erthe of alle the world, as wel undre as aboven,
and turnen agen to his contree, that hadde companye
and schippynge and conduyt : and alle weyes he scholde
fynde men, londes, and iles, als wel as in this contree.
For yee wyten welle, that thei that ben toward the An-
tartyk, thei ben streghte, feet agen feet of hem, that dwellen
undre the transmontane ; als wel as wee and thei that
dwellyn undre us, ben feet agenst feet. For alle the
parties of see and of lond han here appositees, habitables
or trepassables, and [yles] of this half and bezond half.
And wytethe wel, that aftre that, that I may parceyve
and comprehende, the londes of Pestre John, Emperour
of Ynde, ben undre us. For in goynge from Scotland or
from Englond toward Jerusalem, men gon upward alweys.
For oure lond is in the lowe partie of the erthe, toward
the West : and the lond of Prestre John is the lowe partie
of the erthe, toward the Est : and thei han there the day,
whan wee have the nyghte, and also highe to the contrarie,
thei han the nyghte, whan wee han the day. For the
erthe and the see ben of round forme and schapp, as I
have seyd beforn. And that that men gon upward to o
cost, men gon dounward to another cost. Also yee have
herd me seye, that Jerusalem is in the myddes of the world ;
and that may men preven and schewen there, be a spere,
that is pighte in to the erthe, upon the hour of mydday,
whan it is equenoxium, that schewethe no schadwe on
no syde. And that it scholde ben in the myddes of the
world, David wytnessethe it in the Psautre, where he
seythe ; *Deus operatus est salutem in medio terre.* Thanne
thei that parten fro the parties of the West, for to go toward
Jerusalem, als many iorneyes as thei gon upward for
to go thidre, in als many iorneyes may thei gon from
Jerusalem, unto other confynyes of the superficialtie of the
erthe bezonde. And whan men gon beyonde tho iourneys,
toward Ynde and to the foreyn yles, alle is envyronynge

the roundnesse of the erthe and of the see, undre oure contrees on this half. And therfore hathe it befallen many tymes of o thing, that I have herd cownted, whan I was yong ; how a worthi man departed somtyme from oure contrees, for to go serche the world. And so he passed Ynde, and the yles bezonde Ynde, where ben mo than 5000 yles ; and so longe he wente be see and lond, and so enviround the world be many seysons, that he fond an yle, where he herde speke his owne language, callynge on oxen in the plowghe, suche wordes as men speken to bestes in his owne contree : whereof he hadde gret mervayle : for he knewe not how it myghte be. But I seye, that he had gon so longe, be londe and be see, that he had envyround alle the erthe, that he was comen agen envirounynge, that is to seye, goynge aboute, unto his owne Marches, gif he wolde have passed forthe, til he had founden his contree and his owne knouleche. But he turned agen from thens, from whens he was come fro ; and so he loste moche peynefulle labour, as him self seyde, a gret while aftre, that he was comen hom. For it befelle aftre, that he wente in to Norweye ; and there Tempest of the See toke him ; and he arryved in an yle ; and whan he was in that yle, he knew wel, that it was the yle, where he had herd speke his owne langage before, and the callynge of the oxen at the plowghe : and that was possible thinge. But how it semethe to symple men unlerned, that men ne mowe not go undre the erthe, and also that men scholde falle toward the hevene, from undre ! But that may not be, upon lesse, than wee nowe falle toward hevene, fro the erthe, where wee ben. For fro what partie of the erthe, that man duelle, outher aboven or benethen, it semethe alweys to hem that duellen, that thei gon more righte than ony other folk. And righte as it semethe to us, that thei ben undre us, righte so it semeth hem, that wee ben undre hem. For gif a man myghte falle fro the erthe unto the firmament ; be grettere resoun, the erthe and the see, that ben so grete and so hevy, scholde fallen to the firmament ; but that may not be : and

16

therfore seithe oure Lord God ; *Non timeas me, qui suspendi Terra ex nichilo ?* And alle be it that it be possible thing, that men may so envyronne alle the world, natheles of a 1000 persones, on ne myghte not happen to returneñ in to his contree. For, for the gretnesse of the erthe and of the see, men may go be a 1000 and a 1000 other weyes, that no man cowde redye him perfitely toward the parties that he cam fro, but gif it were be aventure and happ, or be the grace of God. For the erthe is full large and fulle gret, and holt in roundnesse and aboute envyroun, be aboven and be benethen 20425 myles, aftre the opynyoun of the olde wise astronomeres.

VII. FOREIGN HABITS

(*p.* 201) FROM that Yle, in goynge be see, toward the southe, is another gret yle, that is clept Dondun.[1] In that yle ben folk of dyverse kyndes ; so that the fadre etethe the sone, the sone the fadre, the husbonde the wif, and the wif the husbonde. And gif it so befalle, that the fadre or modre or ony of here frendes ben seke, anon the son gothe to the prest of here law, and preyethe him to aske the ydole, gif his fadre or modre or frend schalle dye on that evylle or non. And than the prest and the sone gone to gydere before the ydole, and knelen fulle devoutly, and asken of the ydole here demande. And gif the devylle, that is with inne, answere, that he schalle lyve, thei kepen him wel : and gif he seye, that he schalle dye, than the prest gothe with the sone, with the wif of him that is seeke, and thei putten here hondes upon his mouthe, and stoppen his brethe, and so thei sleen him. And aftre that, thei choppen alle the body in smale peces, and preyen alle his frendes to comen and eten of him, that is ded : and thei senden for alle the mynstralle of the contree, and maken a solempne fest. And whan thei han eten the flessche, thei taken the bones, and buryen hem, and syngen and maken gret melodye. And alle tho that ben of his kyn, or pretenden

[1] One of the Andaman Islands.

hem to ben his frendes, and thei come not to that feste, thei ben repreved for evere and schamed, and maken gret doel ; [1] for nevere aftre schulle thei ben holden as frendes. And thei seyn also, that men eten here flesche, for to dely-veren hem out of peyne. For gif the wormes of the erthe eten hem, the soule scholde suffre gret peyne, as thei seyn ; and namely, whan the flesche is tendre and megre, thanne seyn here frendes, that thei don gret synne, to leten hem have so long langure, to suffre so moche peyne, with oute resoun. And whan thei fynde the flessche fatte, than thei seyn, that it is wel don, to senden him sone to Paradys ; and that thei have not suffred him to longe to endure in peyne.

VIII. THE VALLEY PERILOUS

(*p.* 280) BESYDE that yle of Mistorak, upon the left syde, nyghe to the ryvere of Phison, is a marveylous thing. There is a vale betwene the mountaynes, that durethe nyghe a 4 myle : and summen clepen it the vale en-chaunted ; some clepen it the vale of Develes, and some clepen it the Vale perilous. In that Vale, heren men often tyme grete tempestes and thondres and grete murmures and noyses, alle dayes and nyghtes : and gret noyse, as it were sown of tabours and of nakeres and trompes, as thoughe it were of a gret feste. This vale is alle fulle of develes, and hathe ben alle weys. And men seyn there, and it is on of the entrees of Helle. In that Vale is gret plentee of Gold and Sylver : wherefore many mys-belevynge men, and manye Cristene men also, gon in often tyme, for to have of the Thresoure, that there is : but fewe comen agen : and namely of the mys belevynge men, ne of the Cristene men nouther : for thei ben anon strangled of Develes. And in mydde place of that vale, undir a roche, is an hed and the visage of a devyl bodyliche, fulle horrible and dreadfulle to see, and it schewethe not but the hed, to the schuldres. But there is no man in the world so hardy,

---

[1] woe.

Cristene man ne other, but that he wolde ben a drad for to beholde it ; and that it wolde semen him to dye for drede ; so is it hidouse for to beholde. For he beholdethe every man so scharply, with dreadfulle eyen, that ben evere more mevynge and sparklynge, as fuyr, and chaungethe and sterethe so often in dyverse manere, with so horrible countenance, that no man dar not neighen towardes him. And fro him comethe out smoke and stynk and fuyr, and so moche abhomynacioun, that unethe [1] no man may there endure. But the gode Cristene men, that ben stable in the feythe, entren welle withouten perile. For thei wil first schryven hem, and marken hem with the tokene of the Holy Cros ; so that the fendes ne han no power over hem. But alle be it that thei ben with outen perile, yit natheles ne ben thei not with outen drede, whan that thei seen the Develes visibely and bodyly alle aboute hem, that maken fulle many dyverse assautes and manaces in eyr and in erthe, and agasten hem with strokes of thondre blastes and of tempestes. And the most drede is, that God wole taken vengeance thanne, of that men han mys don agen his wille. And yee schulle undirstonde, that whan my fellows and I weren in that vale, wee weren in gret thought, whether that wee dursten putten oure bodyes in aventure, to gon in or non, in the proteccioun of God. And some of oure fellowes accordeden to enter, and somme noght, so there weren with us two worthi men, Frere Menoures, that weren of Lombardye, that seyden, that gif ony man wolde entren, thei wolde gon in with us. And when thei hadden seyd so, upon the gracyous trust of God and of hem, wee leet synge masse, and made every man to ben schryven and houseld : and thanne wee entreden fourteen personnes ; but at oure goynge out, wee weren but nine. And so wee wisten nevere, whether that oure Fellowes weren lost, or elle turned agen for drede : but wee ne saughe hem never after : and tho weren two men of Grece and three of Spayne. And oure other fellows, that wolden not gon in with us, thei

[1] almost.

wenten by another coste, to ben before us, and so thei were. And thus wee passeden that perilouse vale, and founden thereinne gold and sylver and precious stones and riche jewelles gret plentee, both here and there, as us semed : but whether that it was, as us semede, I wot nere : for I touched none, because that the develes ben so subtyle to make a thing to seme otherwise than it is, for to disceyve mankynde : and therfore I towched none ; and also because that I wolde not ben put out of my devocioun : for I was more devout thanne, than evere I was before or after, and alle for the drede of fendes, that I saughe in dyverse figures ; and also for the gret multytude of ded bodyes, that I saughe there liggynge be the weye, be alle the vale, as thoughe there had ben a bataylle betwene two kynges and the myghtyest of the contree, and that the gretter partye had ben discomfyted and slayn. And I trowe, that unethe scholde ony contree have so moche peple with in him, as lay slayn in that vale, as us thoughte ; the whiche was an hidouse sight to seen. And I merveylled moche, that there weren so manye, and the bodyes all hole, with outen rotynge. But I trowe, that fendes made hem semen to ben so hole, with outen rotynge. But that myghte not ben to myn avys, that so manye scholde have entred so newely, ne so manye newely slayn, with outen stynkynge and rotynge. And manye of hem weren in habite of Cristene men : but I trowe wel, that it weren of suche, that wenten in for covetyse of the thresoure, that was there, and hadden over moche feblenesse in feithe ; so that hire hertes ne myghte not enduren in the beleve for drede. And therfore weren wee the more devout a gret del : and yit wee weren cast doun and beten down many tymes to the hard erthe, be wyndes and thondres and tempestes : but evere more God of his grace halp us : and so wee passed that perilous vale, with outen perile and with outen encombrance. Thanked be alle myghty Godd,

IX. PARADISE

(*p.* 303) OF paradys ne can not I speken propurly :
for I was not there. It is fer beyonde ; and that for-
thinkethe me : and also I was not worthi. But as I
have herd seye of wyse men beyonde, I schalle telle you
with gode wille. Paradys terrestre, as wise men seyn,
is the highest place of erthe, that is in alle the world :
and it is so highe, that it touchethe nyghe to the cercle
of the mone, there as the mone makethe hire torn. For
sche is so highe, that the flode of Noe ne myght not come
to hire, that wolde have covered alle the erthe of the
world alle aboute, and aboven and benethen, saf Paradys
only allone. And this Paradys is enclosed alle aboute
with a walle ; and men wyte not wherof it is. For the
walles ben covered alle over with mosse ; as it semethe.
And it semethe not that the walle is ston of nature. And
that walle strecchethe fro the southe to the northe ; and
it hathe not but on entree, that is closed with fyre brennynge ; so that no man, that is mortalle, ne dar not entren.
And in the moste highe place of Pardys, evene in the
myddel place, is a welle, that castethe out the 4 flodes,
that rennen be dyverse londes.

And yee schulle undirstonde, that no man that is mortelle,
ne may not approchen to that Paradys. For be londe no
man may go for wylde beștes, that ben in the desertes,
and for the highe mountaynes and gret huge roches, that
no man may passe by, for the derke places that ben there,
and that manye : And be the ryveres may no man go ;
for the water rennethe so rudely and so scharply, because
that it comethe doun so outrageously from the highe
places aboven, that it rennethe in so grete wawes, that no
scripp may not rowe ne seyle agenes it : and the watre
rorethe so, and makethe so huge noyse, and so gret tempest,
that no man may here other in the schipp, thoughe he
cryede with alle the craft that he cowde, in the hyeste
voys that he myghte. Many grete lordes han assayed
with gret wille many tymes for to passen be tho ryveres

toward Paradys, with fulle grete companyes : but thei
myghte not speden in hire viage : and manye dyeden
for werynesse of rowynge agenst tho stronge wawes ; and
many of hem becamen blynde, and many deve,[1] for the
noyse of the water : and sume weren perisscht and loste,
with inne the wawes : So that no mortelle man may
approche to that place, with outen specyalle grace of God :
so that of that place I can seye you no more. And therfore
I schalle holde me stille, and retornen to that that I have
seen.

X. A MEDIEVAL SIEGE

*Service abroad often meant a dreary period of inaction before some
walled city, or a still more terrible period of inaction within its walls.
The* Brut *gives us the following account of the siege of Rouen in* 1418.

(*p.* 400) AND tho it drewe nere Cristemesse ; and by
that tyme her vitailis scarsid sore [2] with-ynne the Cite,
for they hade nothir bred, ale, nor wyne, but watir and
vynegur, that was her [3] drynke. And flesshe nor fisshe
they had non, but eten hors, doggis, mis, rattis and cattis ;
for an quarter of an horse, were he lene or fatte, was tho
sold in the Cite amonge the pepull for an hundred shillings
good payment, and an hors hede for xx. s., and a Ratte
for xl. d. ; and for xiij. s. iiij. d. thei sold a Catte, and a
mows for xx. d. ; and these wormys weren bought and eten
so faste that unnethe [4] thei fonde eny for to selle for no
money. And tho was a ferthynge lof boght in the Cite
for a ffranke. And thanne hem failid bothe whete, and
mele, and alle othir graynys that thei myght make of eny
brede ; but branne and broken wortis,[5] and nepe-rotis,[6]
and lekis, was to hem mete of grete valewe ; for a leke was
sold for twelvepence, and an Egge for ninepence, and an
appull for tenpence : Siche merchaundyse was there with-
ynne the Cite a gret while ; and ther was many a carefulle
creature, for her vitailis were alle wastid and spent, and

| [1] deaf | [2] were very scarce. | [3] their. |
| [4] scarcely. | [5] plants. | [6] turnips. |

they myght come to no new by no maner wey; for the sege [1] that lay withoute, rounde aboute the Cite, wold suffre no vitaile come in, to hem, neythir by watir neythir be londe.

And thanne be-ganne the pepull with-ynne the Cite to deie faste, bothe, smale and grete, for the passynge hungur and enfamen [2] that was amonge hem, by two hundred personys and moo day by day; and there as was firste joy and pryde, and grete boste, tho was there amonge hem weylynge, sorow and care, and wepynge, and wryngynge with hondis. And though a child shuld deie, the modir wold geve it no brede ne nought ellis of othir fode, ne wold not departe [3] no morselle though she myght save the lif of her child of hir body borne, but wold save her selfe while she myght; for love and hertly kyndenesse was tho from hem passid. Nor the child wold not profir the modir, for eche of hem caste hymself to leve; [4] for alle kyndenesse and love tho was sette beside; for evyr the childe wold hide his mete and his drynke fro his modir and from all his other ffryndis, [5] for his mete thei shuld not see, for thei ete hit alle in pryvete. And we may preve by that pepull there, that houngir passithe kyndenesse and eke love, that made her unrightwesnesse and her cursid levynge and pryde that regnyd amongis hem in tho dayes, wherefore God sent hem a yerd [6] of chastisement. But yet thei that kept the wallis and touris of the Cite rounde aboute, be-cause the pepull withoute shuld not knowe nor wete [7] of her grete nede and myschef that thei weren ynne, evyr [continued] to hold her courte and contynaunce of opyn werre, bothe with shot of gounnys and quarellis. [8]

But amonge ther issewid [9] summe pepull of the Cite oute; and they come forthe, and weren take of the wacche-men without eat the sege Cite. And they affraynyd [10] hem how it stode with the pepull that weren lefte with-ynne the Cite. And they ansuerid and told to the Enge-

---

[1] siege. [2] famine. [3] give away.
[4] live. [5] friends. [6] rod. [7] weet. [8] cross-bowbolts.
[9] issued. [10] questioned.

lisshe pepull of the grete nede, scarste, hungir and dethe, that was evyry day amongis hem. But our folke wold not beleve nor truste hem, be cause that the pepull with-ynne hilde alle tymes contynaunce like in werre, day be day, as thei did beforne upon the sege withoute ; wherefore thei had hem in no truste in no degre.

And thanne with-ynne a litull while aftur, the worthi men that weren with-ynne the Cite, gederid alle the pore pepull that tho were with-ynne the Cite, man, woman, and child, and brought hem to the gatis, and put hem oute at evyry porte by an hundred personys on a rowte,[1] and had hem helpe hem-self in her beste maner that thei myght, for there thei shold no lenger abyde yn no wyse with hem. And thanne thei come forthe toward the Engelisshe seege, knelynge on her kneis, and wepynge sore, bothe man, and woman with yonge sowkynge children in her armys, and olde febull men knelynge besyde hem, makynge there a dilfull [2] crye ; for alle they cryed there atonys [3] ' Have mercy on us, ye good and Cristen and worthy men.' And thanne oure Kynge had rewthe on hem and pite, and yaf hem brede and drynke, and made hem turne ayen to the Cite ; and there thei kepte hem in the diche, that thei shold not knowe nor here the ordynaunce nor counseile of the seege, ne of her wacche in no wyse, for trayne [4] and treson that myght falle.

And whanne these pore pepull shuld turne ayen, thei made high sorough and grete murmuracion amonge hem-self, and seyden they had levyr byn sleyn there thanne go ayen into the Cite, and dilfully, with high voycis bannynge and cursynge her owne nacion ; for thei, that weren with-ynne the Cite, wold not suffre hem come in ayen ; wherefore y trowe thei diden grete synne and myschieff to hem-self ; for meny of him deiden there for colde, that, and [5] thei had byn with-ynne, her lifis might have byn savyd and kepte.

And tho was come the tyme of Cristmesse, in whiche oure Kynge did the grete mercy and relef to his enemyes, at

[1] at a time.   [2] doleful.   [3] at once.   [4] betrayal.   [5] if.

the reverence of that glorious feste of the byrthe of oure
Lorde Jhesu Criste and of his blessid modir, oure Lady
Seynt Marye, that gracious and mercifull virgyne. For,
of high pite, mercy and grace, and at the reverence of
that tyme of the holy feste, the Kynge, of high compascion
that he had in hert, and of his worthi and excellente manhode, sent oute his heraudis in good araye, bothe to hem
that weren wyth-ynne the Cite as welle as with-oute the
Cite, on the Cristemesse day self, to hem that lackid vitaile,
that thei shold come and have mete and drynke ynow, in
worship of the Feste, and sauf-condite to come and to
goo.   And thei seiden alle ' gramersis ' [1] lightly, as thei
had no nede there-to, and set no pryce by his sonde.   And
unnethe [2] thei wold graunte space unto the pepull of her
owne nacion to ben relevyd that layn in the diche undir
the Cite wallis, that thei had droven and put oute of
grete myschieff.   But [they allowed] two preestis and
four servauntis for to brynge hem vitailles, mete and
drynke ; and if ther come eny moo personys, thei wold
shete to hem and sle hem to dethe.   And thanne weren
alle these pore pepull set arowe ; and these two preestis
with her four servauntis broughten hem plente of mete
and drynke, of the Kyngis gracious almys ; and so thei
weren at that tyme made welle at eese ; and replete of
mete and drynke.   And as thei sete her mete to fonge, [3]
this talkynge thei had amongis hem.   ' A almyghty God,'
thanne thei seide, ' the Engelisshe-men be of good and
treue herte !   Lo, how here this excellent Prynce and Kynge
that we thought nevyr to obey unto, ne nevyr profre ne
don hym homage, now hathe he on us more pite and com-
passion by a thousand [fold] thanne hathe oure owne
nacion.   Therefore, oure Lord God, that art full of myght,
graunte hym grace to wynne and get his trewe right ! '
Thus the pore pepull for the Kynge prayde ; that God
kepe and mayntene hym in alle his nedis.   Whanne thei
had thus servyd alle the pore pepull with mete and drynke,

---

[1] gramercy, i.e. graunt mercy : many thanks.   [2] scarcely.
[3] took up their meat.

and were welle reffresshid, oure folke turnyd agen to the
Kynge, for the trewse lastid no lengur but that same day.

And whanne the nyght be-ganne to apere and shewe,
thanne thei on the wallis beganne newe werre ayen upon
the seege, and wacchidden a ward that full streyte bothe
day and nyght with hungir smerte, for that tyme her
vitaill weren alle wastid and spente.   And meny a worthy
body for defaute of lyvelod of mete and drynke was spent
and ded, for evyr grete houngir brekithe herd stonen wall
yn hir grete nede ; for evyr the lif is dere and swete.

XI. MORE MEDIEVAL SIEGE OPERATIONS

The next extracts, taken from Romances, will serve two purposes
First they illustrate the scenes incident on campaigning, both at home
and abroad, and give us a series of pictures of the medieval warrior ;
and secondly they will enable the reader to form (perhaps too favourable)
an opinion of the medieval romance.   The passages are all taken from
Metrical Romances of the XIII, XIV, and XV Centuries, *ed. H.*
Weber, 1810, 3 *vols.*

The Lyfe of Alisaundre.

[*Vol. I, p. 54, lines* 1201-38.]

HE touchith his horn, and forth rideth,
Mony mon him went myde.
The ryghte way they nome,
That heo to the cite come.
Heore drawbrugge they drowe ate
And sheotten faste heore gates :
Alisaundre heom asailed fast,
And with mangnelis [1] to heom cast.
They into the walles stowe,
And defended heom with howe ;   10
With albastres,[2] and with stones,
They slowe men, and braken bones,

----

[1] a mangonel was a machine which threw stones and was com-
monly used in medieval siege operations.   [2] cross-bows.

With hot water, and other engyn,
They defended heom therynne.
Ac [1] Alisaundre quic hoteth his hynen, [2]
Under heore walles to myne,
With strong gynnes, [3] and deth werres,
The whiles the mynoris.
Ac, by strenthe no by gynne,
No myghte he heom that day wynne ;   20
No that other, no the thridde,
No the feorthe he ne spedde
  Ac tho Alisaundre seygh this
He stopped heore way, y-wis, [4]
That ther no myghte, to heore fode,
Come to heom no gode ;
Knyght, no swayn, ne heore stren, [5]
No none wise myghte fleon,
The folk, and the poraile, [6]
Weoren an-hungred, saun faile ;   30
And al day on the richer gradden. [7]
Theo riche of heom reuthe [8] hadden,
And saide they hadden, sekirliche,
Leovere steorve aporteliche, [9]
Than thole [10] soche wo and sorwe :

II

Richard Coer de Lyon.

[Vol. II, p. 171, lines 4295-4415.]

SER Fouke broughte good engynes,
Swylke knew but fewe Sarazynes :
In every half [11] he leet hem arere,
Hys enemys a new playe to lere.
A mangenel [12] he leet bende,
To the prys-tour [13] a ston gan sende.

---

[1] But.   [2] ordered his men.   [3] engines.   [4] indeed.   [5] progeny.
[6] poor people.   [7] cried out.   [8] pity.   [9] openly.   [10] suffer.
[11] side.   [12] See above.   .   [13] chief tower.

That stone whanne it out fleygh,
The Sarezynes that it seygh,
' Allas ! ' they cryede and hadde wondyr.
It routes as it wer a thondyr !   10
On the tour the ston so hytte,
That twenty feet away it smytte.
To another a ston he threw,
For to make hem game newe ;
Al that on syde he smot away,
And slowgh dogges off faloun fay.[1]
They beet doun the toures alle,
In the toune and on the walle.
A prys-tour stood ovyr the gate,
He bent hys engynes and threw therate   20
A great stone that harde droff,
That the tour al to-roff,
The barre, and the burdys ; [2]
The gate burste and the portecolys.
Therto he gaff another strok,
To brek the bemes al off rok,
And slowgh the folk that therinne stood,
The other fledde and wer nygh wood.[3]
And sayde it was the devylys dent !
' Alas, Mahoun ! what has he ment,   30
Thys Inglyshe dogge, that hyghte Fouke ?
He is no man, he is a pouke,[4]
That out off helle is i-stole !
An evyl deth mote he thole !
For us he beseges fast,
If he moo stones to us cast,
Alle this toun wole be doun bete,
Stondand hous wole he non lete ! '
    Ser Fouke gan hym apparayle,
With hys folk the toun to assayle.   40
Or [5] he the toun with strengthe wan,
Ther was slayn many a man !

[1] felon, i.e. heathen faith.   [2] beams.
[3] mad (with fear).   [4] puck, spirit.   [5] ere.

The toun dykes on every syde,
They wer depe, and ful wyde,
Ful of grut, no man myghte swymme ;
The wal stood fast upon the brymme,
Between hem myghte no man stande.
The archers alle off this lande
Schotte in with arwes smale,
The toun folk he gaff no tale.   50
The Sarezynes went upon the walles,
And schotte with arweblaste and spryngalles,[1]
And with quarelles [2] they gan hem stonye,
Of our folk they schotte monye,
Envenymyd ther takyl was.
But when Fouk Doyly seygh that cas,
That hys men scholde be slawe,
He bad hem to withdrawe,
And bryngys trees and many a bowgh.
To don hys wylle folk com inowgh ;   60
Crystene men made hem a targe
Off dores, and off wyndowes large ;
Some caughte a bote and some an hach,
And broughten to tymbyr and rach,[3]
And grete schydes, and the wood.
And slunge it into the mode,
And the thach abone theron,
That Crystene men myghte on gon
To the walle, and stande sekyr,
And hand by hand to geve bekyr.   70
A sorye beverage ther was browen !
Quarelles and arwes thykke flowen,
The Ynglyssche slewe that they off-took,
Durste no man over the walles loke,
That the Crystene hem ovyr-threw,
And wylde-fyrr ovyr the walles they blewe.

[1] both military engines for throwing missiles.
[2] a square-headed cross-bow bolt.
[3] rushes for the thatch mentioned below.

Many an hous anon ryght
Bycome upon a fuyr hyght;
Many a lane and many a streete.
The Sarezynes thoo, for heete,   80
Drowgh out godes and faste gan flye:
Allas! and helpe! loud gan they cry,
They wer strong and wel hardy,
To wynne the toun weel they wende.
They withinne weel hem deffende:
Though it wer soo that one doun falle.
Another styrte upon the walle,
In the slede ther he stood,
And weryd it well with herte good.

   Among the toun folk was no game,   90
To counsayl they gaderyd hem insame.
Then sayde the chef amyrayl,
' Lordynges, lystnes to my tale,
This sege is gret, this fyrr is stronge.
Thus may we noughte dure longe.
To sleyn us they have gret desyre,
They have set our toun affyre.

  . . . .

Beter it is that we out renne,
Then as wreches in house to brenne,
And frye inne oure owne gres!   100
Ynglysshe be flynte and herteles;
Of mete and drynke they have defawte,
We shal hem sley alle inne assawte,
And felle hem alle in the feelde;
Hangyd be he that this toun yelde,
To Crystene men, whyl he may leve!'

XII. A VICTORY

The Lyfe of Alisaundre.

[*Vol. I, p.* 93, *lines* 2147–82.]

THUS they passeth ost by ost,
Withoute fyghtyng, other bost,[1]
Till heo comen, saun faile,
To the kynges ost of Tysoile.
This gan Alisaundre segge,[2]
And furst him mette with speris egge ;
Through brunny [3] and scheld, to the akedoun,[4]
He to-barst atwo his tronchon ;
Ac Alisaundre hutte him, certe,
Thorugh livre, and longe, and heorte.   10
Areches he hutte ; now he is ded,
N'ul he no more ete bred.
Alisaundre'is folk gan crye,
And saiden in gret melodye,
' Oure kyng hath this freke [5] y-felde ;
Oure is the maistry of the felde ! '
Now rist grete tabour betyng,
Blaweyng of pypes, and ek trumpyng,
Stedes lepyng, and ek arnyng
Of sharp speres, and analyng [6]   20
Of strong knighttes, and wighth metvng :
Launces breche and increpyng ;
Knighttes fallyng, stedes lesyng ;
Herte and hevedes [7] thorough kervnyg ;
Swerdes draweyng, lymes lesyng,
Hard assaylyng, and strong defendyng,
Stif witthstondyng, and wighth fleigheyng, [8]
Sharp of takyng armes spoylyng :
So gret bray, so gret crieyng,
For the folk there was dyeyng ;   30

---

[1] or noise.   [2] to see.   [3] breast-plate.
[4] a quilted jacket worn under armour.   [5] fellow.
[6] ? killing.   [7] heads.   [8] rapid retreating.

So muche dent, noise of sweord,
The thondur blast no myghte beo herde !
No the sunne hadde beo seye,
For the dust of the poudre !
No the weolkyn seon ne myght,
So was arewes and quarels flyght !

XIII. SINGLE COMBAT

[*Vol. I, p.* 302, *lines* 7369–7421.]

ALISAUNDRE com into the feld,
Wel y-armed undur scheld ;
And syt, so a noble knyght,
On a stede wel y-dyght ;
He ryt [1] his spere braydyng [2]
Pors also, come flying,
Y-greithed so a riche kyng.
Y-armed wel in knyghtis wise,
N'is [3] no nede heore armes to devyse.
Ac eythir lette go theo reyne,   10
And smyten togedre with gret mayne.
Heore speris barsten ageyn theo sheldis,
They dasschen over into the feldis.
They turned ageyn, doughtiliche,
With drawen sweordis sikirliche.[4]
Eythir on other laith on,
So does the mason on the ston ;
Ac as they skirmed [5] to the cors,
Ayther slough otheris hors.
Tho [6] they were on fote bothe,   20
They foughte togedre with heorte wrothe.
Getith nought of reste to preche ;
Aither gan so areche,
With 'saylyng, and with smytyng,
And keputh heom with fair werryng.

---

[1] rode.   [2] sticking out.   [3] There is
[4] surely.   [5] skirmished.   [6] Then.

Wel they foughte in the playn,
With target,[1] and with reremayn,
With overhed, and with stoke,
Ayther on othir sweordis schoke ; [2]
Yet wiste no mon, heom bytweone,   30
Who scholde maister beone ;
For heore armes, riche of mounde,[3]
Hole they weoren in that stounde.
    Ac listeneth now ! After restyng,
They bygynneth togedre flyng.
To kerve heore armes, and heore schelde,
Tho peces flowen into the feldis.
No say never men yet knyghtis two
So manliche togedre go !
Aither othir faste gan spye ;   40
To don othir vilanye,
Othir with stoke, othir with dent,[4]
Therto is al heore entent.
While they were so in mangle,
Theo Indiens gan gangle ; [5]
Pors gan abak renne,
And nom thiderward yeme,[6]
And loked toward heore crye.
Alisaundre was sone him bye ;
And smot him, in the discoverte,   50
Ryghte with the strok into the heorte,
Faste by the chyne bon :
Pors theo kyng feol ded anon.

[1] shield.
[2] reremain and overhead are two of the strokes used in combat.
[3] value, power.   [4] blow.   [5] to make a noise.
[6] and paid attention thither.